LAW & OTHER THINGS

LAW

&

OTHER THINGS

By

THE RT. HON.

LORD MACMILLAN

(HUGH PATTISON MACMILLAN)

Essay Index Reprint Series

BOOKS FOR LIBRARIES PRESS

FREEPORT, NEW YORK

First Published 1937
Reprinted 1971

To K.

INTERNATIONAL STANDARD BOOK NUMBER:
0-8369-2196-8

LIBRARY OF CONGRESS CATALOG CARD NUMBER:
76-152195

PRINTED IN THE UNITED STATES OF AMERICA

CONTENTS

PREFACE

It would have been pleasant if I could have said, in the conventional phrase, that these papers have been collected and republished in response to numerous requests. But it would not have been true. One or two friends did indeed suggest that I should arrest these fugitives *in meditatione fugæ*, but the responsibility for doing so is my own. Parental partiality must be my excuse for wishing to have a family group of my offspring and perhaps any who care to look at them may find some interest in tracing a certain consistency in their features.

M.

LAW AND POLITICS

The Henry Sidgwick Memorial Lecture
Delivered at Newnham College, Cambridge, November 1935

THERE is much to commend the institution of an annual namesake Lecture as a means of keeping fresh among us the memory of our departed masters. It ensures that each year one person at least, the chosen lecturer, shall give some thought to the life and work of the great man under whose auspices he is to speak; and his audience, too, if he is fortunate enough to have one, will for a passing hour recall the merits of him who is gone if only to compare them with the shortcomings of the speaker on whom his nominal mantle has fallen. Many such memorials have been founded in our Universities but in no instance more fittingly than in that of Henry Sidgwick, for it was in the lecture room that his incomparable gift of exposition found its most congenial atmosphere. In his case the appropriateness of this annual commemoration is enhanced by its association with Newnham College, itself an imperishable monument to his chivalrous crusade and under whose roof he spent the last and happiest years of his life.

Already the generation which knew Sidgwick has passed away in the thirty-five years which have elapsed since his death. The lecturer of to-day belongs to the next generation. But as in pious duty bound I have not failed to read the admirable Memoir of his life which we owe to his brother and his wife. I read it not only in order to be able to picture what manner of man he was, as he appeared to those who knew him best, but also in order to recapture, if I could, the intellectual mood of his day, to appreciate the nature of the problems which then confronted the thinker, and to estimate the measure of success which he achieved in their solution.

Fortunately we have still with us one of those who knew Sidgwick intimately. In his altogether delightful volume of reminiscences entitled *For my Grandson*, Sir Frederick Pollock tells us that "Henry Sidgwick was a born philosopher, ardent in the pursuit of truth, capable of sacrificing worldly advantage to his conscience, yet always judicious and abhorring dogmatism to the point of enjoying suspense of judgment for its own sake....In speculation he was sceptical, in action cautious but not timid." In a later passage he says of Sidgwick and Jackson, whom he describes as "the leading captains of modern and ancient philosophy" during his residence at Cambridge, that "they taught younger men to seek for themselves and to seek with an exacting conscience". And then he adds these words, so characteristic of the learned expositor of Spinoza: "Even if you consider philosophy merely as an intellectual game, there is no fun in playing with people (including yourself) who fudge their conclusions."

This is the testimony of one who saw and heard Sidgwick. But we, who are unhappily confined to the written record, can well confirm it, for it is just this spirit of conscientious candour and courageous diffidence which is exhaled not only from his more intimate diaries and letters but also from his published writings. In describing, in a moment of self-examination at the age of twenty-six,

Law and Politics

"that particular aggregate of psychological phenomena" which he called himself, he exclaimed: "For my part, I have determined to love the Ideal only." To that dedication of his spirit he remained true to his last breath.

Now it may seem more than a little odd after this preamble that in choosing a topic for this year's lecture I should have selected a subject so arid and so apparently alien to Sidgwick's genius as *Law and Politics*. What right have lawyers and politicians, those noisy and mercenary persons, to invade these quiet cloisters? But in truth I have ample justification, for Sidgwick all his days was intensely preoccupied with this very theme of my choice, as those can best testify who, like myself, have studied his great work on *The Science of Politics*, that "heavy book" as he not unjustly characterises it. Let there be no mistake, however. I do not use the word "politics" in the sense in which it is so often used by chairmen of public meetings who reassure their audiences by informing them that the cause they are met to promote has nothing to do with politics. It is remarkable, by the way, how invariably this announcement is greeted with applause when one reflects how vitally the happiness and prosperity of everyone of us are concerned in the conduct of our Government. But of course the disclaimer is always understood to refer to party politics in the sinister and derogatory sense of that expression, and this aspect of politics, which Sidgwick once described as a "blind free fight", was as distasteful to him as it would be out of place for a person in my judicial position to discuss it.

No. What interested Sidgwick supremely, and what must always be of interest to every thinking citizen, was politics in the sense of the science of associated humanity.

3 I-2

He was essentially a moral, rather than a metaphysical philosopher. Hence he treated politics as a branch, indeed as the main branch, of ethics. There are no doubt problems of ethics which affect the individual and the individual only and which would exercise the mind of the solitary denizen of a desert island in the conduct of his daily life. But most of the problems of ethics, and certainly the most vexed ones, concern our relations with our fellow-men. Few of the moral virtues could be practised by us if there were no other human beings towards whom they could be exhibited.

It is easy to see the pathway by which Sidgwick was led from ethics to politics. Most of us have traversed it, though some of us in the opposite direction. For politics in the scientific sense is the art of organising and managing human beings in the associations into which they are brought by their common membership of a city, a nation, or some larger social unit. This art, inasmuch as it has to deal with human beings endowed with moral consciences, cannot confine itself merely to economic or disciplinary regulations. It must ultimately concern itself with the fundamental considerations of ethics.

The very first sentence of Aristotle's *Politics* takes one at once into the moral sphere. "Seeing", he says, "that every State is a sort of association and every association is formed for the attainment of some Good—for some presumed Good is the end of all action—it is evident that as some Good is the object of all associations, so in the highest degree is the supreme Good the object of that association which is supreme and embraces all the rest, in other words of the State or political association." Observe that the word "Good", the key word of ethics,

4

occurs no less than four times in that opening paragraph.

Thus the moral philosopher sooner or later cannot escape from the consideration of political science. The human being who is the subject of his study is a social being, whose activities for good or for evil are in large measure determined for him by the society in which he lives, and that society in turn derives its character from its political constitution. True, politics may be said to deal rather with the setting than with the substance of the moral life, with the conditions under which the citizen lives rather than with the ethical quality of his individual life. But the interaction between the citizen and the political medium in which he lives is so close and constant as to affect his moral nature profoundly. And so the moral philosopher finds himself discussing politics—in their ethical aspect, no doubt, but with a full appreciation of the truth that the extent to which the individual can attain the ideal of the moral life is deeply affected by the character of the social organisation, in other words, of the political system, under which he lives. It is difficult, as Sidgwick indicates, to sort out the elements in social life which may properly be called political because they are so intimately combined with the other elements. Still, it is possible to make at least a theoretical analysis of our social life and to isolate for special study its political components.

What Sidgwick sought was to give precision to our political concepts as a contribution to the art of moral government, and he defined the scope of his study as being "concerned primarily with constructing, on the basis of certain psychological premises, the system of relations which ought to be established among the persons governing, and between them and the governed, in a society composed of civilised men as we know them". While not a few of the questions to which he addressed himself in pursuing this study now seem to us somewhat dimmed by the distance which we have so swiftly travelled since his day, Sidgwick's discussion of the proper functions of Government remains still full of instruction and guidance for us. To his treatment of this topic Professor Marshall paid the tribute of saying that it was admitted to be by far the best thing in any language. For us to-day it has a special value for it furnishes us with the wisdom of a singularly balanced mind on what has become the cardinal problem of political science, which when Sidgwick wrote was already beginning to come into prominence; I mean the conflict which has since grown so acute between Individualism and State Socialism—to use his own terms—as rival theories of civil government. The economic doctrine of *laissez-faire*, the doctrine that enlightened self-interest if left to itself best conduces to the social well-being of the community, had held sway in this country since the time of Adam Smith and was still cherished by many adherents of one of the great political parties with almost religious fervour. With them it was a far greater achievement to secure the repeal than to secure the enactment of a statute. But already there were ominous signs of change and presumptuous hands were already being laid on the ark of the covenant. "It is universally recognised", says Sidgwick, "that the present drift of opinion and practice is in the direction of increasing the range and volume of the interferences of government in the affairs of individuals." So he wrote some forty years ago. I wonder what would have been his comment on our legislation of the past two decades! In the ninety-second chapter of his great work on the American Commonwealth, Bryce describes the inception of a similar process in the United States. More and more the main issue in political science has come to be—not whether the State should intervene at all in the regulation of our daily lives but where the frontier line ought most wisely to be drawn between the province of State activity and that of individual enterprise. On all hands it is now recognised that the policy of *laissez-faire*, which gave us no doubt our industrial and commercial supremacy but also gave us our slums and many other attendant evils, must give place to a new regime. The contest has now shifted to a new ground on which those who are all for State regimentation do battle with those who defend what they regard as the rightful strongholds of individual initiative. The definition of the sphere of government has become the main preoccupation of the student of political science. We have travelled far since Tom Paine —that early champion of the people's rights—proclaimed that "The more perfect civilisation is, the less occasion has it for government...it is but few general laws that civilised life requires".

This changed attitude of mind has come about not only through a revulsion from the old theory and its attendant evils, but also as a consequence of the increased complexity of modern life. Politics are concerned with the regulation of the contacts of human beings with each other, and the enormous changes which have come about in the mechanism of life have infinitely increased these contacts and consequently the necessity for their regulation. Let me quote side by side a passage from Sidgwick's *Science of Politics* and one from the Archbishop of York's broadcast lecture on "Faith and Freedom" on 30 May last. "It is easy", says Sidgwick, "to see how new occasions for this kind of interference may continually arise: either because the mischief in question has been increased or newly introduced through the closer massing and more complicated relations of human beings which the development of industry and civilisation brings with it; or because mischiefs of long standing have been unveiled by the increased insight of advancing science, or possible remedies hitherto unknown have been pointed out." In my parallel passage from the Archbishop, His Grace declares that "with the development of centralisation which the new means of communication have made possible and the growth of planning which mass-production has made necessary it has been natural that the State should invade spheres hitherto left to voluntary effort".

The same insight which enabled Sidgwick to discover this new movement of political thought enabled him also to perceive its dangers. He recognised that a crowded world cannot safely be left to its own devices and that in such a world a certain amount of what we now term social legislation is essential to the preservation of the liberty of the individual. Such measures, he saw, may promote rather than diminish freedom. This is essentially true. I am not less but more the captain of my soul in a city which is well sewered, well paved, well policed, and free from slums and the diseases they breed, and in which the education, the health and the welfare of my fellow-citizens are promoted by sensible measures.

But the defect of all social policies, as Sidgwick saw, is their tendency to run to extremes, and now we hear on all sides a warning that if we do not take heed we may wake up some fine morning to find all our liberties gone, overwhelmed by a mass of legislation which by depriving life of all its individual initiative will rob it of all its happiness and interest. Just as the unrestrained policy of *laissez-faire* wrought many evils which we are now slowly redressing with much cost and labour, so there is a risk that the opposite policy may in turn bring in its train no less, though different, evils, if not vigorously guarded.

That serious alarm as to the present trend of political thought is entertained in many quarters is manifest, and the danger which is threatened is danger to our liberties. "Freedom, our traditional treasure, is threatened," says the Archbishop of York, "how can it be saved?" Before me as I write lie the writings of four authors, nurtured in very different pastures, who have discerned the same impending menace. First I open a book which hails from the land of the free, entitled *The Challenge to Liberty*. There I find ex-President Hoover impelled to vindicate the cause of liberty in his country with almost passionate eloquence against the encroachments of regimentation. His opening words are: "For the first time in two generations the American people are faced with the primary issue of humanity and all Government—the issue of human liberty." No less trenchant language is employed elsewhere by my friend the President of Columbia University. But Europe is evidently in no

9

better case, for here is General Smuts, in his Rectorial Address on "Freedom" at St Andrews University, telling us that: "In many if not most European countries the standard of human freedom has already fallen far below that of the nineteenth century. Perhaps I do not exaggerate when I say that of what we call liberty in its full human meaning—freedom of thought, speech, action, self-expression—there is to-day less than there has been during the last two thousand years." Let us come nearer home. The third of my books is entitled *The New Despotism*, and here I find the Lord Chief Justice of England once more buckling on the armour of Sir Edward Coke and, in the sacred cause of the Rule of Law, offering battle to that ancient foe of freedom—the executive. And finally in one of the last of his public utterances, when at the Royal Institution last April he traced the history of *Liberty under the Common Law*, my lamented colleague Lord Tomlin, with the studious moderation which characterises the utterances of Lords of Appeal, permitted himself "a sigh over the ever increasing tendency, due perhaps to the ever increasing complexity of modern life, to limit in so many fields the freedom of action of the individual" and ventured still "to proclaim the importance above all else of the freedom of the mind, to recall that through the history of our law's development...there runs a romantic thread of passionate attachment to freedom of thought and speech and to maintain that only when that freedom is accorded and in the atmosphere created by it, can the mind of man develop and display its finest flowers". Such quotations from such responsible leaders of thought in very diverse spheres—and I could multiply them indefinitely—plainly indicate that something is amiss.

There are many diagnoses of the mischief and indeed the causes are manifold. But there is one which to my mind is plainly among those at work, and it brings me at last to the special topic with which I have promised to deal—the relation of law and politics.

In a limited sense law may be said to be merely the vehicle of politics, for it is by legislation that the politician gives expression and effect to his policy—at least in countries which enjoy—perhaps I should rather say possess—representative government. The statute book reflects in its contents the prevalent political theories of the time. No one can study its recent volumes without being struck by the extent to which they are nowadays almost monopolised by immense masses of elaborate social legislation. And the counterpart of this is the growth of our annual expenditure on these social activities in England and Wales from 31 millions to 430 millions in the course of the last thirty years or so, an expenditure which is still rising. Our country is not alone in this new development of legislative activity. I have a volume of nearly nine hundred pages in which the Labour Office at Geneva published in 1933 the results of its International Survey of Social Services, covering twenty-three other countries as well as our own.

But while law in the sense of legislation is merely a means of enforcing policy, there is another sense in which law is, or ought to be, the master of policy. Law is something much greater and nobler than the contents of any statute book, of any code, of any volume of judicial decisions. It is the guardian and vindicator of the two most precious things in the world—justice and liberty. It may well be that at any particular time its manifestations in the governance of our daily lives may fall lamentably short of attaining its ideals. It may even be perverted, for it is an instrument confided to fallible, it may even be to wicked, human agencies. But its ideal remains constant and unchanging. By the standards of justice and liberty which it sets up all governments, all political theories, must ultimately be judged and must ultimately stand or fall.

It should then be the aim of the science of politics to devise, and of the art of politics to promote, such a system of government as will ensure the fullest enjoyment of justice and liberty by all who come within its scope. "I suppose", says Dean Inge, "politics consists in choosing always the second-best." I should be sorry to subscribe to this depressing doctrine, though I should equally be the first to admit that in an imperfect world the perfect ideal is not attainable. But to cease to strive for the best and to decline in disillusioned lethargy on the second-best is in the statesman the unpardonable sin.

Let us examine a little more closely these great conceptions of justice and liberty. In political science justice may be said to have a rather wider significance than in its ordinary legal application. To the lawyer the essence of justice is that the law shall be the same for all, that it shall be administered without fear or favour and that it shall secure for each citizen that to which by the law of the land he is justly entitled. But the student of political science asks the more fundamental question— is the law itself just? And here he enters upon much more difficult and controversial ground. For while all would have the laws to be just, there are almost infinite variations in the conception of what is just—every citizen has his own idea about it. Nor is there any absolute standard of justice. The idea of justice which each one of us entertains is affected by our training, by our economic position, by our sentiments, by our prejudices. What may seem just to one man in one age may seem to another man in another age the very quintessence of injustice. The historian can supply us with any number of political measures which at the time were conceived and honestly conceived by their promoters to be just but which now outrage our sense of justice. Yet there is in every age a public conscience which according to its lights is alive to particular injustices, even if it cannot define justice in the abstract, and the efficiency of a Government is judged by its success in removing these. Each age seems to have its own problem. At one time it is the injustice of slavery, at another the injustice of woman's position, which awakens the nation's conscience. At present I should say that the kind of injustice which most exercises the world is economic injustice.

It follows from this constant expansion, I hope I may say progress, in our conception of justice that the law which is the framework of our social structure can never be static. "Respect for the law", a present-day writer has said, "depends in the long run on the power to change it." But there will always be a lag in the process of change, for the law cannot be altered without careful consideration. There is a principle of justice itself which forbids inconsiderate change in response to gusts of public sentiment, for the people of a country arrange their lives and their affairs in reliance on the stability of the law, and every change in the law involves a certain amount of disturbance and often even some injustice. So it is the part of the wise politician to weigh well the measures for the alteration of the law which he is urged to undertake in the interests of justice, lest his well-meant efforts may work an injustice greater than that which he has set out to cure. He was a wise statesman who said: "Where it is not necessary to change it is necessary not to change."

Here I may venture to emphasise a distinction which is apt to be lost sight of in these days; I mean the distinction between justice and philanthropy. Justice requires that each man shall receive his deserts, the reward of his merits and the penalties of his demerits. "Whatsoever a man soweth, that shall he also reap", says St Paul. There are those who find this a hard doctrine and who would destroy the whole relation between merit and reward on which our moral as well as our legal system is based. Herbert Spencer discerned the beginnings of this mood over forty years ago when he said that "daily legislation betrays little anxiety that each shall have that which belongs to him, but great anxiety that he shall have that which belongs to somebody else". Where social justice finds its true sphere is in securing that each shall have a fair and equal chance of winning the rewards of life. Justice may equalise the opportunities of life but it cannot equalise the ability to take advantage of these opportunities. It has been suggested that material things might be divided equally and shared equally in common, leaving special merit to find its reward in immaterial things, such as fame and public approval, but there may be and often is as much injustice, and consequent ill feeling, over the distribution of intangible as over the distribution of tangible rewards. However, I am not considering how ideal justice would re-shape the world. I am trying to think out how law may best serve the cause of social justice in the world as we find it; and I suggest that a good working test is that such measures as tend to remove unfair and man-made handicaps and to promote equality of opportunity for all may be deemed to be just measures; while those which tend to deprive of adequate reward those who have displayed merit in using the opportunities afforded to them are unjust measures. An acute commentator has observed that we are "confronted with the paradox that man is at once a social being and therefore co-operative, and an individual personality and therefore competitive". We cannot eliminate this duality and so we come back to the central problem of where the line should be drawn between co-operation whose rewards are shared, and competition whose rewards are monopolised. But I am getting perilously near controversial topics.

I have bracketed justice and liberty as the supreme ends which the spirit of law prescribes for political science. In truth, however, justice and liberty are not and cannot be isolated from each other, for there can be no real justice without liberty, no real liberty without justice. A much graver wrong is done to a man in unjustly depriving him of his liberty of action, of thought or of speech, than in unjustly depriving him of his material possessions. The supreme injustice is the coercion of the soul. The history of civil government in this country has been the history of the slow but sure achievement of civil liberty for its citizens, and it is because in other less happy lands around us we see liberty being not only threatened but destroyed that we must take heed that this menace does not reach our shores.

Now it is by the law that our liberty is assured. "To be free", said Lord Mansfield, "is to live under a government by law." The badge of servitude is subjection to the arbitrary will of another and the law is the sworn foe of arbitrariness. The first of the direct guarantees of civil liberty in this country is "the open administration of justice according to known laws truly interpreted and fair constructions of evidence". These are the words of Hallam in his *Constitutional History*, as quoted by Lord Justice Farwell in a famous case. That the law shall be certain and the same for all, that no person shall be deprived of his liberty save by due process of law, that all charges must be founded upon and formulated in accordance with existing law, that the prosecutor must prove his case by competent evidence, that the accused must have every opportunity of defending himself and that the trial must be conducted by an independent and impartial judge and, not least important, that the accused can only be detained on a definite charge and must be brought to trial within a definite time—these are the bulwarks of liberty—and so, as Heraclitus said five hundred years before Christ: "The people ought to fight in defence of the law as they do of their city wall."

But this hard-won liberty which the law assures to us is ever at the mercy of politics. Where the political system of a country breaks down, as it has broken down in several of the great countries of Europe, then the rule of law, which needs a sound political structure for its support, collapses in turn and there is substituted for it

that horrid arbitrariness which is the negation of law
and of which we have had such painful examples of late.
Thus it is true that law and politics are indissolubly
linked together. The government of a state must be
based on sound theories of political science or at any
moment it may be overthrown and anarchy or tyranny
take its place, and in its downfall justice and liberty alike
will perish. What particular form of government will
best ensure the preservation of these essential rights it is
the province of the political scientist to discuss. Probably it will vary in its constitution according to the
stage of progress which the nation has reached and according to the genius of its people. But the fact that in
this country of ours, almost alone in the world, freedom
still survives undiminished may justify us in main-
taining that its best safeguard for us at any rate is the
democratic system of representative government which
we have devised for ourselves. It has a theoretical as
well as a practical justification. Liberty is not licence
and it can only be enjoyed in obedience to laws which
involve some restrictions of individual freedom of action.
But if these restrictions are imposed by our own choice
and can be altered by our own will they lose their irk-
someness. No one will be bold enough to say that a representative democracy is the final product of political
wisdom, but it at least has the merit of giving effect to
the will of the majority of the people and thus of en-
suring that only such limitations on liberty shall be imposed as the majority are willing to accept in the general
interest. Professor Whitehead reminds us that "a doctrine as to the social mingling of liberty and compulsion
is required. A mere unqualified demand for liberty is

the issue of shallow philosophy, equally noxious with the antithetical cry for mere conformation to standard pattern." The task which is common to law and to politics, each in its own province, is so to reconcile the freedom which is necessary if the individual is to give of his best to mankind with the compulsion which is necessary if the community is to exist in which alone he can enjoy his freedom.

When so much depends for all of us on the due discharge of their duty by our lawyers and our politicians to whom we have confided the guardianship of those precious treasures—justice and liberty—are we quite just in so constantly deriding their character and their activities? I am not going to indulge in platitudes about the quality of British justice and it would hardly be seemly for me to vindicate the merits of the profession to which I belong. But I may bespeak a more charitable, a more appreciative—I will say, a more just—attitude to those who devote their lives to politics. Perhaps the politicians are themselves in no small measure responsible for the distrust which they so often incur, for far too large a part of their energy is spent in abuse of each other. If you think of it, it seems a strange and ironical arrangement that when the country has entrusted to a particular group of men the arduous and delicate task of conducting the business of the nation, we at the same time expect and permit them to be harassed by every form of obstruction and vituperation. It is as if we had employed a surgeon to perform a difficult operation and then had arranged that his elbow should be jogged at the most critical moments.

You have probably all read F. S. Oliver's Political

Testament in the third volume of *The Endless Adventure*
published after his death. "The hardest chapter to write
about Politicians", he says, "is that which deals with
their morals." But his next words are: "Let me say
again what I said at the beginning—that in my view
'politics is the noblest career that any man can choose...'.
Stout must be the hearts of those who take so great a risk
and who dedicate themselves—souls as well as bodies—
to the service of their country." And then he quotes
Montaigne, than whom, as he justly says, few if any
writers have been freer from illusions: "I am of opinion",
says that sage, "that the most honourable calling is to
serve the Public and to be useful to the many." When so
much is at stake in these days I think then that we might
be a little more generous in our criticisms of those upon
whom we place the burden of decisions which we shirk
ourselves. We are more likely to get good work from our
politicians if we expect good work from them, for praise
and confidence are much better stimulants to wise effort
than abuse and mistrust. Fair criticism is another
matter. I hope we shall always have that.

I cannot say that I conclude this lecture with much
satisfaction, for I have an uncomfortable feeling that I
have stirred far more questions than I have answered.
I suppose this must always be the case when one seeks to
explore fundamental principles. Indeed I doubt if any
fundamental principles are susceptible of precise formulation. At any rate none of the doctors and sages whom,
not only in my youth, I have eagerly frequented has expounded any social theory to my complete satisfaction.
I console myself, however, with the reflection that in my
avoidance of dogma I have perhaps proved myself for a

2-2

brief hour a not unworthy disciple of Sidgwick, that least dogmatic of philosophers.

After all, the things that matter most are always the most elusive. They derive from instinct rather than from reason. So I shall resort to a poet, and not to either a lawyer or a politician, for the noblest expression of that ideal which is the aspiration alike of law and politics. It is four hundred years since the words were written, but never has there been better cause to realise their truth than in these days:

> Ah! freedom is a noble thing;
> Freedom makes man to have liking,
> Freedom all solace to man gives,
> He lives at ease that freely lives.

LAW AND ORDER

Address delivered at the Annual Meeting of the Canadian Bar Association, Regina, Saskatchewan, August 1928

WE have left behind us for a little the cares of the Bench and the Bar, the office and the desk, and are met to talk of the things that concern our great profession in its wider aspects. It is well for us thus to step aside from time to time out of the traffic of our daily business and from some coign of vantage, such as our meeting here affords, to scan the way by which we have come and the destination to which our steps are bent. The strenuous routine of the lawyer's day is so engrossing as to leave little time for reflection. Yet even to the busiest of us there come moments when we ask ourselves what is the purpose of all our manifold activities and, baffled for an answer, are apt to be depressed by a sense of our futility. At such moments we seek a reassurance that our labours are not in vain and that our calling can justify itself by some worthier measure than the record of our fee books. "There is nothing better", says the worldly wise Preacher, "than that a man should rejoice in his own works; for that is his portion." But to have joy in his work a man must be satisfied that what he is doing is worth while and that he is rendering service of real value in his day and generation. I decline to acquiesce in Voltaire's policy of despair: "Travaillons sans raisonner, c'est le seul moyen de rendre la vie supportable." In

21

the legal profession, as in every other vocation, the "imponderables", to use Bismarck's striking word, count for much and perhaps I owe it to my Scottish upbringing that as a lawyer I seek for justification by faith as well as by works.

To those who share with me this need I commend the comfort to be found in the words which I have chosen as the text of this address—"Law and Order". The conjunction of law and order in common parlance is not fortuitous. It embodies a fundamental truth. The purpose of the law is the creation and maintenance of order. In the ultimate analysis you will find that this is the true objective of the lawyer's vocation, the cardinal tenet of his faith.

This conception of order as the end and aim of all our endeavours is an inspiring one. In the world around us there have from all time been two great contending forces arrayed against each other, the force of order and the force of disorder, and the history of civilisation is the history of the gradual triumph of the former over the latter. "Order governs the world," wrote Swift, "the Devil is the author of confusion." In this secular struggle I claim that our profession, notwithstanding all the gibes levelled at us, has been and still is on the side of the angels.

There is in all well-regulated minds an instinctive love of order. It has an aesthetic as well as a practical appeal to us, for order is the basis of beauty and harmony as well as of efficiency. The mere physical process of arranging, sorting and classifying a miscellaneous heap of objects affords a certain pleasure. An untidy drawer, a cupboard of confused odds and ends, a littered desk,

22

rouse in us at least an aspiration—not always, I fear, realised—to put things straight. I suspect that no small part of the fascination of such games as Patience and other pastimes which consist in arranging cards or pieces in sequence is to be found in the satisfaction of this primitive instinct. And the pleasure of producing order out of chaos among our possessions, if we really set ourselves to the task, is never-failing. Like so many other words, such as "straight" and "right", which we have transferred from the physical world and applied in the sphere of conduct, the word "Order" retains the sense of the metaphor buried in it. Such words are "fossil poetry" in Emerson's phrase, or better, as Trench puts it, "fossil ethics". The idea of order still carries with it the visual suggestion of its origin in the Latin word for a symmetrical row or arrangement of objects as opposed to disarray and confusion. To the mind's eye the conception of order will never lose the attractiveness which it borrows from its etymological origin in physical symmetry and fitness.

If, then, "Order is Heaven's first law", in Pope's fine phrase, the task of the lawyer in setting the affairs of men in order may well claim to be in harmony with the increasing purpose which runs through the ages. The particular aspect of order with which our profession is concerned is order in one of the highest of all spheres, the sphere of human relationships. In every human community, large or small, the family, the village, the city, the nation, all the elements of strife and anarchy are present which we owe to our brute inheritance of selfishness, greed and passion. In every transaction of daily life the possibility of conflict lurks. And all strife, all conflict, is disorder. Happily, amidst these many occasions of provocation, there is implanted no less deeply in the breast of mankind a craving, however dim, for justice, that is to say, for such an ordering of human life as that each shall have his due rights and that those who infringe the rights of others shall receive condign punishment. The sentiment which condemns a breach of the orders, the categorical imperatives, of justice is inherent in human nature. To quote Herbert Spencer's illuminating study: "One who has dropped his pocket book and turning round finds that another who has picked it up will not surrender it, is indignant. If the goods sent home by a shopkeeper are not those he purchased, he protests against the fraud. Should his seat at a theatre be usurped during a momentary absence, he feels himself ill-used. Morning noises from a neighbour's poultry he complains of as grievances. And meanwhile he sympathises with the anger of a friend who has been led by false statements to join a disastrous enterprise or whose action at law has been rendered futile by a flaw in the procedure." (*Justice*, p. 35.) The extent to which the ordering of our simplest doings is based upon implicit legal sanctions is entertainingly exhibited in von Ihering's little book on *Law in Daily Life*, in which he contemplates with a legal eye the hundred and one delicate problems of jurisprudence to which the simplest occurrences of everyday existence may give rise.

As society advances and the relations of life become more complicated, the forms and causes of disorder become more subtle and the task of the forces of order in counteracting them becomes correspondingly more arduous. The maintenance of the equilibrium between the rights and liberties of each and the rights and liberties of all grows increasingly difficult, while the failure to maintain it becomes at the same time more disastrous.

Here, then, is the lawyer's place in the social economy. It is his privilege, as it is his duty, to promote that kind of order in the community which results from the formulation and administration of just laws. The necessity for the formulation of rules regulative of conduct and for their due enforcement to secure order is exemplified in every branch of human activity. Why, you cannot start a new golf club without framing a constitution for it and providing rules for the use of the links. A company cannot start business till it has got its memorandum and articles of association. A church must have its formulas and articles. We are, every one of us, making laws daily for the ordering of our homes when we fix the hours for meals and determine the order of precedence for the morning bath. The lawyer's business is concerned with those rules which have been prescribed by the State for ordering the activities of its citizens in their public and private relations with each other.

In this city my theme is indeed an apposite one, for history has no nobler record than the annals of the North-West Mounted Police, the Riders of the Plains, that force of intrepid pioneers of law and order first raised here half a century ago. Recognising that lawlessness must be put down if civilisation was ever to conquer the vast region of the Territories, the far-sighted administrators of those days instituted this dauntless band, whose name soon became and has ever remained a synonym for romantic courage and endurance, and whose tradition, under their new name of the Royal

Canadian Mounted Police, is still worthily maintained in all the outposts of the Dominion. I cannot refrain from quoting a sentence or two from the last published Report of the Commissioner. Speaking of the patrols carried out by his men, he tells us that "a small party recently concluded a stay of nearly two years in the extreme north of British Columbia, on the upper reaches of the Liard River, suffering much from the severity of the winter, moving about in a wild, remote and imperfectly known region and doing much at once to enforce obedience to the law and to relieve distress and mitigate suffering". "For grimness, few occurrences could surpass the four hundred and fifty mile journey of a constable in Baffin Island, conveying to his detachment, amid great difficulties of travel, the body of an unfortunate fur-trader for decent burial after due investigation into the causes of his death." "Nor are the patrols", says the Commissioner, "confined to these faraway regions. Farther south, in forests, along the rivers and on the prairies, by steamboat, power launch, canoe, motor car and saddle horse, at times on foot, our men traverse regions where their presence serves at once as a reminder that laws must be obeyed and governmental regulations observed, as a means of carrying on the administration of the country and as a proof that the Government can and will extend its aid to people in distress." I note with pleasure that he speaks of the cordial and happy relations of the Royal Canadian Mounted Police with other police forces of the British Empire, paying a special tribute to the assistance received from the Metropolitan Commissioner of Police in London and the various departments of Scotland Yard.

Law and Order

It is not our lot to share the labours of these executive officers of the law, but it is very much indeed our province to see that the laws which they enforce are just and certain. Let us consider for a little the function of the lawyer in promoting good order in the State. The public are too apt to regard us as merely contentious persons engaged in venal controversies and disputes. There could be no greater misconception. In truth, I should rather say that every dispute on a point of law which finds its way into the law courts is a confession of the lawyer's failure, for it demonstrates that the law has been imperfectly framed or imperfectly applied to some relationship or transaction. Every law is but the expression of a principle of order, and if it fails to express that principle with clearness and precision the people suffer. The loftiest of the lawyer's duties is to assist in the formulation of the law, in clarifying and amending the rules which the State prescribes to govern our daily life and business. In the legislative process he is indispensable. The drafting of a statute is a task involving the highest form of legal skill and requiring both technical equipment and learning. To all lawyers who have to engage in this form of work I should like to take this opportunity of commending a remarkable and too little studied volume on *Practical Legislation*, by Lord Thring, an acknowledged master of the art. He quotes two sentences from Austin's *Jurisprudence* to the truth of which every parliamentary draftsman will subscribe. "I will venture to affirm", says Austin, "that what is commonly called the *technical* part of legislation is incomparably more difficult than what may be called the *ethical*. In other words, it is far easier to conceive justly what would be useful law, than so to construct that same law that it may accomplish the design of the lawgiver." And again: "Statutes made with great deliberation and by learned and judicious lawyers have been expressed so obscurely or have been constructed so ineptly that decisions interpreting these provisions or supplying and correcting the provisions *ex ratione legis* have been of necessity heaped upon them by the courts of justice. Such, for example, is the case with the Statute of Frauds which was made by three of the wisest lawyers in the reign of Charles II, Sir M. Hale (if I remember right) being one of them." Lord Thring gives some amusing examples of how not to draft. A statute, for example, of George the Third's reign (52 Geo. III, c. 146) enacted that the penalties under the Act were to be given one-half to the informer and one-half to the poor of the parish. As the only penalty prescribed by the statute was fourteen years' transportation, neither the informer nor the poor would be likely to be grateful for this benefaction. A ludicrous instance of faulty drafting is to be found in a Darlington Improvement Act of 1872, which defines a "new building" as meaning "any building pulled or burnt down to or within ten feet from the surface of the ground". An amendment proposed by a certain Q.C. to a Bill brought forward in 1865 reaches the high-water mark of ineptitude. It proposed that "Every dog found trespassing on inclosed land unaccompanied by the registered owner of such dog or other person who shall on being asked give his true name and address may be then and there destroyed by such occupier or by his orders." No one who attends to Lord Thring's experienced and practical teaching is likely to fall into such absurdities.

Law and Order

Neglect of the art of accurate and orderly drafting has of late tended increasingly to bring the law into disrepute. Legislation by reference, the besetting sin of the parliamentary draftsman, has become so rife that it is often impossible to ascertain the existing law without going through the process of collating half a dozen statutes. Mr Justice Rowlatt, whose unhappy lot it is to spend his days unravelling the revenue laws of the United Kingdom, in a recent case dealing with section 31 of the Finance Act, 1927, thus expressed his justifiable exasperation: "That section in five pages of the 'Law Reports' edition of the statutes, makes piecemeal amendments of section 21 of the Finance Act, 1922, which make it perfectly unintelligible to the layman, and to any lawyer who has not made a prolonged study of it with all his law books at his elbow. It is a crying scandal that legislation by which the subject is taxed should appear in the Statute-book in that utterly unintelligible form. I am told by the Attorney-General—and rightly told, I am sure—that it is only in this form that the legislation can be carried through at all. Then all I have to say is that the price of getting this legislation through is that the people of this country are taxed by laws which they cannot possibly understand. This is the worst example that there has ever been upon the Statute-book."

A commentator points out that the same statute contains another egregious specimen of contemporary legislation. Let me read it to you: "*Any individual* upon whom notice is served by the Special Commissioners requiring him to furnish a statement of and particulars relating to any assets in which, *at any time during the period specified in the notice*, he has had any beneficial interest, and in respect of which, within such period, either no income was received by him, *or the income received by him was less than the sum to which the income would have amounted, if the income from such assets had accrued from day to day and been apportioned accordingly*, shall, whether an assessment to super-tax in respect of his total income has or has not been made for the relevant year or years of assessment, furnish such a statement and such particulars in the form and within the time (not being less than twenty-eight days) required by the notice." (Finance Act, 1927, section 33.)

Having recovered my breath, though with a brain still dizzy, I ask you what is the plain citizen to make of such a farrago? Yet he is admonished to remember—I quote Mr Justice Willes—that "every man (who is of sufficient understanding to be responsible for his actions) is supposed to be cognizant of the law, as it is the rule by which every subject of the kingdom is to be governed and therefore it is his business to know it". (*King* v. *Shipley*, 1784, 3 Doug. 177.) I can only oppose to the maxim *Ignorantia juris non excusat* the equally sound maxim *Lex non cogit ad impossibilia*.

I have, as you will observe, judiciously drawn my examples from Imperial legislation, but the privilege which I occasionally enjoy in the Privy Council of considering the Statutes of the Dominions has shown me that this unhappy tendency to complexity and obscurity is not confined to the legislation of the Mother of Parliaments. It is becoming a family disease. Such enactments offend against the principle of my text. What are we to say when the law which is designed to produce order is found itself to be in a state of disorder? The lawyer may seek to throw the responsibility upon the politician, but I cannot absolve our profession of its share. We are experts, and it is our duty to see that the statutes which are the instruments of order are themselves orderly and intelligible. I do not forget the wise words of Aristotle: "As in other sciences, so in politics, it is impossible that all things should be precisely set down in writing; for enactments must be universal but actions are concerned with particulars." (Aristotle's *Politics*, Bk II, Jowett's translation.) Or, as it was put by Portalis, one of Napoleon's Commissioners: "We have guarded against the dangerous ambition of wishing to regulate and wishing to foresee everything. The wants of society are so various that it is impossible for the legislature to provide for every case or every emergency." The *casus omissus* we shall always have with us, but this affords no excuse for slovenly legislation. We may not be able to achieve the fine simplicity which Gulliver found to obtain in Brobdingnag. "No law of that country", he tells us, "must exceed in words the number of letters in their alphabet which consists only of two and twenty. But indeed few of them extend even to that length. They are expressed in the most plain and simple terms wherein those people are not mercurial enough to discover above one interpretation: and to write a comment upon any law is a capital crime." Without adopting remedies so heroic we can do much to cure the statute book of its deformities.

The lawyer's business is with words. They are the raw material of his craft. He must use them not only to enunciate the law in statutes, but also to embody in deeds and contracts and other written instruments the transactions of his clients. In the domain of private practice where most of us occupy our days—for comparatively few of us are called upon to share in the work of legislation—the principle of order should no less be our guiding star. Orderly thinking comes first; then and then only, orderly drafting. The instructions of our lay client must necessarily often come to us in an imperfect state. We have to sort out and arrange in logical order the provisions of the will or contract in which his wishes are to be embodied, to draw attention to omissions, to suggest additions, to ascertain what the law permits and what the law forbids, and then to express in orderly and precise terms exactly what we intend. For myself, I never approach the consideration of a complicated family settlement without first drawing up a genealogical tree with the dates of births, marriages and deaths carefully entered. It is remarkable how with such help one can reduce to order the most confused scheme, and avoid errors which would otherwise be almost inevitable. This art of expressing in orderly and accurate language the transactions of family and business affairs is a high art. Our medium, the technical language of the law, has been perfected through centuries of use. What greater artistic pleasure can there be than to utilise that great medium with the ease of a master, and to attain the happy poise of a successful work?

The lawyer, however, is not confined to the written word. This is a meeting of the Bar of Canada, and in the time that remains to me I should like to emphasise the application of my text to the work of the lawyer in the Courts. The very existence of the Law Courts is the most

signal evidence of the triumph of law and order. The
primitive instincts which formerly found the solution of
all quarrels in violence and bloodshed are here curbed.
For force there is substituted reason. For physical conflict there is substituted orderly investigation of facts
and law, the arguments of counsel, and finally the
judge's decision designed to restore order by rendering
clear and certain the rights of the contending parties.
In this process, daily carried on in our Courts, when you
come to examine it, how large a part is played in sorting
out and clearing up confusion. Once the true facts are
ascertained and marshalled and the precise legal issue
emerges, the rest is comparatively easy. Speaking from
a long experience of presenting controversies for judicial
decision, I find myself daily more convinced that of all
the equipments of the successful advocate a sense of
order is the most valuable. The gift of so selecting and
arranging facts and arguments that the exposition of the
case shall be well proportioned and logical and its pattern harmonious cannot be over-estimated. Orderliness
is itself persuasive. What the mind easily follows the
mind is predisposed to favour. The distraction caused by
the untidy presentation of a case involves loss of time
and temper on the part of all concerned, and may even
lead to the loss of the case itself. You will recall the well-
known admonition of Mr Justice Maule to a blundering
counsel: "It may be my fault that I cannot follow you;
I know that my brain is getting old and dilapidated;
but I should like to stipulate for some sort of order.
There are plenty of them. There is the chronological, the
botanical, the metaphysical, the geographical—even the
alphabetical order would be better than no order at all."

Law and Other Things

The whole department of law which deals with procedure is designed to secure that everything shall be done in our Courts decently and in order, and so as to serve the ends of justice. There is a tendency in these bustling days to be impatient of the niceties of procedure. I may quote a judge of the High Court of Australia, who, in a recent case, stated that "Procedure to-day in all departments of life is regarded as of secondary importance. The result is the main thing. In Courts it tends more and more to discard the trappings that often cause Justice to stumble on the way, and it moves towards simplicity, directness and economy of time and money that leave the tribunal free to concentrate on the real problem before it." (Isaacs, J., in *Gray* v. *Perpetual Trustee Co., Ltd.*, 1927, 39 C.L.R., 473.) But this contempt for procedure may well be carried too far. No one would willingly revert to the bad old days when the merits of a case were entirely subordinated to the formalities of pleading or revive the elaborations of the old criminal procedure whose pitfalls for the prosecutor enabled so many accused persons to escape without "resorting to the clumsy expedient of proving innocence", as the Professor of Scots Law in Glasgow University once wittily put it. On the other hand in the Temple of the Law, if anywhere, order must be maintained. There must therefore always be rules to regulate the steps whereby actions are brought and proceedings conducted in Court. The aim of these rules should be to facilitate, not to embarrass, the course of justice, and this aim can only be accomplished if our codes of procedure are framed on principles of orderly simplicity. Reform of procedure is always a ticklish business, for we

34

grow accustomed to the paths we have long trodden, however tortuous, and vested interests are apt to grow up around them. But the task must be undertaken from time to time if the vehicle of law is to keep pace with the changing requirements of the age. If you care to study Sir Walter Scott in the unfamiliar rôle of a technical lawyer—remember that he was a member of the Bar and for twenty-four years a Clerk of Court—you will find in the *Edinburgh Annual Register* of 1806 a remarkable dissertation by him on the changes then proposed in the administration of justice in Scotland, in which he discusses with acumen the principles which should govern all reforms of this nature.

The vast disturbance of the world war from which Western civilisation is only now emerging has brought about a new passion for peace and order. We have learnt that strife means not only disorder but also loss. The national strike in Great Britain in 1926 reinforced the lesson in the domestic sphere. No right-minded person can fail to note with satisfaction the steps now being taken towards industrial peace, which have for their goal the elimination of disorder from our economic system. There is great work here for the lawyer in aiding the accommodation of conflicting interests and bringing order out of chaos. For in the observance of the principles of law and order alone are to be found the conditions of national efficiency and prosperity.

Order, when all is said and done, is the true handmaid of justice and of liberty, the great causes to which we have sworn allegiance; and if the law fails to achieve order in our midst, then neither justice nor liberty can prevail.

3-2

LAW AND ETHICS

Inaugural Address delivered to the Associated Societies of the University of Edinburgh, 1933

JUST forty years have passed since I bade farewell to the classrooms of the University of Edinburgh, the proud possessor of a parchment which testified to the world at large that I had satisfied—or deluded—the examiners in the seven subjects which in those days were thought to comprise a liberal education. To-night I return to these halls of learning much less assured that I am a Master of Arts or indeed of any art, but with a new pride in the honour which you have conferred upon me by electing me to the presidentship of the Associated Societies of my Alma Mater. It is a high distinction, as I well realise, to hold an office which in the course of the past century has been adorned by such eminent precursors as Lord Brougham, Lord Moncreiff and Lord Ardmillan, of my own profession, and, in the sphere of more polite learning, Aytoun, Ruskin, Browning, Morley, Masson and Chesterton—all names so familiar that they have no need of conventional prefixes. It is a circumstance of special interest that my term of office will include your centenary year, an occasion which I understand you are already taking steps to mark with fitting celebrations.

I feel it to be all the more generous of you to have thus honoured me when I have to confess that during my days at the University I did not take the share which I ought to have taken in the life and work of the Societies —perhaps from a premonitory sense that I should have more than enough of discussion and debate in my later life.

Your secretary was good enough to send me for my admonition a copy of Professor Masson's presidential address of 1896. I learn from the words of wisdom of my old professor that for the composition of an essay such as I am offering you to-night there are three rules. The first is that the subject ought to be one which the author himself likes; the second is that there should be some novelty in its treatment; and the third is that there ought to be no introduction—the author should get down at once to his subject, without any beating about the bush.

So I shall not further transgress the third of these counsels of perfection, only adding that it will be for you to judge whether I have complied with the second; while as for the first, I can claim at once that my subject to-night, the relationship between law and ethics, is one which has always interested and attracted me.

The division of the whole field of human thought into compartments, which we designate with the specific names of religion, metaphysics, ethics, law, sociology, economics, and so forth, marks the first effort of our intelligence to master the vast domain of knowledge by a process of classification, the primary instinct of the orderly mind. *Divide et impera* is the inspiration of this process, and that it serves a useful end thus to isolate for the purposes of study the various departments of science and philosophy I should be the last to deny. But frontiers are always apt to become the occasion of controversy, if not of conflict, and the professor of each subject

37

is always prone to cast covetous eyes on the debatable territory which separates him from his neighbour, doubtless on the analogy of the legal maxim that it is the part of a good judge to amplify his jurisdiction. Much time and much labour have in consequence been wasted in seeking to delimit artificially the confines of the various provinces of thought, and the disputes of the rival competitors have often degenerated into mere futile logomachies. There comes to all of us a time when we feel that analysis has done its work and that synthesis is what we crave. We realise that life is really an organic whole and that, while for working purposes and by reason of the limits of our individual capacity arbitrary divisions of study and investigation are essential, we can never be satisfied unless we can relate our special work to wider conceptions of the world's activities and find its justification as contributory to universal progress. The truth of this is perhaps becoming better appreciated in these present times than ever before. The barriers between the sciences are showing a remarkable tendency to become impalpable. Chemistry and mathematics in their higher spheres are found to be branches of the same learning; the biologist and the politician are beginning to invoke each other's knowledge in the promotion of social services; and even those sworn foes of Victorian days, physical science and religion, are showing a tendency to kiss mutually. I may perhaps be allowed to congratulate my audience to-night on having been in the vanguard of this movement, for I take it that the conjunction of the very varied intellectual interests represented by the different societies which during the past hundred years have been members of this Association was not dictated solely by the shortage of accommodation in the University premises, but was also due to a recognition of the benefit to be gained from the meeting of men engaged in very diverse pursuits, and to an appreciation of the essential unity of all true learning.

I have noted with special satisfaction that the Scots Law Society is one among the present Associated Societies, for I venture to think that there is no subject the study of which benefits more than does the law from the liberalising influence of contact with other spheres of life and knowledge. It has always been a favourite reproach against the lawyer that his intellect is hidebound and his interests narrow, technical and professional. It is an odd reproach, for there is no profession which touches human life at so many points as the profession of the law. And yet the reproach has not been without some justification, for the legal mind in its absorption in formalism has an undoubted tendency to forget the spirit in the letter and to regard the law as an end in itself instead of merely a means to the much wider end of the well-being of human society.

The lawyer of these days can no longer afford to keep his eyes glued to his desk and to limit his intellectual horizon to the Law Reports and the textbooks. A change, at first almost unobserved, but now thrusting itself prominently on our attention, is taking place in the sphere assigned to law in the community. Formerly, apart from matters of crime, the law was chiefly concerned with the technique of real property, conveyancing and succession, and the domestic relations, the application to particular cases of fairly well-established principles of contract and delict, and the settlement of mercantile

39

disputes. Nowadays, largely as the result of the industrial revolution and its consequences, the law is being
made the instrument through the Legislature of vast
social and economic changes, and whether we like it or
not we have to recognise that the lawyer of the future
will have to accommodate himself to this altered outlook. The law reports themselves afford the best evidence of the change that is taking place. I wonder what
Stair or Erskine or Bell would have made of the last
volume of the Session Cases!

This growing use of the statute book as the vehicle
of a new political and social gospel raises some of the
most interesting problems in the mutual relations of law
and ethics. Perhaps I should at once explain that I am
confining myself to-night to the ethical aspect of law on
its civil as distinguished from its criminal side. The relations between the criminal law and morality raise
issues of a different order, and I do not propose to enter
upon the topic, which would lead me far afield, of the
legal conception of crime as contrasted with the moral
conception of wrong-doing or the religious conception
of sin—fascinating as that topic is.

It has always been recognised that the fields of law
and ethics closely adjoin each other. Their respective
areas never have been, and probably never can be, precisely delimited, for it would be more accurate to say
that they overlap rather than adjoin each other. The
lawyer and the moralist are both intimately concerned
with human conduct, but the verdict which each passes
on a particular case may be very different. The lawyer
may acquit where the moralist condemns. The main
difference between them is that the criteria of the law

are objective while those of the moralist are subjective. The primary concern of the lawyer is with acts and their consequences, with the conformity of conduct to external standards prescribed by authority. The moralist is preoccupied rather with motives and objects and with the estimation of conduct as satisfying the conscience.

But while this broad distinction is true, the contacts between 'ethics and the law are constant and close. Historically they both derive from an origin in the remote past when their spheres were not differentiated, and to this day they share many conceptions in common. The Courts are constantly discussing questions of motive and good faith, essentially ethical topics, and the moralist no less frequently finds himself considering the problems of individual conduct in relation to general law. The Lord Chancellor of Great Britain is not only the head of the judicial hierarchy, but he is also the Keeper of the King's Conscience. My object to-night is to show that that picturesque conjunction is symbolic of a fundamental unity, and that, widely different as the spheres of law and of morality may to outward semblance appear, there is, nevertheless, behind their differences an essential sympathy and identity of aim.

From the broadest point of view I find the relationship between law and ethics most significantly attested in the fact that Courts of Law exist for the administration of justice and that justice is one of the cardinal virtues of moral philosophy. But, you will say, the justice of the Law Courts is a very different thing from the ideal virtue of Aristotle's Ethics. That is true, and yet I maintain that the ultimate justification of the law is to be found, and can only be found, in moral considerations.

You will have noticed that all our early writers on law seek to justify its precepts as based either on divine revelation or on the moral and rational nature of man. Let me commend you to read the first title of Stair's *Institutions of the Law of Scotland*, wherein he treats of the common principles of law, if you wish to see the lofty claims which the father of Scots law made for his science. No doubt there is a prosaic school which has sought to explain all laws as the product solely of expediency and utility, but I have always found their doctrine as unconvincing as it is uninspiring. The truth is that in the ultimate analysis the basis of the law is ethical, at first perhaps dimly perceived and concealed under much that is irrelevant, but increasingly realised as civilisation advances and becomes self-conscious. I have instanced already the profession which, by the inscription over their doors, our Courts make to the world that they are temples of justice, a conception which the law shares with moral philosophy; but the coincidence of their vocabulary goes much further than this, for they share also such words of fundamental ethical significance as "right" and "wrong", which are as often on the lips of the lawyer as they are on those of the moral philosopher. The appeal of law is in the last resort to the conscience of mankind, and to commend itself to our conscience the law must be righteous and just. When Justinian, at the outset of his *Institutes*, proclaimed that the precepts of the law were these—to live honestly, to injure no one, and to give every man his due—he used the language of ethics in order to state the true aim of the great system of law which he formulated and which still provides the rules of conduct for a great portion of the human race. And so with our own institutional writers. I have already referred to Stair. Let me quote also Bankton who, on the first page of his *Institute*, describes law as "the rule of voluntary actions of rational beings, prescribing what ought to be done or forborne; what it commands is just, right, and good, and what it forbids is unjust, wrong, or evil". And Erskine in his *Institute* (i, i, 3) declares that "as the end of law is an equal distribution of justice, on which the happiness of every society depends, all laws ought to be in themselves just". If I had not told you their source, you might well have imagined that my quotations were derived from a treatise on ethics instead of from two well-known law books.

All this you may say is very fine and high-sounding, but what has it to do with law as we encounter it in our daily lives? What great ethical principle is involved in the regulations of the Burgh Police Act, the provisions of the Income Tax Acts, or the relics of "Dora" which still hamper our freedom? The answer is that in every civilised community there must be a large number of rules of conduct of a purely conventional character which have as little ethical content as the rules of a cricket club—though even these, it would appear, may be provocative of much feeling and may evoke criticism of their justice. I am not concerned to deny that a large part of the law lies outside the sphere of morals and is the product of mere expediency and convenience, just as there is a large part of ethics which lies outside the sphere of law, for there are many things which morality enjoins but with which the law takes no concern. It is in their principles and aims that law and ethics find a meeting ground rather than in the particular rules of conduct which each prescribes.

Even in rules of the law which might appear to be morally indifferent, such as those to which I have alluded, there is an ethical element. They may seem often to be merely artificial and irksome, but they are prescribed, ostensibly at least, in the interest of the community, in order to ensure the order and safety of our daily lives. In approving or condemning them we constantly apply ethical standards as well as the standards of utility. How often we hear some rule complained of because it is not "fair", which just means that in some way it offends our sense of justice. And the sanction which lies behind even the most trivial obligations laid upon us by the law is truly an ethical one, the sense that it is right to obey them because they have presumably been imposed for the common benefit, and, while we may sometimes not believe in their wisdom or necessity, yet we still feel somehow that it is wrong to disobey them. If you read the debates on any measure which comes before Parliament, you will find that its promoters and its opponents alike constantly invoke moral considerations of justice and fairness in supporting or attacking it.

To my mind the ethical aspect of legislation is of supreme importance, and more than ever now that Parliament is concerning itself to an increasing extent with matters which were formerly regarded as outside its sphere. There is nothing more detrimental to the moral order of society than that its laws should not commend themselves to the conscience of the people. We have had an object lesson from across the Atlantic of what it means when an Act of the Legislature is derided and flouted and its evasion is regarded as a subject for jest or a source of profit. It was doubtless with this example so near to his hand that Dr Nicholas Murray Butler, the courageous and outspoken president of Columbia University, declared that "The law whose infraction calls out the overwhelming disapproval of public opinion is a good law. The law that does not call out that disapproval is a bad law. When conduct and the law are at odds the fault may be with the law."

It is no new complaint that the laws which the Legislature enacts often fail to be consonant with the principles of justice. It is now over forty years since Herbert Spencer, in his volume on *Justice*, exclaimed that "daily legislation betrays little anxiety that each shall have that which belongs to him, but great anxiety that he shall have that which belongs to somebody else". Perhaps it is fortunate for that eminent philosopher that he did not survive to these present days. If he had, he would have had to retain permanently the cotton wool with which, his biographer tells us, he used to stuff his ears against unwelcome communications.

We have no right to point the finger of scorn at the Prohibition laws of the States when we have in our own country laws which a large majority of the people think it quite legitimate to disregard. The whole system of our laws against betting and gaming, in its futility and disingenuousness, calls out for candid and courageous reform, and we look forward to the recommendations of the very able committee which is now examining the whole matter in the hope that means may be evolved to bring the law into a shape acceptable to the enlightened conscience of society.

45

Law and Other Things

So long as the makers of our statutes confined themselves to the topics which formerly were regarded as
suited to legislative treatment, there was less risk of the
law being brought into contempt; but when Parliament
proceeds to deal with all the details of our daily lives
there must inevitably be grave danger of the law losing
its moral sanction. Such measures must often fail to obtain the approval of large sections of the community
who are opposed to their policy or injured by their interference, and those who dislike them do not hesitate
to do their best to frustrate their operation. A spirit
most damaging to the morale of the body politic is thus
engendered. When a community ceases to be "law-
abiding" in spirit as well as in fact, a very serious social
degeneration soon ensues. I was struck in the States
with the lack of respect which was entertained for what
was rather contemptuously designated "only statute
law" as compared with the almost exaggerated respect
expressed for the common law. But I fear that this
attitude towards the statute book must be difficult to
avoid in a country which, as I am credibly informed,
has in a space of five years produced no fewer than
60,000 Acts. Before such achievements the Mother of
Parliaments must hide her diminished head, but our
own record of some 2070 statutes passed between 1895
and 1930, covering 15,540 pages of print in the Law
Reports edition, may make us at least pause to reflect
whether we are not tending in the same direction.

I have said enough, however, on the ethics of legislation, a subject perhaps unsuited to judicial treatment,
for are not the judgments of the Courts full of tributes—
I trust, sincere—to the wisdom of Parliament which no

occupant of the Bench ventures to question? I only desired to make my point that the essence and the justification of all good legislation must be ethical, or, in
other words, that it ought to be satisfactory to the conscience of the community.

I now turn to the ethical aspect of that great body of
legal principles which we call the common law and
which has grown up by a slow process of evolution in
answer to the needs of civilised life. Here we find the
collective wisdom of all those who, in determining the
controversies to which human relationships give rise,
have sought to ensure that right should be done as between man and man. In this spontaneous growth we
may find much clearer evidence than in Parliamentary
enactments of the operation of ethical forces, for among
the motives which have inspired the formation and the
acceptance of the principles of the common law the
motive of justice, that is, of fair dealing, has undoubtedly
been the predominant factor. Of course, you can point
to many defects and shortcomings, for man is constantly
deflected from the paths of virtue by self-interest and
ignorance, and those from whom we have inherited our
common law have not been exempt from these and
other human frailties. I am not so complacent as to echo
the dictum of Mr Justice Bacon, in a case in 1670, when
he roundly declared that "law and conscience are one
and the same". But when all is said and done the common law has always set justice before it as its aim.

That it does not always achieve this aim is unhappily
evidenced by the contrast so often drawn in popular
parlance between *law* and *justice*. "It may be the law",
says the indignant citizen smarting under a judicial

decision, "but it is not justice." And in more dignified language how frequently do we find judges saying that they regretfully find themselves compelled by the law to pronounce a particular decision which obviously offends their sense of fairness and giving a strong hint that it is for the Legislature to intervene and redress the law's injustice. But in these very complaints and criticisms I find my thesis vindicated, for they show that the public and the judiciary alike instinctively apply a moral standard of justice to the law, to which they expect it to conform, and that they regard the law as defective in so far as it fails to satisfy their conscience. It was one of the greatest masters of our law, Lord Macnaghten, who said: "It is a public scandal when the law is forced to uphold a dishonest act."

Fortunately, for our reassurance, it is the special virtue of the common law that it possesses powers of growth and adaptation to the changing conditions of society and to new standards of good conduct. As Mr Justice Holmes puts it in his classic treatise on *The Common Law*: "The law is always approaching, and never reaching, consistency. It is forever adopting new principles from life at one end, and it always retains old ones from history at the other, which have not yet been absorbed or sloughed off. It will become entirely consistent only when it ceases to grow." Judges, as they often remind us, have to administer the law as they find it, but all the time they are themselves slowly shaping and developing it. In almost every case, except the very plainest, it would be possible to decide the issue either way with reasonable legal justification. It must be so in view of the large number of decisions which are arrived at only by a majority of judicial votes, for I assume that the dissenting judges are just as convinced of the soundness of their law as are their brethren in the majority. It is thus clear that the judiciary are constantly confronted with the necessity of making a choice among the doctrines of the law alleged to be applicable to the particular case, and the choice which they make in the particular instance results inevitably in the expansion or restriction of the doctrine applied or rejected. It is at this point that what may, I think, quite properly be called ethical considerations operate and ought to operate. I hope I shall be acquitted of any suggestion that judges should allow themselves to be swayed by sentiment to wrest the law, and I should deprecate as strongly as any the admission of the motives of the social reformer into the counsels of the Bench. I am no friend of that spurious kind of equity which Lord Bramwell robustly denounces as consisting in "A disregard of general principles and general rules in the endeavour to do justice more or less fanciful in particular cases". Other eminent judges in equally vigorous language, to which I am quite prepared to subscribe, have condemned the impropriety of allowing other than purely legal considerations to influence the decisions of the Courts. But when, as happens from time to time, the law itself presents a choice, and when it is a question whether one or other principle is to be applied, then it seems to me that it is impossible, as it is undesirable, that the decision should not have regard to the ethical motive of promoting justice. I may here make another, and perhaps indiscreet, quotation from Mr Justice Holmes: "The very considerations", he says, "which judges most rarely mention, and always with an apology, are the secret root from which the law draws all the juices of life. I mean, of course, considerations of what is expedient for the community concerned."

Let me give an example of what I mean, for it is always so much more easy to understand a concrete case than an abstract principle.

I shall choose for my illustration a very human problem which has actually come before the Courts both in Scotland and in England. It is a well-established rule that you cannot get damages for an injury done to you through another person's negligence if you have by your own negligence contributed to the casualty. This is what lawyers call the doctrine of contributory negligence, and it seems quite a fair, common-sense rule. And there is another rule which lawyers, with their fondness for Latin, express in the maxim *volenti non fit injuria*—you cannot complain of an injury which you have brought upon yourself. That, too, seems quite just and proper. With these two principles of the common law in your minds, how would you deal with a case in which a person is injured through voluntarily exposing himself to danger in order to save another from being injured by a third party's negligence? The Court of Session had to deal with this very question in 1897, and that it raised a nice point is best shown by the fact that three judges took one view and four took the other (*Wilkinson* v. *Kinneil Cannel and Coking Co., Ltd.*, 1897, 24 R. 1001). What had happened was that a truck had been negligently allowed to run away down an incline and was about to collide with another standing truck on which a man and a boy were trimming coal. The boy saw the truck coming, jumped off his own truck, and succeeded in stopping the on-coming truck by spragging one of its wheels with a pit prop. In so doing the boy was injured. If he had not done what he did, he himself would have escaped injury, but there would have been a serious collision between the running and the standing truck and his fellow-workman on the latter might have been seriously injured, if not killed. All the judges obviously thought that the boy had done a meritorious and courageous act, but three of them took the view that as he had chosen voluntarily to place himself in danger without any legal obligation to do so he could not complain of the consequences. The four other judges held that there was no principle of law which prevented the boy from recovering damages. Lord Young, who, as one would expect, was of the majority, said: "If it is proved that there was fault on the part of the defenders in having that wagon sent along that lye at a dangerous rate of speed and that the pursuer's son interposed, although not in pursuance of a legal duty, but only as doing what was right and reasonable in the circumstances and thereby met with an accident, he is not precluded from claiming damages because he was in safety and put himself out of safety in order to save another." And Lord Kinnear, also of the majority, said that he was not "prepared to hold as matter of law that if one is exposed to danger by the fault of another he has failed to exercise reasonable care and prudence for his own safety merely because he has paid regard to the safety of another as well as to his own and so brought himself into further peril which he might have escaped if he had thought of nobody but himself".

Law and Other Things

An English judge, Mr Justice Swift, found that decision helpful when he had to decide a case where a man and his wife were standing in a shop when a skylight was broken by the negligence of contractors who were carrying out repairs and some of the glass fell and struck the husband causing him a severe shock (*Brandon* v. *Osborne, Garrett and Co.*, [1924] 1 K.B. 548). The wife was not herself struck, but seeing her husband in danger instinctively clutched his arm and tried to pull him away from the spot. In so doing she strained herself and suffered injury. The judge observed: "I do not say that there is a legal duty to risk one's own life to save that of a stranger; indeed, I should unhesitatingly say there was not; but there may be a nearer approach to such a duty to save the life of one's child or wife or husband. In any event there may be a moral obligation which would so act upon the mind of any ordinary reasonable man that he would instinctively rush to the assistance of one in immediate peril through the negligent act of a third party." In the result it was held that the devoted wife had not been guilty of any contributory negligence and she got £25 damages. Finally, just to show that my citations are up to date, I observed in last Wednesday's *Times* that a jury returned a verdict for £150 damages at Leicester Assizes in favour of a man who, seeing a little girl in danger of being run over by a motor lorry, dashed from the footpath and pulled her out of the way, but was himself severely injured (*Gregory* v. *Miller*, 8 February 1933; *The Times*, 9 February 1933). I observe that Mr Justice Macnaghten is reported to have said: "When you see a small child in peril you do not think of anything else." That is an echo of the

statelier language of Chief Justice Cockburn who in
1880 observed in one of his judgments that "the im-
pulsive desire to save human life when in peril is one of
the most beneficial instincts of humanity".

This particular problem of the law, so far as I know,
has never yet been considered by the House of Lords
and, therefore, it would be most unfitting for me to say
whether I think these cases were rightly decided or not.
I leave the question to the jury of my audience. But this
at least I may say, and I am sure you will agree with me,
that these cases of the judicial recognition of the moral
virtue of altruism demonstrate my thesis that, within the
law, ethical considerations do influence the judgments
of our Courts when they are free to give effect to them,
and you will probably also think that they ought to
do so.

The occasions when such problems present themselves
are probably not so frequent nowadays in this country
where the law has reached a high stage of development
and of adaptation to all the phases of civilised life, but
in other less settled parts of the Empire the judicial duty
of so applying the law as to promote "peace, order, and
good government" is a matter not only of conscience
but of obligation. The cases which come from remote
regions to the Privy Council often afford examples of the
necessity of resort to the principles of justice where no
positive law is available. Even in the highly civilised
legal system of India I find in the Letters Patent con-
stituting the High Courts of the Provinces a reference to
"the law or equity and rule of good conscience" to be
applied, while the Civil Procedure Code expressly
enacts that "nothing in this Code shall be deemed to

limit or otherwise affect the inherent power of the Court to make such orders as may be necessary for the ends of justice". After all, there is probably no better instance historically of the contest between the letter and the spirit of the law than is exhibited in the secular contest across the Border between law and equity, now happily composed. Though no such contest has marred the history of Scots law, we can trace throughout its development the same antagonism and the same process of accommodation between the rigour of the rule and the claims of conscience. Here, as in England, the law is a living organism constantly readjusting itself to its environment, and it is in that power of constant readjustment that its supreme merit resides, as compared with the stereotyped codes of other nations.

And now I must conclude these random reflections. I do not profess to have placed before you any thought-out theory of the relation between the legal and the ethical view of life. My purpose has been the more modest one of trying to show you that there is no ultimate or necessary conflict between these two ways of looking at things, and that the surest hope of promoting the welfare of the individual and of the community lies in the wise co-operation of law and ethics.

LAW AND RELIGION

*Inaugural Address delivered to the Edinburgh
Philosophical Institution, October 1933*

WHEN you honoured me with an invitation
to speak to you to-night in this historic
Assembly Hall, I could not but recall that
within these walls thirty-six years ago I listened to my
father as he delivered his Moderator's address. And so,
as I cast about for a subject of discourse, it occurred to
me that I might not unfittingly discuss with you the
associations and the contrasts between the two great
branches of human thought which my father's vocation
and my own represent. My selection of a topic, however, has more than a merely personal or sentimental
justification. For centuries law and religion have been
the staples of Edinburgh's intellectual commerce and
the whole of Scottish history has been coloured by the
relation which has subsisted between them in our
national life. Nor do I forget that by a happy coincidence the eminent judge who occupies the chair is at
once a Doctor of Divinity and a Doctor of Laws, thus
providing in his own person an interesting illustration
of the reconciliation of the law and the prophets.

Between the concepts of law and religion, as we now
see them, there may well appear to be a wide gulf fixed.
Law, we are reminded, is concerned with external behaviour, with acts and forbearances and their consequences or, as it has been put, with "rules of civil con-

duct enforced by the State". Its sanctions are secular. It does not presume to deal with things of the spirit, but confines itself to mundane matters of contract and delict, property and succession, and the maintenance of order by the suppression of crime. As a modern writer has expressed it, criminal law "has no mission beyond the preservation of physical quiet. The peace of the soul is not its concern", and civil law is equally indifferent to the spiritual side of life. Anything less reminiscent of the language of inspiration than a modern statute it would be difficult to conceive. Here all is hard and practical. Religion, on the other hand, concerns itself not with the things which are seen and temporal, but with the things which are not seen and eternal. Its essence is to be found in faith and devotion, in an attitude of the soul, though, no doubt, by works faith may be made perfect. The dictates of religion are not those of this world and its rewards and punishments lie hereafter.

Yet far apart as would thus seem to be the spheres of religion and law in our day, historically this was not always so. Indeed, these apparent opposites spring from a common origin in the human mind. They both alike share that mysterious word "ought", which is significant of so much that is distinctive of man's higher life and which ever reminds us that we owe to a power outside ourselves the obligation to obey the commands of duty, that "stern daughter of the voice of God". Religion, after all, means etymologically only something by which we are bound, which is also the root conception of law. The duties which the law prescribes have by a slow process of evolution separated themselves from

those which religion inculcates; but the obligations of
religion and of law were originally indistinguishable;
they derived from a common source and, as I shall show,
there are countries where they still remain to a large
extent identical, while in all countries they retain traces
of their early association. I put forward no pretension
to being learned in the researches which have been
made by students of primitive religion or in the science
of legal origins. I have no doubt that those who have
pursued these studies could give you a much more
critical and reliable disquisition on my theme. I have to
content myself with the obvious commonplaces of the
theologian and the lawyer, but these will serve my purpose quite well. And let me say at once, to remove all
apprehension, that the purpose I have in view is not to
stir again the embers, happily almost extinct in Scotland,
of the age-long controversy regarding the relations of
Church and State. My purpose is rather to trace the
religious element in law and the legal element in
religion.

It is perhaps the earliest, as it is one of the most inveterate, of human instincts to refer to some supernatural agency outside ourselves the control of our lives
and destinies. In primitive times this agency is invoked
by the ruler as the source of the laws which he prescribes
and the decisions which he pronounces, by the medicine
man as the spirit to be influenced by spells and incantations, by the priest as the dispenser of good and
evil who must be propitiated by worship and sacrifices.
The deity whom the savage instinctively conceives is at
once his lawgiver, his physician, and his providence, a
power to be obeyed, to be propitiated, to be worshipped.

57

Law and Other Things

In the famous first chapter of Sir Henry Maine's classical work on *Ancient Law*, he speaks of "the persuasion which clung so long and so tenaciously to the human mind of a divine influence underlying and supporting every relation of life, every social institution. In early law, and amid the rudiments of political thought, symptoms of this belief meet us on all sides. A supernatural presidency is supposed to consecrate and keep together all the cardinal institutions of those times—the State, the Race, the Family." Speaking a little further on of the early codes of Eastern and Western law, he points out that they "mingled up religious, civil and merely moral ordinances without any regard to differences in their essential character; and this is consistent with all we know of early thought from other sources— the severance of law from morality, and of religion from law belonging very distinctly to the later stages of mental progress".

Among all peoples of whom we possess early records, we find traces of the belief that the law is in some way divinely inspired. "Themis", the Homeric word for a judicial award, was personified in the Greek mythology as a goddess, the daughter of Heaven and Earth, the spouse of Zeus, and the mother, according to Hesiod, of good laws, justice, and peace. The dooms of our Anglo-Saxon forefathers equally derived their authority from the mysterious source of supernatural inspiration to which they were ascribed. In Rome, even after the idea of law in its modern sense had developed, we still find a large area of human conduct ruled by what was known as "fas"—"the will of the gods—the laws given by heaven for men on earth". Breach of what was "fas"

58

rendered the offender *impius* and entailed religious penalties which had serious social consequences: such breach was a sin which required to be expiated rather than a crime to be punished.

Perhaps the most striking extant instance of the identification of law with religion is to be found among the Mohammedans. "In Islam"—as Viscount Bryce tells us in his illuminating essay on *The Relations of Law and Religion*, to which I am much indebted—"In Islam, Law is Religion and Religion is Law, because both have the same source and an equal authority, being both contained in the same divine revelation." The Koran contains for the Mohammedan the revelation of "a monarch both temporal and spiritual, Mahomet, the Prophet of God", a revelation which covers "the whole sphere of man's thought and action. Being divine it is unerring and unchangeable." Obedience to the law is still for the Mohammedan not a matter merely of ethical duty or of social expediency, but a matter of religion. In his account of the great Mohammedan University of El Azhar at Cairo, Viscount Bryce describes a system of education resulting from this identification of law and religion which seems very strange to us of the Western world, where we have long ago learned the undesirability of confining education within the bonds of creed. But at least the teaching at El Azhar is thorough. One who aspires to be a kadi or judge of the Sacred Law must undergo a course of fourteen years' training, while a *mufti* or doctor of the law must spend an even longer time at the university.

In India to this day a large part of Hindu family law is regarded as of divine origin. Among its main sources are the Vedas, which are believed to contain the very words of the Deity, and the Codes or Institutes of Manu and other sacred texts which embody the recollections of the precepts of God handed down by the sages of antiquity. The law has been in large part developed by commentators on these Codes, whose works have acquired the highest authority. Only the other day I took part in the hearing of a case in the Privy Council where we had to consider a question deeply embedded in the religious life of the Hindus. It related to the power of a widow to adopt a son to her deceased husband. The adoption of a son has important civil consequences in India in the matter of succession to property, but we were reminded that its religious significance is of even greater importance. In the judgment prepared by my learned colleague, Sir George Lowndes, you will find extensive quotations from the Code of Manu attesting the religious element in the Brahminical law which it was our duty to ascertain and apply. It seems strange to read in a modern law report such a passage as this: "The father by the birth of a son discharges his debt to his progenitors; through him he attains immortality; by a son a man obtains victory over all people; by a son's son he enjoys immortality; and afterwards by the son of that grandson he reaches the solar abode; a son is called 'putra' because he delivers his father from 'put' [that is, from Hades]. In the Dharma Sutra of Bandhayana, which is probably older than the Christian era, the formula prescribed for adoption is: 'I take thee for the fulfilment of my religious duties: I take thee to continue the line of my ancestors'." Thus, where a Hindu has no son of his own, adoption is a matter of vital concern in order that there may be someone to perform the necessary ceremonial rites for him and secure for him and his ancestors those spiritual benefits which are denied to the sonless. In the same month the Judicial Committee decided that they could not proceed with a case relating to the possession of a plot of land in Oudh because it involved a question of the dedication of the land to a certain idol and the idol or his representative had not been made a party to the suit. So closely is law interwoven with religion in India, as these two illustrations show, that one of the highest Courts of the realm, sitting in Downing Street in London, has to this day constantly to have regard in its decisions to ordinances that are divine rather than secular.

But, of course, the example of the intermingling of law with religion that is most familiar to us all is to be found in the Old Testament. The first five books composing the Pentateuch are predominantly law books. Lord Coke claimed Moses as "the first reporter and writer of law in the world"; and Sir Frederick Pollock says of the leading case of Zelophehad's Daughters that it is the earliest recorded decision which is still of authority. You remember how, when these five young women, who to-day would doubtless be in the vanguard of the feminist movement, claimed a right of succession to their father who had left no sons, they pleaded so movingly that Moses brought their cause before the Lord and judgment in their favour was pronounced by the Lord Himself: "The daughters of Zelophehad speak right: thou shalt surely give them a possession of an inheritance among their father's brethren; and thou shalt cause the inheritance of their father to pass unto them."

Law and Other Things

Here you have an admirable example of a civil dispute determined by divine law. But not only were particular judgments divinely inspired. The whole law of the ancient Hebrews was God-given. The two "tables of testimony, tables of stone" which Moses received on Mount Sinai, and which contained the ten commandments which to this day we repeat in church, were "written with the finger of God". They present a most interesting stage in the development of human institutions, when the distinction between law and religion scarcely existed. Several of the commandments are now part of the criminal law—"thou shalt not kill", "thou shalt not steal"—but others of them remain in the sphere of religion. It is no part of the law of the land that we should honour our parents or refrain from coveting our neighbour's property. It is wrong, but it is not illegal, not to honour our parents or to covet our neighbour's goods. Yet in the ten commandments these matters which we now relegate to distinct spheres were all alike made the subject of positive law.

"Sin" and "crime" now convey to our minds two quite distinct conceptions, the one subjective, the other objective; but the distinction is of comparatively late growth, and they have still a meeting ground. The same act may still be both a sin and a crime, but we have learned to discriminate between its two aspects. We punish the crime; we leave the sin to be answered for before another tribunal.

The Pentateuch, indeed, contains a full legal code of conduct, prescribing rules in the most minute detail for all branches of human activity. Its sanitary regulations almost rival the provisions of our present-day Public

62

Health and Burgh Police Acts. And the whole was invested with divine authority: it was binding because it was the law of God divinely revealed to His chosen people. The rules there laid down have lost their sanction for us, although I may remind the lawyers in my audience that certain texts in Leviticus still form part of the law of Scotland, but the important thing to realise is that in the quite advanced stage of civilisation reached by the Israelites the conception of law was still the conception of a series of divine ordinances. Law was sacred, not secular. In the words of Moses: "Behold, I have taught you statutes and judgments, even as the Lord my God commanded me" (Deut. iv. 5).

It is remarkable that in the Old Testament not only were what we should now describe as crimes treated as sins, but a whole category of civil wrongs were also so treated. Let me quote the sixth chapter of Leviticus: "If a soul sin, and commit a trespass against the Lord, and lie unto his neighbour in that which was delivered him to keep, or in fellowship, or in a thing taken away by violence, or hath deceived his neighbour; or have found that which was lost, and lieth concerning it, and sweareth falsely; in any of all these that a man doeth, sinning therein: then it shall be, because he hath sinned, and is guilty, that he shall restore that which he took violently away, or the thing which he hath deceitfully gotten, or that which was delivered him to keep, or the lost thing which he found, or all that about which he hath sworn falsely; he shall even restore it in the principal, and shall add the fifth part more thereto, and give it unto him to whom it appertaineth, in the day of his trespass offering. And he shall bring his trespass offering

63

unto the Lord, a ram without blemish out of the flock, with thy estimation, for a trespass offering, unto the priest: and the priest shall make an atonement for him before the Lord: and it shall be forgiven him for any thing of all that he hath done in trespassing therein." Here you have a whole group of civil wrongs relating to deposit or bailment, partnership, deceit, trover and detinue, and trespass treated as the subject not only of legal reparation but also of spiritual atonement and forgiveness.

Have you ever considered the extent to which the whole of the Bible is permeated with legal phraseology? The very titles of the Old Testament and the New Testament are legal, for the word "testament" means a covenant, or bond entered into between two persons, in this instance between God and man. The whole conception of the relationship between God and man is legal. God enters into a covenant with man whereby He contracts that in consideration of man performing certain stipulated duties He will bestow upon him certain rewards. The God of the Old Testament is essentially a lawgiver and a judge, and it is this aspect of the Deity that is constantly emphasised. Even in the Psalms, one of the least legal of the books of the Old Testament, I found the words "judge" and "judgment" employed over eighty times, the word "statutes" twenty times, and the word "law" some thirty times. In the new dispensation of the Gospels the formal legal aspect of religion has fallen into disrepute, but the terminology of the law still survives. It is only a new content that is given to the conception of the law. Love, we are told, is henceforth to be the fulfilling of the law. But the relations of God and man are still described in legal phraseology, or at least by legal metaphors. Man is still called upon to obey the laws of God; our Lord is described as our advocate; and the final climax of human destiny is the Day of Judgment. The topic would be an attractive one to pursue. I have no doubt it has been pursued by theologians, but my studies have not lain in theology. The point I wish to make is that the whole fabric of the sacred books of our own religion is interwoven with the phraseology of law and that legal terms are used throughout to express its most solemn conceptions. While nowadays we distinguish between the duties of religion and the duties of law, in Bible times the distinction was only beginning to be appreciated. Perhaps the distinction first began to be realised as regards that least divine department of law which is concerned with taxation. It is difficult to believe in the inspiration of the income tax, and while we are enjoined in the Gospels to render unto Caesar the things that are Caesar's, this would seem to be reckoned a secular rather than a sacred observance. If you care to pursue this subject of the legal element in the Bible, I may refer you to two books which are not very well known— *Leading Cases in the Bible*, by David Werner Amram, of the Philadelphia Bar, and *Studies in Biblical Law*, by Harold M. Wiener, a barrister of Lincoln's Inn.

There is probably no country in the world which can exhibit so remarkable a blending of theology and law as we find in the history of Scotland, especially in the sixteenth, seventeenth and eighteenth centuries. The political controversies and contests of Scotland in former times were ecclesiastical and theological to a degree

which to us in these Laodicean days seems almost in-
comprehensible. The language of the perfervid religion
of Knox and the Covenanters is permeated with legality,
and the whole relations of God and man are conceived
in terms of legal transactions. The matter could not be
better put than it is by Miss Haldane in her latest book,
The Scotland of Our Fathers, published only this week.
"Calvin", she points out, "had been trained in the law,
and his doctrine was above all things legal and logical
and thus it appealed to the Scottish people and gave
immense power to the clergy and other office-bearers
who were appointed to carry out its teaching and discipline. A logical, systematic view of life permeated the
whole social outlook; its influence on religion was profound and the very language of religion became technically legal." I think it is possible to find an explanation
of this curious phenomenon in our history. It seems to
me to be the outcome of one of the most characteristic
and one of the most persistent qualities of the Scottish
genius, its instinctive love of principle, which has earned
for us an unenviable reputation for metaphysical disputatiousness. The Scot has always had a distaste for the
easy-going and untidy opportunism of his southern
neighbours. With him the principle has always been the
thing and no argument contents him which does not go
back to first principles. The history of Scots law affords
an admirable instance of this tendency. In early times,
and before the national consciousness had awakened,
such law as there was in Scotland was English law.
Then came the time when the enmity between England
and Scotland turned the commerce of Scotland towards
the Continent and not only her commerce in com-

modities but also her commerce in ideas. The young
men of those days who were destined for careers in
politics and law frequented the great Universities of the
Continent—Bologna, Paris, Utrecht, Leyden, and many
others, in whose archives their names may still be found
inscribed. There they came into contact with the great
teachers of the Roman law, then flourishing in all the
splendour of its renaissance. This majestic system at once
appealed to them by its logical precision and its philosophical principles, and they became imbued with its
doctrine. When they returned home, they brought back
with them the learning which they had acquired at the
feet of the famous civilians of the Continent, and as a
result the law of Scotland became impregnated with
the principles and the spirit of the Roman law. The influence of this importation remains with us to the present
day. While outwardly in many respects our law does not
differ substantially, except in certain departments, from
the law of England, its historical background is profoundly different. What I wish to emphasise is that the
ready and almost ardent reception which the Roman
law met with in Scotland was due to the sympathetic
reaction which it evoked in the Scottish mind. Here
was a great logical system ready to hand which seemed
to satisfy all the cravings of the Scot for a code of law
based on eternal principles of reason and justice—no
haphazard collection of precedents, but a philosophical
and rational structure.

The same natural instinct which in the legal world
found such congenial satisfaction in the Roman law as
taught in the great Universities of the Continent found
in the theological world an equal satisfaction in the

Genevan doctrines of Calvin. The first edition of Calvin's
Institutes was published in 1536. Even the title of his
work was borrowed from the law. And his whole system
of religious doctrine was essentially legal. It was based
upon the central principle of the absolute sovereignty of
God and the utter worthlessness of man; its fundamental
tenets were determinism and predestination. However
much our hearts may nowadays recoil from what
Froude describes as the paradox "that the creatures who
suffer under the accursed necessity of committing sin are
infinitely guilty in God's eyes for doing what they have
no power to avoid and may therefore be justly punished
in everlasting fire", nevertheless the rigid and uncompromising logic of the Calvinistic theology unquestionably possessed an extraordinary fascination for the Scot
of the Reformation period. The certainty of its principles, however harsh, and its unassailable, if brutal,
coherence seemed to him to furnish a sure and reliable
guide for human life and to satisfy his craving for a religion which should be able to justify itself at the bar of
reason. As we now look back upon it, it was a hideous
system, but its very vigour and harshness appealed to the
robust and Puritanical element in the Scottish character,
revolted by the latitudinarian abuses of the pre-Refor-
mation Church. It may seem an odd paradox of history
that while Scotland was adopting in her legal system the
doctrines of the Roman law, she was in her religious life
combating and rejecting with equal vigour the doctrines
of the Roman Church. But the paradox disappears
when we reflect that the law of Rome had through the
ages preserved its integrity while the Church of Rome
had sadly degenerated from the primitive faith.

Law and Religion

Perhaps the most distinctive feature of Calvinism from the legal point of view was that it once more practically obliterated the distinction between sin and crime, thereby reverting to the Old Testament doctrine. The Law and the Gospel were one and the same. You remember John Buchan's delightful description in *Witch Wood* of the meeting of ministers in 1644 in the Manse of Woodilee, when the Rev. Mungo Muirhead declaimed that "The Solemn League and Covenant bound all Scotland in a pact with the Lord" and that "there would be soon that comfortable sight which had been foretold by their godly Fathers, a uniform Kirk and a pure Gospel established by law from London to the Orkneys and a covenanted Sion to which all the peoples of the earth would go up." " Mr Muirhead was eloquent, for he repeated a peroration which he had once used in the General Assembly." Under the dispensation of these seventeenth-century days the true faith was the concern of Parliament. On 26 May 1690 we read that the Confession of Faith was "produced and read in the presence of Their Majesties' High Commissioner and the Estates of Parliament and being voted and approved was ordained to be recorded in the books of Parliament".

Probably the most illuminating case on the change which has come over opinion in modern times in the relation between law and religion is the famous judgment of the House of Lords in *Bowman* v. *The Secular Society, Ltd.*, in 1917. The question was whether the law would support a bequest in favour of a society whose professed object was to promote the principles of rationalism and whose tenets were treated as involving a denial of the Christian religion. Lord Finlay, then Lord Chan-

69

cellor, held that the legacy could not be upheld, but his colleagues all took the contrary view. Statements by many great judges were cited to the effect that Christianity is part and parcel of the law of the land, and the great names of Lord Chief Justice Kenyon, Chief Justice Hale, Lord Chancellor Hardwicke, and others were invoked. The famous pronouncement of Chief Justice Best in 1828 was quoted: "There is no act which Christianity forbids that the law will not reach: if it were otherwise, Christianity would not be, as it has always been held to be, part of the law of England." A modern writer's comment on this passage is brief but pointed. "This is nonsense. For example, a man may do a selfish and malicious act on his own land on purpose to injure his neighbour and the common law does not forbid it, so long as it is not a public nuisance. In like manner he may take advantage of the un-Christian doctrine of *caveat emptor*." In *The Secular Society's* case Lord Sumner more courteously dismisses these celebrated pronouncements as rhetoric, not law. Henry Crabb Robinson disposes of the matter by an anecdote of Rolfe, afterwards Lord Chancellor Cranworth, who, on someone remarking that "Christianity is part and parcel of the law of the land", rejoined: "Were you ever employed to draw an indictment against a man for not loving his neighbour as himself?" Stair puts it even better and more pithily when he quotes the Scottish proverb: "We cannot poind for unkindness."

But the traces of the ancient identity between law and religion die hard. The law has long ceased to rely for proof of guilt on an appeal to divine revelation by the ordeals of hot iron, of water, of *peine forte et dure*, or of wager of battle. With the disappearance of the ecclesiastical element originally predominant in the judiciary, reliance gradually ceased to be placed on the special interposition of Providence as a guide to just decision. But while the law, as its administration passed more and more into lay hands, became increasingly secular, it retained, and still retains, many religious elements. Of these none is more familiar than the oath. Not only does the judge on assuming office invoke the Deity when he swears faithfully to administer his office, but no evidence is receivable in Court except upon oath. The witness who holds up his right hand in Court and swears by the Almighty God, as he shall answer to God at the Great Day of Judgment, that he will tell the truth, the whole truth, and nothing but the truth, invokes one of the most ancient of all religious sanctions. In the first book of the Old Testament we read that Abraham, in swearing that he would take nothing from the King of Sodom, used the words: "I have lift up mine hand unto the Lord, the most high God, the possessor of heaven and earth"; while in the last book of the New Testament the angel whom St John saw in his vision "lifted up his hand to heaven, and sware by him that liveth for ever and ever, who created heaven, and the things that therein are... and the sea, and the things which are therein, that there should be time no longer". Down through the ages the invocation of the Deity by an oath in order to give sanctity to a transaction or credit to a statement has been one of the most persistent of legal ceremonies. Formerly the breach of an oath entailed the most serious spiritual consequences and resulted in the excommunication of the offender. Now perjury is a crime and is visited with the ordinary penalties of the criminal law, but the law still relies on an appeal to the supernatural to ensure that evidence is truly given.

The whole history of the part played by oaths in the evolution of legal doctrine is of remarkable interest. It is almost inconceivable to us that in primitive times the modern conception of a contract was almost entirely absent. Its place was taken by the use of oaths by which the parties bound themselves. There were no damages for breach of contract, but spiritual penalties for breach of faith towards the Deity. The bond was created not by the agreement of parties, but by the oath which they had taken. There is much learning on this subject of the development of contract which it would be out of place to discuss here, but for my purpose it is sufficient to draw your attention to the part which the invocation of supernatural powers has played in it. I may, in this connection, remind you also of the potency attached to curses, the calling down of divine vengeance on the wrongdoer, a subject of special interest in connection with primitive law among Celtic peoples and not least in the Highlands of Scotland.

There is another respect in which the law still bears traces of its early associations with religion and that is in the importance which it attaches to the use of particular words and phrases. One of the most fascinating chapters in folk-lore is concerned with the superstitions which attached to certain names and words. They were thought to have a virtue in themselves and must be used with careful circumspection. The sanctity with which religion has always invested its formulas was reflected in the early Roman law in the legal sanctity accorded to particular forms of words which were essential to constitute a binding obligation. In English law the requirements of formalism were originally peculiarly stringent and there were many words of style which Maitland described as "sacramental phrases". The slightest slip in the use of the covenanted words was fatal. In Scots law we are familiar with the same doctrine. The omission or even the writing on an erasure of certain words destroyed the binding force of an entail, however clear was the intention to create it; and I need not remind the legal members of my audience that it is only comparatively recently that the mystic word "dispone" has ceased to be essential to a conveyance of heritage. So lately as 1901 an English judge was constrained to decide that a title to land was defective because a conveyance was expressed to be "in fee" instead of "in fee simple", although he was in no doubt as to what the parties intended. I have no doubt that in attributing a special solemnity to certain written or spoken words the law has been influenced by the primitive belief in the potency of spells and incantations.

Yet another link between law and religion is to be found in the extent to which they both alike made use of symbols. The symbolic element in religion is familiar to us. I may instance the token and the pillar covenants of the Old Testament. Of the former the rainbow is the most poetical example. God said to Noah: "I do set my bow in the cloud, and it shall be for a token of a covenant between me and the earth." Of the pillar covenant the first example is that between Laban and Jacob, when they set up a stone pillar and gathered together a heap of stones in order that the pillar and the cairn should be a witness of their treaty. In our own law symbols have also played an important part. I need only remind you of the ceremony of taking sasine with its formal delivery of earth and stone or other symbols appropriate to the subject of transfer.

The law of sanctuary, long a familiar part of the law of Scotland and the subject of much learning and many decisions, is of course directly borrowed from the Old Testament. This topic, by itself, would furnish material for a whole lecture. I shall only record in passing that the Scots statute of 1469, which excepted murderers from the privilege of sanctuary, employs the terms of the Vulgate (Exod. xxi. 14) in describing malice aforethought.

I must not, however, weary you with further instances of the early association between law and religion and of the survival in the law of the vestigial traces of religious sanctions and supernaturalism. I have already furnished you with a sufficiently miscellaneous selection. I am really concerned with something of deeper significance. While our legislators no longer claim divine sanction for their enactments and our judges no longer claim that their decisions are divinely inspired, the law, I make bold to say, is still something more than a merely secular code of conduct and its administration something more than a mere matter of mundane business. I quote and adopt Professor Jenks's definition in his recently published work, *The New Jurisprudence*: "Law", he says, "may be defined provisionally as the force or tendency which makes for righteousness." The conventional boundaries which we have drawn between things human and things divine are after all only the expedients of con-

74

venience. Although law and religion have severed their original conjunction on which I have dwelt with so much insistence to-night, we cannot by our arbitrary divisions destroy the essential unity of man's nature. So long as we believe that man is spirit as well as matter, so long as we believe that peace, order and good government concern our souls as well as our bodies and our estates, the law will continue to possess for us a certain divinity, and a certain authority derived from higher sources than the statute book or the volumes of the Law Reports. Justice can never shed her majestic and godlike attributes no matter to what humble details she may condescend in the regulation of the affairs of our daily lives, for justice is never trivial. In these times we have lost the art of eloquence and so for my peroration I am constrained to borrow the language of more spacious days. "Of Law", wrote Richard Hooker three hundred years ago in his *Ecclesiastical Polity*—"Of Law there can be no less acknowledged than that her seat is in the bosom of God; her voice the harmony of the world. All things in heaven and on earth do her homage, the very least as feeling her care and the greatest as not exempting her power—all things whatsoever, though each in a different sort and manner, admiring her as the mother of their peace and joy."

TWO WAYS OF THINKING

*The Rede Lecture delivered before the University of
Cambridge, May 1934*

THE eminent Chief Justice of the Common Pleas
who is responsible for my presence here this afternoon directed that the lectures which bear his
name should be devoted to humanity, logic and philosophy. So generous a field of choice even in the days of
Henry VIII must have occasioned some difficulty to the
lecturer in search of a suitable subject. To the lecturer
of the present day the embarrassment of selection is im-
measurably greater. I can only plead—and you will
judge whether I make good my plea—that the subject
I have chosen has at least some relation to all three of
Sir Robert Rede's trinity of topics.

A well-known adage of the law pronounces a warning
against the deceitfulness which lurks in generalities.
Like many other warnings, it has more often proved an
incitement than a deterrent, for the tendency to gener-
alise is inveterate and every thinker has experienced its
attraction. In sorting out the disordered data of experience, derived from our observation of the present
and our study of the past, we are inevitably impelled to
look for some general principles of discrimination to
guide us in the process. So, undismayed by the attendant risks, I propose to discuss to-day a generalisation
of the widest order, no less than the thesis that all human
minds, in their ultimate assortment, fall into one or other

of two classes or types, each characterised by a fundamentally different and distinctive way of thinking.

I am sensible of the audacity of one who, while not professing to be either a philosopher or a psychologist, yet ventures to air his theories on such a topic in this home of scientific learning. But, as Mr H. A. L. Fisher says in his charming biographical sketch of one of Cambridge's most distinguished scholars, "We are a nation of bold amateurs". These words, I need scarcely say, were not applied to F. W. Maitland, the subject of the biography, but to one who had temerariously challenged his accuracy. You will concede to me that the bold amateur may at least have his uses as a target for the expert's practice.

I have this further excuse—or perhaps it is an aggravation—that there is nothing really new in the broad classification which I offer you of the ways in which the human mind thinks. In truth it is as old as thought itself, for it is founded on the familiar distinction between the theoretical and the practical mind, between the study and the laboratory, between the Aristotelian and the Baconian, or, to put it in the language of the logician, between deduction and induction. But while I have thus nothing new to enunciate, I can at least put before you some verifications of this classical division and some reflections on its far-reaching significance in the world of affairs.

It was a personal experience in my own professional sphere which first made me realise the wide cleavage between the two types of mind of which I have spoken. It has been my fortune, after practising Scots law for a quarter of a century in the Parliament House in Edinburgh, to have found myself called upon during the past ten years to study and latterly to administer the entirely different system of the law of England. Superficially these two systems of law, except in a few important departments, have in modern times become to a large extent assimilated, owing to the constant inter-communication between the two nations and to the fact that for over two hundred years they have shared a legislature and an ultimate court of appeal in common. But I was not long in discovering how entirely different are the historical backgrounds of the English and the Scottish law. I found myself encountering the fundamental distinction between the methods of two of the greatest products of the human intellect which the world has ever seen, the civil law and the common law. In the contrast between these two famous systems there is evidenced, and nowhere better, the cardinal difference I am seeking to vouch, and for that reason I should like to dwell for a little on this topic.

When Justinian in his palace in Constantinople 1400 years ago enacted the Corpus Juris, he promulgated to the world a systematic code of the whole law which was destined to be the basis of the modern continental codes of Europe. Only the other day it came once again into its own in the land of its birth by Turkey's adoption of the Swiss code, which is pre-eminently Roman in character. The most finished product which we owe to Justinian's inspiration is *The Institutes*, composed by Theophilus and Dorotheus under the direction of Tribonian and published in A.D. 533. "No law book", says Lord Mackenzie, "has been so much admired for its method and elegant precision and none has been so

78

frequently printed, translated, imitated and commented on as the Institutes of Justinian." Indeed so early as 1701 a learned professor published a work on the Excessive Multitude of the Commentators on the Institutes. I am not concerned to discuss the success of Justinian's enterprise; it is the nature of his conception which I wish to emphasise. This consisted in the recognition that all human relationships could be assorted and rationalised in accordance with certain fundamental principles. From these principles the whole law could be deduced, and with the aid of these principles the law could be methodised and arranged. It is the conception of order, logic and reason in the regulation by law of human affairs. The influence of this conception has prevailed down to the present day in a large portion of the civilised world. Rome, in the words of the great French Chancellor D'Aguesseau, continued to rule by her reason long after she ceased to rule by her authority.

In England the process of legal development has been entirely different. No doubt in early times Roman law was studied in this country, both at Oxford, where Vacarius lectured in the twelfth century and incurred an injunction from King Stephen against teaching Roman law in England, and here at Cambridge, where a Regius Chair of Civil Law was established by Henry VIII. But although the civil law has survived in our Universities as a subject of academic study, there were potent causes at work which prevented it from becoming the law of England. I do not intend to pursue these causes so far as they were political, but I find in the failure of the civil law to establish itself in England highly significant testimony to the fact that the English genius has always had a strong aversion for and distrust of theory and principle. In England a native growth of law more consonant with the national temperament and proclivities surely and steadily ousted what Wyclif called the "doubly alien" importation from Rome, till it came to be the fashion to disclaim any debt whatever on the part of the law of England to Roman law. In England the common law grew up out of practice. It was never promulgated as a complete system. It developed as occasion arose, for the Englishman prefers not to anticipate. "Sufficient unto the day is the evil thereof" is a text which has always appealed to him. The judges of England were said by Bentham to have made the common law as a man makes law for his dog—by waiting until he has done something wrong and then beating him for it. Thus the law of England was the product of the work of practitioners, not of professors, of practical men, not of philosophers. The famous system of the forms of action arose out of the necessities of pleading. You had no right unless you could find a writ for its enforcement. And writs were invented as they were required. In 1570 there were seventy varieties of them to embarrass the plaintiff's choice. It seems an odd idea that law should be what you can find a writ to fit, but it is eminently characteristic of the English disposition. Discussing the medieval law of England, Maitland observes that "Legal remedies, legal procedure, these are the all-important topics for the student. These being mastered, a knowledge of substantive law will come of itself. Not the nature of rights, but the nature of writs, must be his theme." Again to quote Wyclif—"The laws of England have only a few principles and leave the rest

to the reasonableness of the wise." Such a system naturally lent itself to the development of the method of precedents. What had been done before should be done
again. The question came to be "What did we do last
time?" Not, "What would it be right to do this time?"
And so grew up in England

> ...the lawless science of our law,
> That codeless myriad of precedent,
> That wilderness of single instances.

The two great systems of law which thus divide the
civilised world between them, the system of code law
and the system of case law, exemplify the two main
types of mind, the type that searches for the principle
and the type that proceeds on precedent. The two
methods are the results of widely divergent temperaments. The formulation of principles with accuracy and
precision is a peculiarly difficult task. It is much easier
to appeal to previous experience. Constitutionally the
Englishman has always in the practical affairs of life
been suspicious, often rightly so, of the apostle of principles. If he does not roundly declare him a crank, he
more politely terms him a doctrinaire. He has found
that life is unconformable to any fixed theory and that
principles always fail because they never seem to fit the
case in hand, and so he prefers to leave theory and principles alone. Of that most typical of English statesmen,
Lord Salisbury, his daughter tells us that his mind dis-
trusted "large conceptions" in lawmaking as leading to
the "sacrifice of realities to the symmetry of cherished
theories". It was an Englishman who ventured to speak
of us "Englishmen who never clean our slates", and it

was another Englishman who described the law of England as an "ungodly jumble". But, says Sir Frederick Pollock, "being an illogical folk we do well enough on the whole with our anomalies". "I suppose"—again to quote Sir Frederick, for I am sure this sentence in that delightful book *The Etchingham Letters* came from his pen —"I suppose this is the only country in Europe where quite a large proportion of important affairs, from the Constitution downwards, are worked by just doing the thing you want and saying as little as possible about it even to yourself." *Solvitur ambulando* is the Englishman's motto and he might quote Seneca to justify the path he has chosen—*longum iter est per precepta, breve et efficax per exempla.* Thus the law of England exhibits what Lord Westbury calls "that distinctive peculiarity of the English mind—a love of precedent, of appealing to the authority of past examples rather than of indulging in abstract reasoning".

All this is constitutionally repugnant to the continental disciples of the civil law. To them the principles of the law are what matters. The particular case must be decided not by invoking previous decisions but by logically subsuming it under the appropriate general proposition applicable to it. The principles of the law of torts, which in this country must be gathered from an innumerable series of decisions, are embodied for France in five brief articles of the Code Civile. Here we have the logical and the empirical methods in their most extreme contrast.

But let me bring my comparison and my contrast nearer home. It was, as I have said, my study of the legal systems of England and Scotland which first set me thinking on my present subject, and I venture to suggest that no better illustration could be found of the difference of mental outlook on which I am insisting than is afforded by the contrast between the legal history of England and that of Scotland. In the days when Scotland was first beginning to emerge from her rude and primitive beginnings, political and economic reasons alike directed her sons to the Continent of Europe rather than across the border to the south in their search for education and enlightenment. The ancient alliance with France, close trading associations with the Netherlands and the fame of the Universities of Italy led to a constant migration of the aspiring youth of Scotland to the great law schools of Paris, Utrecht and Leyden, Bologna and Padua. There they found the civil law in the full tide of its renaissance. The philosophical system of jurisprudence taught in these and other great continental schools made a strong appeal to the natural proclivities of the Scottish students, who readily imbibed the tenets of the famous masters of the civil law. When they returned to practise and administer law in their own country they brought with them not only much of the substance of the civil law to make good the deficiencies of their native system but also the inspiration of its principles. It is not without significance that Viscount Stair, the father of Scottish jurisprudence, visited Holland twice in his earlier days and that it was to Holland that in 1682, the year after the publication of his famous *Institutions of the Law of Scotland*, he fled for refuge and there found solace for his exile in the sympathetic atmosphere of Utrecht and Leyden. Stair's great treatise has no counterpart in England. In evidence of the spirit in which he undertook his task I may quote a sentence from the dedication of the *Institutions* to King Charles II. He proposes, he says, to offer to the view of the world the laws of the Scottish nation "in a Plain, Rational and Natural Method; in which Material Justice (the Common Law of the World) is in the first place orderly deduced from self evident Principles"; and he prides himself on the fact that "the nauseating burden of Citations are (*sic*), as much as can be, left out". It has been well said of "this comprehensive survey of legal relations common to all systems" that "the constant search after principles, the philosophical analysis and the thorough technical knowledge have given to a large part of his treatise a vitality and width of application unexampled, we think, among works of the same class".

I have dwelt at such length on the form of intellectual activity exhibited in the evolution of the two great schools of law for the reason that the predilection on the one hand of the continental and the Scottish mind for the code law system and the predilection on the other hand of the English mind for the case law system serve to throw into relief the two ways of thinking of which these systems are the respective products. To proceed from principles to instances is the characteristic of the one school; to proceed from instances to principles—or perhaps not to proceed beyond instances—is the characteristic of the other. It is true that in Scotland the Courts now attach almost as much importance to precedents as do the English Courts, for the edges of distinction have been blurred by constant contacts; yet well on in the eighteenth century Erskine, the second of Scotland's great legal institutional writers, is found saying: "Decisions...though they bind the parties litigating, create no obligation on the judges to follow in the same track, if it shall appear to them contrary to law." He proceeds, however, to add that decisions "are frequently the occasion of establishing usages, which after they have gathered force by a sufficient length of time, must, from the tacit consent of the state, make part of our unwritten law". France has in the past resolutely rejected the principle of case law, but it is noticeable that even in that country there has been a tendency of recent years to resort to the authority of precedents, and lately there has appeared a volume of French leading cases collected by Professor Capitant, which may be regarded as almost a portent. To those who wish to pursue the study of the philosophy of precedents I cannot do better than commend a recent article by Professor Goodhart on "Precedent in English and Continental Law" in the January number of the *Law Quarterly Review*. One of the most acute criticisms which he makes of the precedent system is that it is really not entitled to the praise, commonly accorded to it, that it enables the law to benefit by growing experience, for, as he truly says, after the first precedent has been created it excludes experience. So it is a case of freedom not broadening, but narrowing, down from precedent to precedent. But, for your reassurance, you must also read the reply which Professor Goodhart has evoked, I must not say provoked, from the Vinerian Professor. Sir William Holdsworth will suffer no aspersions on the English method; he claims for it that it "keeps the law in touch with life and prevents much unprofitable speculation upon academic problems which serves only to illustrate the ingenuity of the speculator".

85

Law and Other Things

I hope I have not allowed my professional bias to lead me to over-elaborate the legal aspect of my thesis. I am indeed tempted to say that there has in the past been far too little appreciation of the law as a liberal science, too little recognition of its place in intellectual and social history as distinguished from its merely technical functions. A more enlightened view is gradually beginning to be taken of its human interest and, for myself, I confess that I find more and more significant the contribution which its study can make to the discussion and the solution of the problems of mental and social development.

Quitting the law, I proceed to pursue my distinction between the logical and the empirical mind into other regions, and here again I find that the Tweed is an intellectual as well as a geographical boundary. The love of dialectic, degenerating, I fear, sometimes into an unattractive argumentativeness, permeated in former times the whole outlook of Scotland, religious, philosophical and political. There can be little doubt that this spirit was largely fostered in Scotland in the seventeenth and eighteenth centuries by the system of religion which then prevailed. Religious polemics were during this period the staple diet of the Scottish mind. While I was writing these sentences I happened to have at hand Buckle's *History of Civilisation* and found that he had devoted a large part of his treatise to making my point for me. I am sufficiently imbued with the lawyer's respect for authority to be gratified rather than disconcerted by finding myself anticipated by that rather disagreeable author—no lawyer would say, *pereant male qui ante nos nostra dixerunt.* But I may as well demolish at once any claim to originality on my part by quoting a sentence or two from Buckle which I lighted upon when I had got so far in the preparation of this discourse. "Another circumstance", says he, "which operates on the intellectual progress of a nation is the method of investigation that its ablest men habitually employ. This method can only be one of two kinds; it must be either inductive or deductive. Each of these belongs to a different form of civilisation and is always accompanied by a different style of thought, particularly in regard to religion and science. These differences are of such immense importance that, until their laws are known, we cannot be said to understand the real history of past events"; and then he goes on, just as I have been doing, to find an instance of this divergence of method in the history of Scotland as compared with that of England. I would venture, however, to join issue with Buckle when he says that in Scotland men wasted their energies on religious polemics "without the least benefit either to themselves or to others". On the contrary, though I congratulate myself on not having lived in those times, I recognise how greatly Scotland is indebted for its robust and muscular intelligence and for its eager love of education to the intense interest which religious controversy engendered. I find Dicey testifying to the fact that it was "the popular discussion of theological problems in connection with church business" which, in combination with the high standard of education attained by the poorer classes in Scotland, "kept alive among Scottish farmers, labourers and workmen an aptitude for political affairs which was little, if at all, cultivated at any rate before the Reform Act of 1832 among the rural

87

labourers of English parishes or the artisans of English cities ".

No doubt Buckle's lengthy diatribe against the bigotry of the Scottish Church and its gloomy denunciations of all that is happy and beautiful is overdrawn, as usually happens where the historian has a case to make, but the perusal of his painful pages does at least serve to show the undesirable results which ensue from the application of the logical method in the spiritual sphere. I have shown how the rational system of the Roman law made an irresistible appeal to the Scottish mind, undoubtedly to the great benefit of the nation. But when the same instinct demanded in turn that religion should be logical, the results were far from being equally beneficial. Again the Scotsman turned to the Continent and found in Calvin's theology a system which seemed to promise the same precision and certainty in religion as the Civilians had offered in law. Hence the extraordinarily legalistic theory of religion which oppressed Scotland for generations. The *Institutes* of Calvin, a title itself reminiscent of his legal upbringing, became the Scottish textbook of theology as the *Institutes* of Justinian had become the model of their jurisprudence. Thus we find the whole relationship between God and man conceived in forensic terms. God is essentially a judge and lawgiver who administers a necessitarian code to which He is Himself subject. Predestination and election are the foundations of the Calvinistic edifice. Adopted as the basis of the Scottish Reformation, this teaching was developed with relentless logic by a people constitutionally disposed to legal formalism. The religious literature of the period is not pleasant reading, but it is instructive as indicating the extremes to which a ruthless logic may drive men's minds. Salvation becomes a legal transaction and the spiritual experiences of the soul are expressed in the language of the attorney's office. Covenants and bonds become the vehicles of religious conviction and testimony and the believer must subscribe to every article of a code more rigorous than any known to the secular law. Human nature must be regimented by inflexible rules deduced from *à priori* theological tenets. Such a view of man's duty and destiny may conduce to the formation of strong but not of lovely characters and its less happy fruits are intolerance and persecution. Extremes meet; the doctrines of the Church of Rome, deduced with scholastic completeness from infallible principles and as satisfying to the ecclesiastical conscience of the Continent as the civil law was to its legal mind, found their counterpart in the rigour of the Scottish reformers whose minds had the same craving for infallibility and justified the cruelties of their persecutions by the same reasoning as the Inquisitors invoked.

It would of course be wrong to divide the world of thinkers on purely geographical or racial lines. There are no such exact frontiers in the intellectual sphere, and at different periods and in different places one or the other of the two types of thought may predominate. England had her own Puritan period. But while there may be temporary revulsions and sporadic variations, it remains true that the mental cleavage between the two ways of thinking is due to a deep-rooted racial difference, account for it how we may. The Puritan period in England was a phase of English thought when an element generally subordinate became predominant. But it did not endure because it was not truly English. Even Milton, in language almost reminiscent of Omar Khayyám, says that those who

> reasoned high
> Of Providence, Foreknowledge, Will and Fate
> Fixed fate, free will, foreknowledge absolute
> ...found no end, in wandering mazes lost.

The elements that make up the human mind are no doubt much the same the world over; but the proportions in which these elements exist among different peoples vary and racial differences of thought are due to the degree in which these various elements are predominant or subordinate.

Just as the common law is regarded as the most characteristic secular product of the English mind, the Church of England is its most characteristic religious product. What rendered it abhorrent to the logical Scottish reformers was its spirit of compromise, which we now recognise to be the source of its greatest strength. "The Church of England", again to quote the authors of *The Etchingham Letters*, "is the least dogmatic of churches in all things that can by any reasonable construction be considered not of the essence of a Christian commonwealth." "En religion comme en politique la souplesse britannique s'oppose à l'intransigeance romaine", says André Maurois, *à propos* of the Lambeth Conference in 1930.

But I must not tread further on these concealed embers. Let me illustrate the operation of the deductive mind in other perhaps less controversial spheres. Take Scottish Philosophy, for example. It has acquired the sobriquet of the Common Sense Philosophy through a popular misapprehension of the title of Reid's *Enquiry into the Human Mind on the Principles of Common Sense*, but in truth it is in no sense a pragmatic school. The metaphysic of Hume and Reid is essentially *à priori* and it is on that lofty plateau that they join issue, for Reid attacks the sceptical conclusions of Hume, not by Dr Johnson's eminently English answer to Berkeley, but by a rival technique based on deduction from different principles, in which to some extent he anticipated Kant. It is perhaps, however, in political economy that the deductive method in Scottish hands has yielded its most famous results. Adam Smith's great work *The Wealth of Nations* is essentially a deductive treatise; that is to say, it is based on certain fundamental principles which the author assumes to be inherent in human nature. These principles he then proceeds to develop and exemplify with admirable lucidity and from these principles he deduces the economics of human society. How far he was influenced in his method by his three years' sojourn and studies in France it is difficult to say. But while his method is deductive, there is no doubt that his work owed much of its success to the extraordinary variety of practical illustrations which he drew from history and from the world around him. Though never himself engaged in trade, he consorted with the merchants of Glasgow who conjoined strong views on economic doctrine with conspicuous success in business. I find in Walter Bagehot's sketch of his life this passage which is so apt to my theme that I must quote it: "Probably", he says, "in consequence of the firm belief in a rigid theology and of the incessant discussion of its technical tenets there has long been, and there is still, in the south of Scotland a strong tendency to abstract argument quite unknown in England. Englishmen have been sometimes laughing at it and sometimes gravely criticising it for several generations: Mr Buckle wrote half a volume on it: Sydney Smith alleged that he heard a Scotch girl answer in a quadrille, 'But, my lord, as to what ye were saying as to love in the aibstract', and so on. Yet in spite both of ridicule and argument, the passion for doctrine is still strong in southern Scotland, and it will take many years to root it out. At Glasgow in Adam Smith's time it had no doubt very great influence." Mr Bagehot was evidently of opinion that the Scottish passion for doctrine was something to be rooted out, but let that pass. The point he makes is a sound one and we must include *The Wealth of Nations* among the other fruits which the deductive method of thought has yielded.

And so I might go on to trace in almost every sphere of the national life of Scotland the influence of this characteristic habit of thought and to contrast its products with those of the English mind. But it may perhaps be of more practical interest to consider how far the two ways of thinking enter into and affect the practical world of affairs in our own day. I have found it convenient to use, and doubtless to exaggerate, the contrasting mentalities north and south of the Tweed in order to bring into relief the difference between the two types of thought. But of course it is not a mere question of English and Scottish minds. Doubtless there are and have been many deductive minds in England and many inductive minds in Scotland. The difference is something much more fundamental and less localised, and my effort has been to show how pervasive it is throughout the whole history of human thought in all its departments. Indeed it permeates not only thought but action. Let me take an illustration from so unlikely a quarter as a very charming book which has just been published entitled *The Surrey Landscape*. The authors draw an interesting contrast between the ancient Pilgrims' Way which meanders in beauty through the county and the Roman road which traverses it with mathematical precision and directness. "The ancient Way", they say, "came into use naturally as early man followed the line of least resistance from settlement to settlement, but the Roman way was surveyed and made. This point illustrates the difference between the Latin and non-Latin approach to life. The Latin plans intellectually and dominates the scene with his roads and cities, his aqueducts and villas; they are, as it were, a pattern transferred from paper on to the earth. The non-Latin, on the other hand, allows his scheme to develop slowly in conformity with the natural features of the landscape and produces an irregular mosaic of curves which harmonize with the hills, woods and rivers."

Gratefully acknowledging this apt parable, I pass now to consider certain manifestations of the two ways of thinking which we find exhibited in the world around us. We all recognise the two types when we meet them, whatever be their provenance, and as a matter of expediency it is useful to know how to handle them. In public life every board and every committee contains examples of both orders of minds. How well we know the member who is a "stickler for principle" and who insists on arguing out each question on *à priori* lines, while the other and more practical members are trying to devise what is called "a way out". Then someone has the happy thought of proposing that without in any way detracting from their principles they should in the special circumstances of the case make a concession, on the distinct understanding that it must not form a precedent. And so the way out is found and everyone has the pleasant delusion that they have somehow or other contrived to make an exception without infringing their consistency.

In matters, however, of much graver moment than the conduct of our boards and committees it is worth while to study the tendencies to which the two ways of thinking give rise, for we have to deal with them in every walk of life and we encounter them not only in domestic affairs but even more in international discussions.

In the political world there have always been, and there always will be, two parties. By whatever names the rival schools of thought choose for the time being to designate themselves, the real dividing line is between the conservative and the progressive. I use these terms in no party sense but as indicative on the one hand of the type of mind which reverences the past, maintains the *status quo*, and requires the strictest proof of the need for any change, and on the other hand of the type of mind which has scant respect for the past, chafes at the *status quo* and is attracted by change for its own sake. There are no doubt progressive conservatives who recognise that the best means of conservation is a reasonable measure of reform; and there are no doubt reactionary radicals who adhere to their tenets with a diehard persistence long after experience has demonstrated that they are a clog rather than an aid to progress. The para-

dox of the conservative radicalism of Scotland was one
of the most remarkable political phenomena of last
century. I refrain from further instances; they may
occur to you. But it remains essentially true that the
politician inevitably finds himself on one or other side of
the dividing line which I have drawn, according to the
way of thinking which he has inherited or to which his
temperament inclines him. I daresay that "Inductives"
and "Deductives" would not make very popular party
labels or afford very stimulating election slogans, but
they would be more accurate than the designations commonly adopted. The inductive politician tends to support aristocratic government—which we are apt to forget
means government by the best—for his class of mind
relies on tradition and authority. He seeks the justification of his beliefs not in their logic or their conformity to
any predetermined principles, but in experience. Like
the followers of the common law he believes in precedents. The deductive politician on the other hand tends
to support democracy. He derides as unscientific the
system of hereditary government, he is impatient with
the abuses and imperfections of the illogical present; and,
having adopted certain *à priori* doctrines of the equality
and perfectibility of man, he seeks to shape the ends of
society to his theories. Again my analogy holds; he is a
follower of the Civilians and believes in principles. But
in this country of England even the most radically
minded are themselves subject to the *genius loci*. As England preferred to work out her own legal salvation in her
common law, so in her politics all parties, even the most
advanced, have tended to exhibit a certain practical
good sense, a reluctance to push things to their logical

95

extremes. The French Revolution affords the most dramatic example in history of logic applied to government—or did, until Russia afforded us a more modern instance. These two great experiments alike illustrate the working of the deductive mind. "The commonplaces of politics in France", says John Stuart Mill, "are large and sweeping practical maxims from which, as ultimate premisses, men reason downwards to particular applications, and this they call being logical and consistent. For instance, they are perpetually arguing that such and such a measure ought to be adopted because it is a consequence of the principle on which the form of government is founded; of the principle of legitimacy or the principle of the sovereignty of the people." Certain principles are assumed as axiomatic and then all the rest follows.

It has been said that the politics of this country in the past century were dominated by the revulsion of feeling occasioned by the object lesson of the French Revolution, perhaps even more that of 1848 than that of 1789. While the excesses of our neighbours across the Channel were doubtless used to point a political moral, they did not create, though they may well have strengthened, the natural instinct of the people of England to distrust new-fangled theories imported from abroad. The matter is so admirably put by Lord Morley, to whom I am also indebted for my quotation from Mill, that I must give the passage in full. "The influence", he says, "of France upon England since the revolution of 1848 has tended wholly to the discredit of abstract theory and general reasoning among us, in all that relates to politics, morals and religion. In 1848, not in 1789, questions affecting the fundamental structure and organic condition of the social union came for the first time into formidable prominence. For the first time these questions and the answers to them were stated in articulate formulas and distinct theories." These "premature attempts to convert a crude aspiration into a political reality and to found a new social order on a number of uncompromising deductions from abstract principles of the common weal...have had the natural effect of deepening the English dislike of a general theory even when such a theory did no more than profess to announce a remote object of desire and not the present goal of immediate effort".

I doubt if we sufficiently appreciate the totally different approach which the continental, and particularly the Latin, mind makes to every problem as contrasted with what I may call the British approach. It needs imagination to enter into another mentality and imagination is not the strong suit of the English race. "The power of realising and understanding types of character very different from our own is not, I think, an English quality", says Lecky in his discourse on *The Political Value of History*. I believe that the failure of the multitude of international conferences of recent years to achieve the aims which we all profess to have in common is in no small degree due to the incompatibility of the ways of thinking of those who have participated in them. That at least is the view, I gather, which is held by one of the most acute of French observers, who has the advantage of an unusually sympathetic comprehension of the British temperament. In *Mes Songes que Voici*, from which I have already quoted, M. André Maurois confides to us, in a passage of remarkable insight, how he sees the two types of mind at work. "De Rome", he says, "et peut-être aussi d'une longue vie paysanne, la France tient le goût de l'exactitude juridique, des formules, et des textes précis. L'Angleterre mène sa vie politique sans constitution, rend la justice sans code et attend la paix de l'Europe d'expédients contradictoires et d'intuitions hardies. La France veut des chartes écrites et des garanties signées. L'Anglais tient pour dangereux de prétendre endiguer un univers aux crues imprévisables. Le Français croit aux plans, aux édifices symétriques, aux desseins fermes et bien conçus. L'Anglais, s'il rencontre une résistance doctrinale, semble céder, puis revient à la charge dans une autre formation et reprend le terrain perdu. Obligé de concéder à un pays son indépendance, il reconnaît l'indépendance et maintient l'occupation. Un Français eût maintenu le principe au risque de perdre le gage. De tels contrastes entre les idéologies nationales naissent les malentendus qui, depuis la guerre, ont rendu difficile la vie de l'Europe."

My discerning hearers will have observed that M. Maurois finds, as I have done, that it is the same British instinct which expresses itself in "la justice sans code" that animates the British mind in dealing with international affairs, just as it is France's inheritance from Rome which influences her in her very different attitude. I am, again, fortunate in having my point so felicitously made for me.

Professor Graham Wallas has collected for us, in his *Art of Thought*, an interesting anthology of English and French pronouncements on the differing mentalities of the English and the French politician. He declines to accept the common attribution of the difference to racial biology and states it as his own belief that it is "mainly due to a difference of intellectual tradition, transmitted partly by education and partly by political catchwords and legal institutions and strengthened by differences in the political and international history of the two countries". I cannot say that I find this very satisfying but there I must leave it.

Hitherto, as you will have observed, I have confined myself to the exposition and illustration of the two ways of thinking and have sedulously refrained from expressing any opinion upon their relative merits. Perhaps I should be wise to close without doing so, but the temptation to appraise is difficult to resist. If we are to judge by results, by the test of which kind of mind attains the greatest measure of practical success in the art of government and so best promotes human welfare, I am disposed to award the palm to the inductive mind as exemplified in the English race. I speak as a Scotsman whose national and hereditary proclivities may sometimes render him a little critical of the Englishman's way of working out his problems. The Englishman's spirit of opportunism and compromise may sometimes exasperate his logical neighbours across the border and on the continent, but we owe to them Magna Charta and the British Empire. Let me quote the tribute of General Alexandre, one of Joffre's staff-officers, who in the Great War experienced the difficulty of comprehending the English mind. After dwelling on the English habit of refusing to look ahead, of troubling only about the affairs of the current day, of waiting for the event to happen in order to deal with it, he concludes: "Has not the history of a thousand years proved that this manner of doing things has overcome temporary set-backs and has always led to final success."

I recall a conversation I once had with a very eminent continental diplomatist who startled me by declaring that the English were the most revolutionary nation in the world; but then he added that we never noticed that our revolutions were taking place. There is truth in this. Unlike the more spectacular revolutions of other nations, ours are not effected either by syllogisms or machine guns but by gradual and almost imperceptible processes of change, and for that very reason are more fundamental and permanent. It is a merit of our characteristically unwritten constitution that great social alterations can be brought about without destroying the framework of our body politic, and without our ever quite realising what is happening or sustaining the shocks which such changes would give to a more rigid structure. A written constitution compels the revolutionary to face the logic of his policy; an unwritten constitution enables him to avoid it. This again is a source of strength, for it prevents much wasteful conflict, but it is exasperating to the theorist.

When all is said and done, it is the tolerance, the magnanimity, the readiness to compromise and to assimilate, the very illogicality, if you will, that are so typical of the English mind which have always been the secret of England's influence and power and which at this moment, when the whole of the rest of the world is seething with new theories of government, new theories of economics, new theories of everything, have enabled her to retain a stability which is the envy of every other nation.

Two Ways of Thinking

But it may be said that I am applying too utilitarian a test of excellence. Can it be said that a higher ethical value can be assigned to the one type of mind than to the other? Here I find my theme in danger of soaring into the region of the ultimate antinomy between Reason and Authority. In the present day these ancient adversaries once more confront each other, but each is a little less self-confident than it used to be. It is less easy nowadays to be either a convinced rationalist or an impenetrable authoritarian. We are all a little less sure of our ground, a little less supercilious in the assertion of our dogmas. When our most eminent scientists demonstrate the relativity of the laws which their predecessors regarded as absolute, the common man may well wonder where he stands. Intellectually, the recent spectacular developments of science have, oddly enough, engendered a new humility in their exponents, while the mandarins of authority have grown more modest in the assertion of their creeds, as so many of the articles of their faith have been shattered by the world's upheaval. All this is of good augury, for the true answer to the problem I have stated as to the comparative value to mankind of the two ways of thinking is that there is no answer. Neither method is intellectually or ethically better than the other. Both are essential. At different times and in different places, in one race or in another, sometimes the one habit of mind and sometimes the other is found to predominate, lending its distinctive colour, variety and interest to thought and practice, but the world has need of both ways of thinking. Each has its contribution to make to the attainment of the goal of all right ways of thinking—the Truth.

SCOTS LAW
AS A
SUBJECT OF COMPARATIVE STUDY

*Address delivered at the International Congress of Comparative
Law, The Hague, August 1932*

WE have come to this hall from every quarter
of the globe and practically every civilised
system of law has here its representative.
"Variety's the very spice of life, that gives it all its
flavour", as the English poet Cowper has said, and much
of the value and interest of our conference resides in the
diversity of the views which its members can contribute.
But while the nations to which we belong may be far
separated in space and in race, we have in our common
devotion to the science of the law a bond which unites us
all. Without that bond, which enables us to understand
and share each other's problems and aspirations, our
assembly would be as barren of achievement as the con-
course of nations which gathered to build the Tower of
Babel. The unity of creed which makes it profitable for
us to meet and compare our legal doctrines lies in the
faith which we all share that civilisation cannot exist,
far less progress, except in a society based on just laws
justly administered.

I might well adopt as my text the words used by
Viscount Stair, the most illustrious of Scottish lawyers,
in the opening paragraph of his great treatise on *The
Institutions of the Law of Scotland*, first published in 1681.

"No man", he declares, "can be a knowing lawyer in any nation who hath not well pondered and digested in his mind the common law of the world." In formulating the principles of Scots law, as he tells us, he ·derived it "from that common law that rules the world and compared it with the laws civil and canon, and with the custom of the neighbouring nations". I hope to show hereafter how largely Scots law has benefited by the adoption of the eclectic method in its development. Meantime the mention of Viscount Stair, who as a refugee from his native land so long enjoyed the hospitality of Holland, tempts me to digress for a moment to refer to the intimate connection which in former times subsisted between the lawyers of Scotland and their Dutch brethren.

I welcome this opportunity of acknowledging the great debt which Scottish jurisprudence owes to the legal learning of the Netherlands. For it is indeed a great debt. In the formative period of Scots law in the sixteenth and seventeenth centuries Scotland was a land of poverty and strife, and the facilities for the prosecution of legal studies were meagre in the extreme. It was not till 1710 that the first lectures on civil law were given in the University of Edinburgh by a professor for whom no salary was provided, and the first professor of Scots law was not appointed till 1722. In view of her remote situation and the widely divergent races of which her population was composed, it was inevitable that the conception of a national system of law should be of later development in Scotland than elsewhere. When she first began to emerge from the primitive tribal life of early times there was no body of generally accepted customs to form the foundation of a Scottish common law, and when she came to claim her place as a nation she found herself confronted with already formulated systems of law across the border in the neighbouring country of England, and across the seas among the politically advanced nations with which through alliances or trade connections she was brought into contact. Debarred from England by secular hostility, the Scottish student who was ambitious of acquiring an adequate equipment for the practice of the law naturally resorted to the Continent for his instruction. While some went in search of learning to France, some to Germany, and some to Italy, the great law schools of Utrecht, Leyden, Groningen and Franeker especially attracted the young Scottish legal aspirant of those days. Not only was Holland the nearest neighbour of Scotland across the sea, but there were to be found the most erudite and elegant interpreters of the law of Rome on which Dutch law and Scots law are both alike based. Another reason which drew the youth of Scotland to Holland lay in the community of religious views between the two countries and the intellectual freedom which was accorded in Holland to all searchers after knowledge. In that age of intolerance the Netherlands shone out as an example to the world of liberality of thought. The eminent historian, Gilbert Burnet (1643–1715), who ultimately settled at the Hague and became a naturalised Dutch subject, records in the *History of His Own Times*, published shortly after his death, that he "saw much peace and quiet in Holland, notwithstanding the diversity of opinions among them, which was occasioned by the gentleness of the Government and the toleration that made all people easy and happy". And, lastly, the close commercial relations between Scotland and Holland naturally led to an interchange of intellectual as well as of material commodities.

I may refer to one institution as a remarkable example of the intimate mercantile associations between the two countries, namely, the Scottish Staple at Campvere. The word "staple", signifying a storehouse, market or centre of trade, came to be applied to towns which possessed a monopoly of trade in certain leading commodities, and for a long time a Scottish colony of traders enjoyed under this name at Campvere the sole privilege of importing goods free of duty from Scotland into Holland. In the sixteenth century a special court was established there, presided over by an official known as the Lord Conservator of the Scottish Privileges in the Netherlands, to which was granted exclusive jurisdiction to determine according to Scots law all disputes arising among members of the Scottish trading community, who thus, though resident in Holland, *lege Scotica vixerunt.* For the settlement of questions between Scottish and Dutch disputants the Conservator was subsequently empowered to join with the town magistrates in setting up a mixed arbitral tribunal. It was not indeed till 1847 that the title of Lord Conservator was abolished, though the trading monopoly which gave rise to the office had, of course, long previously disappeared. This instance of a foreign tribunal administering foreign law within the confines of another sovereign state is of the greatest interest to students of the history of International law, and serves to indicate the peculiarly sympathetic relations which subsisted between Holland and Scotland in early days.

Linked together as the two countries are thus seen to have been by so many common ties, it is not surprising that for more than two centuries there was a constant migration of Scottish lawyers to Holland to share in the rich stores of legal lore which her famous Universities provided. When Viscount Stair in 1682 had to flee from Scotland to avoid the risk of prosecution for his refusal to comply with the Test Act, inclination and expediency alike combined to draw him to Holland, "the place of greatest common safety", and there he established himself at Leyden, finding congenial society among the learned professors of the University—*illustrissimum et augustissimum illud sapientiae et omnis doctrinae sacrarium maximum orbis museum in quo plures viri summi qui principatum ingenii et eruditionis tenuerunt floruere quam in ceteris omnibus Europae Academiis* (Graevius). To the credit of the States of Holland they refused to expel this distinguished refugee, though called upon to do so, and he continued, in the language of a contemporary tract, "diverting himself with the conversation of the schoolmen and scholars of the two famous Universities of Leyden and Utrecht", until he returned with William of Orange in 1688 to a happier Britain.

At the period of Viscount Stair's residence in Holland the reputation of Dutch legal scholarship was at its zenith. Grotius (1583–1645), Vinnius (1588–1657), Salmasius (1588–1653), Paul Voet (1619–1667), and his son, John Voet (1647–1714), and others scarcely less eminent, had fostered the renaissance of civilian learning and won for the law schools of Holland a paramount position as the custodians and expositors of the great traditions of Roman law. Among the many other

Scottish lawyers who there imbibed their knowledge of the civil law I may mention Lord President Forbes (1685–1747), who proceeded to Leyden in 1705 and stayed there for nearly two years, attaining great proficiency as a civilian, and Lord President Dundas (1713–1787), who studied at Utrecht. Another Scottish judge, well known though less illustrious in the law, who crossed the sea in search of instruction, was Lord Monboddo, the eccentric precursor of Darwin, who spent three years at the University of Groningen. I may conclude my list with the name of James Boswell, of the Scottish Bar, who on Friday, 5 August 1763, set out from London for the University of Utrecht and was accompanied as far as Harwich by Samuel Johnson, whose biography he was subsequently to write. Unhappily Boswell's diary of his stay in Holland has been lost. Were it extant I doubt not that we should have had an entertaining account of his Dutch experiences. I am afraid that if it ever comes to light we shall find that despite his attendance on the lectures of the learned Professor Trotz he fulfilled the parting jibe of his illustrious friend, who said: "He was idle at Edinburgh. His father sent him to Glasgow where he continued to be idle. He then came to London, where he has been very idle. And now he is going to Utrecht, where he will be as idle as ever." Perhaps it is salutary for us to reflect that the fame of this idler is more flourishing at the present day than that of all the learned preceptors whose instruction he neglected.

As late as 1833 there were still advocates in the Parliament House at Edinburgh who had studied at Leyden or Utrecht, but the custom has now long ceased. There is a charming reminder of the ancient amity in one of

Robert Louis Stevenson's novels, in which he tells us of
David Balfour's unsuccessful attempts at Leyden to study
Heineccius in the distracting company of the fair
Catriona.

This digression on the debt of Scotland to Holland,
longer than I intended but not longer than the subject
merits, is not so irrelevant to my theme as it might appear to be. For it is to the close association of Scottish
lawyers with the great civilian teachers of the Continent
that the most distinctive features of the Scottish legal
system are attributable. Hitherto the law of Scotland
has failed to attract to any great extent the notice of
students of comparative jurisprudence, and while this
omission may be regrettable it is scarcely surprising, for
little has been done by Scottish legal writers themselves
to promote interest in it. The history of Scots law has
still to be written but I venture to say that few topics
present a more interesting field of study in legal origins.
Modern Scottish jurisprudence is remarkable in that it
retains so few traces of primitive native custom, and
furnishes an example of a system almost entirely imported from outside sources, and subsequently moulded
and developed to suit the national genius. The earliest
importations were Anglo-Saxon; these were followed by
Norman feudalism; while the Church brought with it
the principles of the canon law. These importations
Scotland shared, though in a lesser degree, with England,
and apart from the Highlands, which long retained their
primitive clan customs, the law administered on both
sides of the Tweed was for a time much the same. But
from the sixteenth century onwards a great change took
place, with the awakening of the national consciousness

by the Reformation. As Scotland geographically and politically began to acquire a new and more definite status she sought to establish her own institutions, and she preferred to seek her models on the continent rather than in England. She borrowed the organisation of her law courts from Paris, as also the constitution of her Church Assembly, while for the substantive principles of her law she found in the system of the civilians, especially as expounded in Holland, a congenial source of inspiration. There was no formal adoption of Roman law in Scotland, but there was a steady infiltration of its influence which profoundly affected both the theory and the practice of Scots law. Where the existing law failed to provide for any particular case the authority of the Roman law was invoked, not as decisive but as persuasive, and generally prevailed. The facility with which the civil law was assimilated in Scotland was due not merely to the circumstance that the leading members of bench and bar alike had received their legal education on the continent, but also to reasons more deep-seated than those of either expediency or familiarity. The Scottish nation has always been credited with a special aptitude for philosophy and a special devotion to logical principle. Consequently the systematic and orderly scheme of the Roman law appealed with an irresistible attraction to the Scottish national genius. The divergence of Scotland from England in matters of jurisprudence was due as much to intellectual as to political causes. As each country went its own way the distinction between their laws became more marked. The formulary system and the fictions of the English common law, the outcome of pure empiricism, find no counterpart in the history of the law of Scotland. In Scotland the search was not for the appropriate form of writ, but for the legal principle involved. Once that was found the forms of process presented little difficulty. To this day the Scottish form of pleading is logical and precise, and adapts itself without technical embarrassments to all the requirements of the pleader. If there is any impatience with it, it is rather because it is too exacting in its logic for the more slipshod ways of modern times.

Apart from the intellectual sympathy which the law of Rome evoked among Scottish lawyers, there was another national characteristic which assisted its influence. "The English lawyer", as Maitland, one of the greatest of English legal scholars, confesses, "knew nothing and cared nothing for any system but his own." The Scot, whether from the poverty of his own land or from a naturally adventurous spirit, has always been more cosmopolitan, and early won for himself the sobriquet of the "gangrel Scot". When he went abroad he took with him an inquiring mind and was ready, in Molière's phrase, to "prendre son bien où il le trouva". He never shared his southern neighbour's resistance to foreign ideas; he preferred to appropriate them if he thought them valuable.

A typical illustration of the difference between the Scottish and the English attitude to jurisprudence is to be found in the fact that thrice in the history of Scots law, in three succeeding centuries, the whole body of the law has been expounded in coherent and systematic form by a great institutional writer. First Stair (1619–1695) published in 1681 his *Institutions of the Law of Scotland*; then in 1773 was published the *Institute* of

Scots Law as a Subject of Comparative Study

Erskine (1695–1768); and, finally, Bell (1770–1843) published his *Principles* in 1829. These treatises, following closely the Roman philosophic model, each cover the whole field of Scots law, and are treated by the Courts as of the highest authority. There is no comparable body of authoritative law in England where the law has "broadened down from precedent to precedent", unaided by such periodic surveys and restatements. The contrast between the two systems is most instructive. Although in these modern times, when law is so largely the creature of statute and is so much more concerned with commercial and social questions on which the two countries have now a common body of legislation, the old distinctions have been much obliterated, the background of the two systems remains fundamentally different. To the student of comparative law an examination of this contrast could not fail to be illuminating, for the contrast is that between the two main schools of legal thought, the logical and the empirical.

The great repository of Scottish judicial decisions, Morison's Dictionary, affords excellent evidence of the familiarity of the Scottish Bench and Bar in the seventeenth and eighteenth centuries with civilian learning. The authorities quoted in Court are largely continental, and chiefly Dutch. Puffendorf, Voet, Bynkershoek, and other famous commentators, are constantly cited. It would be interesting and quite possible to reconstruct from these reports the library of a practising Scottish advocate of those days. But we have fortunately even better testimony to the extent to which Scots law was dependent upon the learning of the Continent in the first catalogue, published in 1692, of the Advocates' Library in

Law and Other Things

Edinburgh which was founded by the King's Advocate, Sir George Mackenzie, in 1682. Of some 1500 "Libri Juridici" entered in the catalogue, there are only about thirty native law books, several of them still in manuscript, while London and Oxford contribute less than ninety. All the rest are continental treatises, and the publications of the press of Leyden are by far the most numerous, including the famous names of Grotius, Vinnius, both the Voets, Salmasius, Matthaeus, Huber, Sotomajor, Puffendorf, and many others. No wonder that in his preface the King's Advocate grows almost rhapsodical in his reference to the civil law as "divinum illud opus quod coelo potius quam Romae debemus, et illuc demissum ut legislatoribus exemplum et gentibus arbiter esset".

But while the civil law thus received the devout homage of the lawyers of the Scottish legal renaissance it would, as I have pointed out, in no sense be true to say that Scots law, either originally or at the present day, is a mere reflection of the law of Rome. Much of its inspiration came from the civil law through continental commentators, and the adherence to principle rather than subservience to precedent which is one of its characteristic features it owed to the same source, but other influences were at work. Transplanted doctrines developed modifications in their new habitat in accordance with the strongly marked idiosyncrasies of the people, and the divergence increased as resort to the Continent diminished. From a very early date the "law merchant" exercised an influence second only to that of the civil law, and the development of mercantile jurisprudence in France which began in the middle of the seventeenth century was undoubtedly observed by her Scottish ally. As Bell points out, the "celebrated Ordonnances de la Marine of 1681 gave a splendour to commercial law which could not fail to make an impression upon the lawyers of Scotland". Moreover, after the union of the Crowns in 1603 the development of trade with England began a process of assimilation of the laws of the two countries in commercial matters which has gone on ever since and is still at work. The law of England came to be much more studied in Scotland as the ancient hostility disappeared. In Bankton's *Institute of the Laws of Scotland*, published in Edinburgh in 1751, the learned author furnishes observations upon the "agreement or diversity between them and the laws of England". I may claim him as an early disciple of the comparative school. In his preface he tells us that he has drawn in his treatise "a kind of parallel between our laws and those of England...showing the conformity or disconformity betwixt the one and the other". "The lord Stair", he says, "had no occasion to observe anything of this kind, nor was it of great use in his time, but now, since the union of the two kingdoms, there is such intercourse between the subjects of South and North Britain, that it must be of great moment that the laws of both be generally understood and their agreement or diversity attended to; so that people, in their mutual correspondence, may regulate themselves accordingly; and the respective laws and usages may likewise receive some light from the comparison." And Lord Kames (1696–1782) in the preface to his *Historical Law Tracts*, speaking of the best method of studying law, says: "I know none more rational than a careful and judicious

comparison of the laws of different countries. Materials
for such comparison are richly furnished by the laws of
England and of Scotland. They have such resemblance
as to bear a comparison almost in every branch; and
they so far differ as to illustrate each other by their
opposition."

The existence since 1707 of a single Parliament legis-
lating for both England and Scotland, the influence of
a common court of ultimate appeal for both countries
in the House of Lords, and the growth of a habit of
citing in the Scottish Courts decisions drawn from the
vastly larger store of precedents in the English Law
Reports, have all tended to bring about a large measure
of conformity in modern times between the legal systems
of the two countries not only in form but in substance.
Yet there still persists in Scotland a distinctive legal attitude of mind and in a few strongholds she still preserves
her own characteristic laws, especially in those always
resistant departments of the domestic relations and real
property.

No one can address himself to the study of comparative
law without being struck with the essential similarity of
the problems of human relationship all the world over
and, despite the diversity in form of the solutions which
each national system of law has devised, with the general
resemblance in substance of these solutions. It is my
fortune to be a member of a Court, the Judicial Committee of His Britannic Majesty's Privy Council, which
has exceptional opportunities of observing and comparing legal phenomena. Possessing a jurisdiction over
the three or four hundred million human beings of every
race who make up the inhabitants of the British Empire,

approximately a quarter of the population of the world, it administers almost every known form of law. While the law of England rules in many parts of the Empire, subject to local statutory modifications, the Judicial Committee may have to apply Hindu and Mahommedan law in appeals from India, French law in appeals from Quebec and Mauritius, Roman-Dutch law in appeals from South Africa and Ceylon, Spanish law in appeals from Trinidad. From time to time the customs and traditions of the most primitive native races come under consideration, for it has always been the British policy to permit the territories added to the Empire to retain their own ways subject only to their not conflicting with peace, order and good government. Every variety of human institution is discussed in this Court, and due observance is paid to the customs of every region of the Empire. Many and strange are the questions which arise for determination, but more and more one is struck, in listening to these disputes from every quarter of the globe, with the essential similarity of the human issues involved and with the vital importance of justice as the prime concern of all good government. My colleagues in this Congress will thus understand the special interest which its discussions must possess for one whose daily business affords him the opportunity of comparing so many diverse systems of law.

It has always seemed to me that to learn another system of law is like learning another language. It not only adds to one's knowledge but renders the system one already knows more intelligible and more vivid. A person who is bilingual is much better able to appreciate the merits of each of the languages he speaks, for each throws the other into relief. I have found this notably in the performance of my duty of administering both the law of England and the law of Scotland in the House of Lords and I do not hesitate to say that the contrasts which emerge in daily debate between the two systems, so very different in their genius and their genesis, enable one better to understand and appreciate the features and the merits of each.

As I have begun with a quotation from the greatest of Scottish lawyers, I shall pay tribute to the catholic spirit of our Congress by concluding with a passage from the most famous commentator on the law of England, which may serve to show that English lawyers are perhaps not quite so insular as my quotation from Maitland might lead one to believe. Describing an ideal exposition of the law, Blackstone proposes, in the Introduction to his *Commentaries*, that the "originals should be traced to their fountains...to the customs of the Britons and Germans, as recorded by Caesar and Tacitus; to the codes of the northern nations on the continent, and more especially to those of our own Saxon princes; to the rules of the Roman law either left here in the days of Papinian or imported by Vacarius and his followers; but above all, to that inexhaustible reservoir of legal antiquities and learning, the feodal law, or, as Spelman has entitled it, the law of nations in our western orb. These primary rules and fundamental principles should be weighed and compared with the precepts of the law of nature and the practice of other countries; should be explained by reasons, illustrated by examples, and confirmed by un-doubted authorities; their history should be deduced, their changes and revolutions observed, and it should be shown how far they are connected with, or have at any time been affected by, the civil transactions of the kingdom." (Edition of 1787, pp. 35–6.)

You will agree that in these sentences Blackstone has well and truly described the spirit of research which should animate the student of comparative law.

LAW AND HISTORY

Address delivered at the Jubilee Meeting of the Scottish Law Agents Society in Edinburgh, October 1934

IT is my first and most pleasant duty this afternoon to offer my congratulations to the Society, whose members I have the honour to address, on the attainment of their jubilee. In celebrating this occasion you are obeying, as I may fitly remind you, the injunction of one of the oldest extant codes of law. In the Book of Leviticus, part of which is still the law of Scotland, the special ceremonies for the observance of the fiftieth year are prescribed. Certain of them, if they were now to receive effect, would be rather disturbing to heritable rights in Scotland, but you will at least recognise the propriety of the Levitical ordinance that the year of jubilee should be ushered in with the blowing of trumpets. To blow your own trumpets would no doubt be distasteful to your modesty, but there is no such consideration to deter me from lauding the progress and success of your Society and the admirable achievements which stand to its credit.

These fifty years have seen your numbers grow from an original membership of some five or six hundred to over two thousand, approximately two-thirds of the enrolled law agents in Scotland, and throughout these years the Society has been a most vigilant guardian of the best interests of the profession. In his inaugural address, delivered in Edinburgh on 29 April 1884, Sir James Roberton, the eminent Professor of Conveyancing in the University of Glasgow and your first president, dwelt on two of the main aims of the Society, namely, first, the promotion of the status of the Scottish law agent by fostering a high standard of education and professional probity; and, second, the maintenance and improvement of the law by an assiduous supervision of all legislative proposals and by the initiation and support of useful measures of reform. In its pursuit of these objects there can be no question of the services which the Society has rendered both to the profession and to the public.

The topic on which I have chosen to address you has, I venture to think, some appropriateness to the occasion. You are to-day in a reminiscent mood. You are naturally casting your minds back over all the changes and developments which the past fifty years have seen in the practice of the law and finding in these vicissitudes much food for interesting reflection. But fifty years is a brief span in the annals of our country and our law, and while you are in this mood it is opportune to invite you to extend your retrospect and to survey more spaciously the landscape of the past.

My subject has two aspects. Law may be looked at in relation to the general history of the country and it may also be looked at in relation to its own history. Both aspects present attractive fields of study.

There are probably few nations more historically minded than our own, and no nation has shown itself more tenacious of its past, not, as with some less happy peoples, in order to foment present grievances, but rather as a source of inspiration for the future. Of all her institutions there is none which has been more closely associated with the history of Scotland than her system of law. The more spectacular features of a country's history are to be found in great events and heroic figures—and Scotland has certainly not lacked either—but we have come increasingly to realise in these modern days that history is not really so much influenced by dramatic incidents and striking personalities as by the social and economic forces which less obtrusively mould and shape the destiny of a nation. It is in this sphere that the law of Scotland has meant so much and stood for so much in the history of our land. The Scotsman has always had a natural turn for the law—I had almost said, a delight in it. If we have been accused of litigiosity and disputatiousness, it is only because we naturally exhibit the defects of our qualities, and those qualities are a strong and vigorous sense of principle and an intolerance of injustice.

I have recently discussed in another place the special attributes of the Scottish intellect particularly in relation to Scots law and I must not repeat myself. But this I may once more emphasise, that the legal way of looking at things has always been characteristic of the Scotsman, and all his intellectual activities—religious, social, and literary—have tended to have a legal tinge. The law to an unusual extent entered into the daily life of the people who loved its phrases and revelled in the battles of the Parliament House. Our two greatest novelists, Scott and Stevenson, were both advocates, brought up in the nurture and admonition of the law, and to the end both of them remained subject to its fascination.

In evidence of the zeal shown in spreading a knowledge of the law among the citizens of Scotland in early times, let me quote from a statute of James IV, 1406,

c. 3, which ordains "all barons and freeholders that are of substance to put their eldest sons and heirs to the schools from they be eight or nine years of age and to remain at the grammar schools till they be competently founded and have perfect Latin: And thereafter to remain three years at the schools of art and 'Jure' so that they may have knowledge and understanding of the laws, through the which Justice may reign universally through all the realm." I have heard some talk recently of the desirability of giving instruction in the elements of law to the pupils in our schools as a preparation for citizenship, and the project has been regarded as rather a startling novelty. Yet here in Scotland, over four hundred years ago, we made provision for training youthful jurists in our grammar schools!

An early Scottish lawyer goes so far as to claim that even our language is peculiarly fitted to be the vehicle of legal exposition. The anonymous author of an entertaining treatise entitled *Pleadings in some Remarkable Cases before the Supreme Courts of Scotland*, published in Edinburgh in 1673, and attributed to Sir George Mackenzie, thus delivers himself: "To me", he says, "it appears that the Scottish idiom of the British tongue is more fit for pleading than either the English idiom or the French tongue; for certainly a pleader must use a brisk, smart and quick way of speaking, whereas the English, who are a grave nation, use a too slow and grave pronunciation and the French a too soft and effeminate one. And therefore I think the English is fit for haranguing, the French to compliment, but the Scots for pleading. Our pronunciation is like ourselves—fiery, abrupt, sprightly and bold."

I fear I have been tempted to digress a little in order to share with you this engaging quotation. But it may serve to enforce my point that there has always in Scotland been a peculiarly close association between the law of the land and the life of the people.

Historians have hitherto paid too little attention to the law. It is only now being realised how faithfully the laws of a nation reflect its history, its genius, its aspirations. Let any one, for example, contrast the contents of a volume of Shaw's Reports with the last volume of the Session Cases, or the statutes of the Victorian reign with those of the present reign. In the nineteenth century the legislature was largely occupied in the adaptation of the law to the needs of a rapidly developing commercial and industrial age. It was the period of the famous Clauses Acts for the regulation of railway, harbour, gas and other enterprises, and of the first of the Companies Acts. Landed property was still an asset and had not yet become merely a liability, and the Courts were still much immersed in heritable disputes. Nowadays the statute book is chiefly occupied with measures relating to housing, town planning, health, welfare, workmen's compensation, and many other similar matters, while the old-fashioned type of litigation has almost entirely disappeared from our Law Reports, showing how profoundly the economic and social preoccupations of our country have altered. There is in truth no better index to the daily life and daily concerns of a people at any given time than the laws which they enact for their regulation and the disputes which they bring to the Courts for decision.

But if the law is of such value to the historian, a topic

which I need not labour further, not less valuable is history to the lawyer. The very subject-matter of the lawyer's daily business is embedded in history. A knowledge of the general history of his country is of constant service to him, but of still greater importance to him is a special knowledge of the history of the law. To the medical man the history of medicine is of little more than antiquarian and curious interest. So also is it with the past history of physical science generally. But with the lawyer it is quite otherwise. The system of rules and principles which he is daily called upon to apply is in large measure an inheritance from the past. It has been slowly built up during centuries of development and its sources are often to be found in the very beginnings of history. How can the lawyer intelligently appreciate the laws with which he has to work unless he knows how they have evolved, the purposes they have been designed to serve, and the mischiefs which they have been designed to meet? A knowledge of the embryology of legal principles is essential to the understanding of them in their present developed form. To take just one instance and that a very practical one: how can any one have any real knowledge of Scottish conveyancing who carries his reading no further back than the statutes of 1868, 1874, and 1924? He may be able to perform well enough the mechanical routine of his office, but he will have no appreciation of why he is doing what he is doing. Take him off the beaten path and he is lost. On the other hand, a sound knowledge of the history of the feudal system will not only impart an entirely new interest to his daily tasks, but will equip him to deal intelligently and effectively with any difficult problems which may arise.

There is no country where the principles of the feudal system survive to this day as they do in Scotland, and there is no country where its theory has been so logically and so practically adapted to serve modern conditions. Consequently, nowhere else can it be studied with more practical profit.

Probably one of the most important and difficult cases I was ever called on to argue in the House of Lords— *The Lord Advocate* v. *The Marquess of Zetland*—turned largely on the interpretation of a conveyancing statute of 1469 and involved the most searching examination of our whole feudal system. I was grateful, in the throes of that contest, for the indoctrination in the historical principles of feudalism which I had received—perhaps a little ungratefully at the time—from Professor Moir in the Conveyancing Classroom at Glasgow University. The proper interpretation of statutes, especially of our old Scots Acts, as that famous litigation shows, is impossible without a knowledge of the circumstances of their enactment and of the course of their judicial application.

It is often surprising how much valuable guidance for the solution of present-day legal problems can be gained from recourse to the wisdom of our forefathers of centuries ago. Nowhere is the vigour of the Scottish intellect better shown than in the works of our great institutional writers who have bequeathed to us a unique inheritance of sound learning. Twice recently in dealing with important questions of principle in the Privy Council, we have had recourse to Stair's *Institutions of the Law of Scotland*. In one instance we had to consider the question of the ownership of an island which had formed itself in the

Rangoon river in Burmah. There was no Burmese law on the subject and we had to decide the question on general principles. I directed the attention of my colleague, Sir George Lowndes, to a passage in Stair which exactly met the case, and in the judgment which he prepared you will find it quoted as the basis of the advice which we tendered to His Majesty. In the other instance we were dealing with the question of the acquisition by prescription of a right of fishing in an Indian river. Here, again, a statement of the law by Stair precisely covered one of the main points at issue, and I quoted it in the judgment of the Board. You will find both these cases in a recently issued part of the Indian Appeals. It is an interesting reflection that the pronouncements of a Scots lawyer of 1681 should be found to aid to-day in the solution of legal problems affecting the affairs of our great Empire in the East. Just before the vacation, when the remarkable question of what constitutes piracy *jure gentium* was being debated and when the laws of many foreign nations were being invoked, I ventured to suggest that it might be worth while to look across the Border, where in other days piracy was not an unknown form of activity in Scottish waters. So Hume and Allison were sent for and they were found to deal fully with the topic. These are surely striking instances of the present-day value of learning which might be thought to be merely antiquarian.

But it is not only on the score of its utility that I would commend the historical study of law. It has an intrinsic attraction of its own. How much of human interest can be derived from apparently the most unpromising material is well shown in the late Dr David Murray's

Law and Other Things

Legal Practice in Ayr and the West of Scotland in the Fifteenth and Sixteenth Centuries, where the protocol book of a remote predecessor of your distinguished president in the town of Ayr is made to throw a flood of light on the conditions of life in those early days.

May I in passing pay a tribute to the memory of my old friend? Few men in recent times have contributed more to legal learning than did Dr Murray. He demonstrated by his own career the fallacy of the idea that scholarship is inimical to professional success, for while few if any have surpassed him in antiquarian learning, he was no mere pedant but an admirable man of business and the head of one of the most important legal firms in Scotland. I am happy in remembering the stimulus which he gave to my early legal studies and, with no less gratitude, the fact that I received from him my first general retainer—for the old Glasgow and South-Western Railway Company.

I would fain demolish the persistent prejudice which has done so much to deter the younger members of both branches of our profession from pursuing literary and historical studies—the prejudice, I mean, which insists that any one who strays outside the pages of the Parliament House Book must somehow be unreliable as a practitioner. The law is no doubt a jealous mistress, but however much she may frown upon the other Muses, she has never objected to sharing with Clio the worship of her devotees. My own experience convinces me that there is no branch of knowledge which does not at one time or another prove of service to the lawyer in his practice. He comes into contact with every kind of human activity and the wider his knowledge the better

126

is he able to advise and guide his clients. Over and over again in the stress of advocacy I have found that information, which, when I acquired it, seemed to have no relation to my daily work, has suddenly come to my aid. And this is especially the case with historical knowledge.

It is no doubt well that the youthful aspirant should not yield to the attraction of alluring bypaths until he has learned to tread with assurance the hard high road. But no one would wish to deter him from the study which I am to-day advocating—the study of the history of our own institutions and our own law, for such study can only serve to enrich his professional knowledge and equip him better for his daily work.

We call ourselves a learned profession. Let me remind you that we are also a liberal profession. The difference between a trade and a profession is that the trader frankly carries on his business primarily for the sake of pecuniary profit while the members of a profession profess an art, their skill in which they no doubt place at the public service for remuneration, adequate or inadequate, but which is truly an end in itself. The professional man finds his highest rewards in his sense of his mastery of his subject, in the absorbing interest of the pursuit of knowledge for its own sake, and in the contribution which, by reason of his attainments, he can make to the promotion of the general welfare. It is only by the liberality of our learning that we can hope to merit the place in public estimation which we claim and to render to the public the services which they are entitled to expect from us.

And now, having opened my case, I fear at inordinate length, let me in orthodox fashion marshal my authorities. I cite first the trenchant exhortation of a great

statesman and man of the world. "I might instance,"
says Bolingbroke, in the fifth of his *Letters on the Study and
Use of History*, "I might instance in other professions the
obligation men be under of applying themselves to certain parts of history and I can hardly forbear doing it in
that of the law; in its nature the noblest and most beneficial to mankind, in its abuse and debasement the most
sordid and the most pernicious. A lawyer now is nothing
more. I speak of ninety-nine in a hundred at least....
But there have been lawyers that were orators, philosophers, historians. There have been Bacons and
Clarendons, my lord. There will be none such any more
till in some better age true ambition or the love of fame
prevails over avarice and till men find leisure and encouragement to prepare themselves for the exercise of
this profession by climbing up to the 'vantage ground',
so my lord Bacon calls it, of science instead of grovelling
all their lives below in a mean but gainful application to
all the little arts of chicane. Till this happen, the profession of the law will scarce deserve to be ranked among
the learned professions: and whenever it happens, one
of the vantage grounds to which men must climb is
metaphysical and the other, historical knowledge."

I found this passage quoted at length in the preface to
Lord Kames's *Historical Law Tracts*, and I commend the
whole of that preface to your reading, for in it Lord
Kames has expressed far better than I can the interest
and attraction of historical studies for the lawyer. He
complains of the neglect of the history of law, which, as
he truly says, is the "more unaccountable that, in place
of a dry, intricate, and crabbed science, law treated historically becomes an entertaining study; entertaining

not only to those whose profession it is, but to every person who hath any thirst for knowledge".

Next let me invoke another high authority, this time one of the most distinguished ornaments of the English Bench, Lord Bowen. When he had occasion, just fifty years ago, as it happens, to address the Birmingham Law Students Society, he took for his subject the value of the historical method as applied to law. "Is it possible", he asked, "to introduce a gleam of sunshine and to furnish a silver thread to guide the law student through the tangled labyrinth of a law library? Wanted, then, a method of studying the law pleasantly. Now, I believe that there exists such a method, absolutely scientific, full of interest, capable of satisfying the finest intellect, because it affords a scope for every power. Law is the application of certain rules to a subject-matter which is constantly shifting. What is it? English life! English business! England in movement, advancing from a continuous past to a continuous future. National life, national business, like every other product of human intelligence and culture is a growth—begins far away in the dim past, advances slowly, shaping and forming itself by the operation of purely natural causes." And then, again, in another eloquent passage, "mere legal terminology", he says, "may seem to you a dead thing. Mix history with it and it clothes itself with life. You have not even to travel far to find the history to mix. Look for it in the legal material itself; and the history, like water in a fertile soil, is ready there at hand and will well up into a spring. There before your very eyes, in the fragmentary decisions of the Law Courts and in the glossaries of commentators, you will see consecutive chapters of the narrative of the progress of the human race."

And, lastly, let me come nearer home and invoke the authority of our own Lord President who has recently rendered so signal a service to legal scholarship by his masterly translation of that Bible of the feudalist, Craig's *Jus Feudale*. In what he modestly entitles the "Translator's Note", Lord Clyde thus addresses his readers: "It is something of a reproach", he says, "that a national system of jurisprudence which justly boasts the pre-eminence of its institutional writers should have no historian. Lord Kames (1696–1782) was keenly alive to the value of historical knowledge in the interpretation of law; and, if adequate materials had been available in his time, he might have filled the vacant place. So also might Lord Hailes (1726–1792). As it was, Lord Kames's philosophical speculations on the origin and history of Scots Law held the field for nearly a century until the recently inaugurated era of modern research—when the labours of Thomson, Robertson, Riddell, and Cosmo Innes (to name but these) promised for the first time to provide authentic means of investigation and synthesis. We are still a long way from possessing the materials for a history of the Law of Scotland; and, unfortunately, our administrators make up for the excellence of their system of registering deeds by a persistent neglect of our national records. But our command over such materials as are now accessible is increasing; and Scottish historical scholarship has made great strides in the last seventy years."

It is in order to aid in the removal of the national reproach to which the Lord President alludes and to foster

and promote the reviving interest in the history of Scots
law that a project has recently been set on foot to establish a Scottish Legal Historical Society, which it is fitly
proposed should be called the Stair Society. The response already received promises an initial membership
in the region of 600, substantially exceeding, I believe,
that of the illustrious Selden Society founded forty-seven
years ago to render a similar service to the law of England. Most of the intending members are naturally
drawn from our own country, but the Dominions, the
United States, and foreign countries are also represented.
Let me instance, by the way, as significant of the growing
interest taken in Scots law in the Dominions that the late
Professor Hunter Marshall, of Manitoba University, has
recently bequeathed the residue of his estate to the University of Glasgow, to be applied *inter alia* to encourage
the study of the history of medieval Scotland, especially
with regard to the history of Scots law and institutions in
that period. I refrain from enforcing the moral of that
generous example.

The main task of the Stair Society will be the editing
and publishing of judicious selections from the early
legal material available in the Register House and elsewhere. It is due to the very circumstance of past neglect
that it is not easy to tell you what should be our first
choice. Unhappily, our records are not so accessible or so
well ordered as those which are under the charge of my
friend, the Master of the Rolls, who has done so much
to arouse public interest in the preservation of the historical archives of England. Incidentally I hope that the
Stair Society will soon be sufficiently influential to bring
pressure to bear in those quarters where so niggardly a

spirit has hitherto been shown towards our national muniments. But at least we know that there is an ample field to explore. We have no year-books in Scotland, but we have in the *Acta Dominorum* a vast quantity of judicial records which may be made to yield valuable contributions to our legal history. What we need, in the first place, is a survey of the material, a *catalogue raisonné* which will let us know what we really possess. Mr Livingstone, in his *Guide to the Public Records of Scotland*, Dr Maitland Thomson, in his Rhind Lectures on *The Public Records of Scotland*, Mr M'Kechnie, in his essays on *The Pursuit of Pedigree*, and Mr Paton, in his paper on the *Scottish Records* read before the Historical Association of Scotland, have all done good work in this direction, but much remains to be done.

Then I should like to see in Edinburgh an exhibition, such as was held last month in the Hungarian National Museum at Budapest, where a remarkable collection of written and printed documents illustrative of the history of Hungarian law was gathered together, the occasion coinciding with the 350th anniversary of the publication of the first printed edition of the *Corpus Juris Hungarici* in 1584. I remember how impressed I was when I paid a visit four years ago to the superb exhibition in the Free Library at Philadelphia of books, documents, portraits and autograph letters illustrative of the growth of the common law of England from the days of Alfred the Great to Sir William Blackstone which had been collected by Mr H. L. Carson, a prominent solicitor of that city.

I am disposed to think that much light might be thrown on our legal history by an examination of the archives of some of the great legal seminaries of Holland, France and Italy to which our early legal students resorted in such numbers and from which they imported so much to this country. Many interesting vistas lie open and await our exploration.

To-day you are looking forward as well as backward, and some of you in these days of rapid and disconcerting changes may be contemplating the future with some dismay. Let history administer her consolations. I was turning over Lord Cockburn's *Journal* the other day and found him on 8 November 1848 indulging in a lamentable threnody on the Court of Session, whose business, he says, "has been long gradually and steadily sinking". He sees salvation only in reform of the "purse-emptying and time-exhausting forms" of procedure. "If the procedure be corrected effectually and speedily, the Court has a chance: if not, half or the whole of it will be quashed." *Adsit omen.* We know how Cockburn's forebodings were belied and how vigorously the Court of Session flourished after the reforms of 1868. This winter the Court begins its work under new rules which have been devised by the best wisdom in the profession under the experienced guidance of the Lord President. I hope that the adage that history repeats itself will once more come true.

But I would not ask you to turn to history only for that rather shabby form of consolation which comes of recalling that times have been just as bad before as they are now. The real practical value of history to the lawyer is to be found in the guidance which it affords in dealing with present-day problems. We think our problems new and unprecedented. Yet almost every one of them has been confronted by our ancestors. Where the lawyer who is grounded in historical knowledge can best help is by bringing to bear on to-day's difficulties the wisdom which comes from the experience of the past. The best progress is that which is based on sure foundations of past experience. And let us not be unduly alarmed by the changes we see around us, for change is essential to progress. As Lord Bowen so well says, in concluding his survey of *Progress in the Administration of Justice during the Victorian Period*: "There is and can be no such thing as finality about the administration of the law. It changes, it must change, it ought to change, with the broadening wants and requirements of a growing country, and with the gradual illumination of the public conscience." I am confident that in this secular process the members of this society will bear an honourable part.

LAW AND LETTERS

Address delivered at the Annual Meeting of the American Bar Association, Chicago, August 1930

I AM happy to have this opportunity of acknowledging in person the distinction which you conferred on me when in 1924 you elected me an honorary member of the American Bar Association, thus enabling me to-day to enjoy the privilege of addressing you as one of yourselves. But indeed a lawyer can never feel himself a stranger at a gathering of the members of his profession in whatever quarter of the globe, for I am convinced that there is no profession which binds its members in a closer fraternity. It is not for nothing that in the law we call each other brethren. We may not succeed in attracting the same measure of popular affection as do certain of the other professions. Nevertheless our services to the community are indispensable and I suspect are valued much more highly than it is customary to avow.

If I were to seek for the explanation of the bond which binds in brotherhood the servants of the law throughout the world, I venture to think that I should find it in our common devotion to a great ideal, the promotion of the orderly progress of civilisation. The famous orders of chivalry in the middle ages dedicated their lives and labours to some noble cause. We in these modern and more prosaic days have no less need, we have indeed more need, of a similar inspiration, and the cause to which we are devoted is truly a worthy one—that justice and truth shall prevail throughout the world. Amidst the daily drudgery of court and office we are apt to lose sight of the lofty aims of our profession. Occasions such as this enable us to recapture the enthusiasm of our high calling, to realise afresh the great and vital interests which are committed to us and in the glow of mutual encouragement and good fellowship to rekindle ideals which, when we separate once more on our several ways, will long continue to illumine our daily path of duty.

I read recently that the great Chief Justice of the United States Supreme Court, John Marshall—*clarum et venerabile nomen*—wore during his life an amethyst ring with the motto *Veritas Vincit* engraved upon it. No minister of the law ever observed more loyally the lesson of that daily reminder. Steadfastly and unswervingly, through good report and through evil report, he pursued the even tenor of his way and proved to the world once more that truth is great and must prevail. His memory is revered not only here in his own country but wherever the law is practised, and his noble judgments will ever continue to echo down the corridors of time. To me, as a Scotsman, it is of peculiar interest that the Chief Justice should have adopted this talisman, for the words *Veritas Vincit* are the motto of the famous Scottish family of the Keiths, the Earls Marischal of Scotland, whose name is associated with many of the most stirring and romantic episodes of my native land. His right to wear it came to him from his maternal grandfather, the Reverend James Keith, a member of this historic Scottish family who fled to Virginia to escape the consequences of his participation in the Jacobite rebellion.

Thus Marshall could count among his ancestors Sir Robert Keith, the commander of the Scottish horse at Bannockburn in 1314, George Keith, the fifth Earl, a famous scholar and diplomatist who in 1593 founded and endowed Marischal College in the University of Aberdeen, and William, the seventh Earl, who saved the regalia of Scotland by concealing them in his castle at Dunnottar. If heredity counts for anything, it is not surprising that John Marshall, coming from such a stock, found himself equally at home in the camp and in the Courts and won distinction in each. And now I must tell you that over the doorway into the law library in the Old Parliament House where the Law Courts meet in Edinburgh there is hung the standard of the Earl Marischal of Scotland which was carried at the fateful battle of Flodden Field in 1513 and which bears embroidered on it, along with the Keith arms, those selfsame words—*Veritas Vincit*. Thus the advocates of the Scottish Bar have ever before their eyes the same admonition which the great Chief Justice of the United States adopted as the key-note of his life work.

There are other pleasant links between the Chief Justice and Scotland besides the fact that some of our best Scottish blood ran in his veins, for he received his first tutoring from a young emigrant Scottish divine, James Thompson, who lived for a year in his father's house, while his second instructor was the Reverend Archibald Campbell, who belonged to a Glasgow family of Virginian merchants and was an uncle of the poet Thomas Campbell, the well-known author of *The Pleasures of Hope*. In the school which Campbell started in Westmoreland County, Virginia, he no doubt imparted to his young pupil the sound classical teaching which he had himself imbibed at a Scottish University. I note, too, that among the earliest books which the Chief Justice bought were the *Lectures on Rhetoric* of the famous Professor Hugh Blair of Edinburgh University and the *Principles of Equity*, a treatise written by the Scottish judge, Lord Kames.

The name and fame of John Marshall lead me easily to the theme on which I should like to say a few words to you to-day, namely, the association between law and letters, for, as I shall show, he exemplified that association in a conspicuous degree. I am convinced, as he was convinced, that no lawyer is justly entitled to the honourable and conventional epithet of "learned" if his learning is confined to the statutes and the law reports. It is the province of the lawyer to be the counsellor of persons engaged in every branch of human activity. Nothing human must be alien to him. "You are a lawyer", said Dr Johnson to Mr Edwards; "Lawyers know life practically. A bookish man should always have them to converse with. They have what he wants." Equally the man of letters has what the lawyer wants, for if he is to fulfil his rôle usefully and wisely he must have a mind not merely stored with the precedents of the law but possessing that width of comprehension, that serenity of outlook and that catholicity of sympathy which can nowise be so well acquired as from consort with the great masters of literature. In such company is found the corrective for the narrowness of mere professionalism. The lawyer does well from time to time to lift his eyes from his desk and look out of the window on the wider world beyond. There can be a too sedulous devotion to the textbooks of the law and I do not commend the example of Chief Baron Palles, who is said to have taken Fearne on *Contingent Remainders* with him for reading on his honeymoon.

Fortunately the law has always been on excellent terms with the Muses. You have only to read the biographies of our great judges and advocates of the past to realise how versed in letters most of them were, and what solace and inspiration they drew from that source. Take Chief Justice Marshall himself. Before he was twelve years of age he had copied out every word of Pope's *Essay on Man* and committed his favourite passages to memory. He bought Mason's *Poems* about the same time as he acquired Blackstone's *Commentaries*, and among his other early purchases were. Chesterfield's *Letters*, the *Life of Clarendon*, Machiavelli's *Works* and translations of Æschines' *Orations* and Demosthenes *On the Crown*—a sufficiently varied intellectual diet. When he was seventy-one years of age he read the whole of Jane Austen's novels, of which he made this perspicacious estimate in a letter to his colleague Joseph Story—"Her flights are not lofty. She does not soar on eagle's wings, but she is pleasing, interesting, equable and yet amusing." In a letter written in 1829 he said: "The plan of my life I had formed for myself to be adopted after my retirement from office is to read nothing but novels and poetry." Alas, in his case, as in that of so many others who have looked forward all their lives to the delights which they have promised themselves on retirement, this happy time never came, for he died six years later still in harness.

Abraham Lincoln in his early days had even greater

difficulties to surmount in the pursuit of learning than John Marshall. I may properly call him also as a witness to my plea, for although his greatest triumphs were in the realm of statesmanship he was also an accomplished lawyer. As a boy "he read", we are told by his step-mother, "every book he could lay his hands on and when he came across a passage that struck him he would write it down on boards, if he had no paper, and keep it there until he did get paper. Then he would rewrite it, look at it, repeat it. He had a copy-book, a kind of scrap-book, in which he put down all things and thus pre-served them." Lincoln diligently borrowed such books as were to be found in the neighbourhood of his early home in Indiana. They were not many, but they in-cluded *Robinson Crusoe*, Æsop's *Fables*, Bunyan's *Pilgrim's Progress*, Weems's *Life of Washington* and a *History of the United States*, while Shakespeare and Burns were his favourite poets. With these he mitigated the perusal of the *Revised Statutes of Indiana*, in those days happily not so bulky as now. Thus Lincoln acquired his marvellous command of clear-cut simple English which reached its perfection of combined brevity and beauty in the dedi-catory speech at Gettysburg and the great Second In-augural. His happy gift of style is illustrated not only in resounding aphorisms, such as the famous "He who would be no slave must consent to have no slave", but also enabled him in more colloquial moments to coin innumerable delightful sayings. Thus when speaking of his difficulties in the organisation of recruits, he said that he felt like "a man trying to shovel a bushel of fleas across a barn floor". Again when he was besieged by office seekers while his own position was highly precarious, he complained that his task was like letting rooms at one end of his house while the other end was on fire. And yet again when he was reproached for the stern measures which war necessitated, he asked—"Would you prosecute it in future with elder-stalk squirts charged with rose water?"

I have given you evidence of the debt which two of the greatest American lawyers and statesmen owed to literature. May I in turn say something of the connection of the Bar of Scotland with the world of letters, for nowhere have law and literature been more closely related? I cannot say how far this may have been due to the fact that the Scottish Bar has for two and a half centuries lived in daily contact with the famous Advocates' Library, the greatest library which ever belonged to any professional body in the world. Founded in 1682 by the famous, some would say notorious, Lord Advocate, Sir George Mackenzie of Rosehaugh—that "noble wit of Scotland" as Dryden called him—it had grown to over three-quarters of a million books and pamphlets, not including its priceless collection of manuscripts, when in 1925 the Faculty handed it over as a free gift to the nation, beyond all comparison the greatest literary benefaction in our country's history. With such resources at hand to inspire them, the Bar of Scotland have always lived in an atmosphere of what used to be called polite learning. It should not be forgotten that Sir Walter Scott was a practising Scottish advocate, and for many years held office as a Sheriff or County Court Judge and as Clerk of the Court of Session, the Scottish Supreme Court. He was a lawyer of no mean attainments and his pen was not solely devoted to poetry and romance. I suppose I am one of the few people of this generation who have read his official disquisition on the technical subject of jury trials. In *Guy Mannering*, Sir Walter has stated my thesis for me in his own inimitable way. You remember the visit which Colonel Mannering pays to the study of his counsel, Mr Pleydell, in the High Street of Edinburgh. "The library into which he was shown", we read, "was a well-proportioned room, hung with a portrait or two of Scottish characters of eminence by Jamieson, the Caledonian Vandyke, and surrounded with books, the best editions of the best authors and in particular an admirable collection of classics. 'These', said Pleydell, 'are my tools of trade. A lawyer without history or literature is a mechanic, a mere working mason; if he possesses some knowledge of these he may venture to call himself an architect.'"

I enjoy for the moment the privilege which the lawyer is so rarely accorded of being as irrelevant as I please and I cannot refrain from referring here to a literary link with the past which may interest you. The late Archbishop of Canterbury told me that Sir Walter tried out his *Tales of a Grandfather* by reading them over to the Archbishop's mother, Mrs Davidson, then a little girl of seven, and according to her verdict retained or rejected what he had written. Dining at Grillion's Club one evening only a year or two ago I sat between the Archbishop and Lord Finlay, who in turn told me that he was reading the *Tales of a Grandfather* to his own little granddaughter. So the ages are bridged.

Another Scottish advocate of our own day has attained a literary fame second only to Sir Walter's. It cannot be said that R. L. Stevenson had much professional associa-

142

tion with the Bar to which he was called as a contemporary of Lord Dunedin, who is with us here to-day. Yet he found the inspiration of some of his best writing in the legal life of Edinburgh, whose characteristic flavour no one appreciated better than he. There is general agreement that his masterpiece was his unfinished *Weir of Hermiston,* in which he gives us with amazing insight and infinite gusto a portrait of a Scottish judge of the old school. I could mention many other names; Lord Jeffrey, for instance, the pungent Edinburgh reviewer who is perhaps best remembered for the petulant "This will never do" with which he greeted the publication of Wordsworth's *Excursion,* and Aytoun, the author of the *Bon Gaultier Ballads* and the *Lays of the Scottish Cavaliers,* who confessed that although he followed the law he never could overtake it. But I content myself with reminding you that the two greatest biographies in the English language—Boswell's *Life of Johnson* and Lockhart's *Life of Scott*—were written by members of the Scottish Bar. So we may accept with becoming modesty Dr Johnson's reluctant tribute—"The Scotch write English wonderfully well!"

The fine scholarship of the Bench and Bar of England is traditional. It has exhibited itself perhaps less in actual contributions to literature than in the professional sphere. The deliverances of the judges of England in the leading cases of the law are distinguished by the highest qualities of literary craftsmanship, witness the historic judgments in which Lord Mansfield enunciated the principles of the common law in their application to commerce, the commanding brevity of Jessel, Master of the Rolls, the elegant irony of Lord Bowen, and those delightful passages in which Lord Macnaghten contrived to illumine with humanity and humour the most accurate exposition of the technical doctrines of the law. Of him it could certainly never be said, as was said of another Law Lord, that he was not only dull himself but the cause of dullness in others. The compilers of anthologies have at last discovered how much admirable literary matter is concealed within the unpromising covers of the Law Reports, and in a recent volume of selections of the best English prose will be found two passages from judgments of Lord Sumner, that incomparable master of the English language, whose retirement from the judiciary even his inadequate successor may be permitted to lament.

While literature for its own sake has always possessed a special attraction for the members of our profession, I venture to suggest that its study has a utilitarian side also. Words, the spoken and the written word, are the raw material of the lawyer's trade, and the possession of a good literary style which enables him to make effective use of that material is one of the most valuable of all professional equipments. Such a style is often a natural gift, but even where it is not so bestowed it may be acquired by study and by practice. We may all at least aspire to such a style as, we are told, characterised the judgments of a well-known American judge—"clear, compact and complete, carrying no immaterial discussions and losing no weight through grammatical leaks or rhetorical cracks". For the attainment of a good English style there is no discipline so admirable as the reading of the Bible, a statement appropriate for a son of the Scottish manse which I take leave to endorse as a Lord of Appeal.

Law and Letters

I have been pleased to observe in the advertisement columns of the *Journal* of the American Bar Association the Bible finding a place among the notices of legal publications. It is there commended to purchasers "bound in high-quality buckram that looks well with other books in your law library. Every lawyer in active practice", says the advertiser, "needs it...you'll find it a wonderful help in your practice." I respectfully agree, though I am not quite sure that we mean exactly the same thing. It was Daniel Webster who said—"I have read the Bible through many times and now make it a practice to read it through once every year. It is a book of all others for lawyers as well as divines; and I pity the man who cannot find in it a rich supply of thought and of rules of conduct." In that delightful and friendly series of letters which those two veteran combatants, Adams and Jefferson, exchanged in their old age and which fortunately has been preserved for our edification, I find Adams on Christmas Day 1813 confessing to his correspondent—"The Bible is the best book in the world. It contains more of my little philosophy than all the libraries I have seen." I am for the moment, however, thinking of the Bible purely as literature, and I am very sure that those who have learned to drink from that well of English undefiled have sought the best source of literary inspiration. If to this you add some generous draughts from the Pierian spring of the classics, you can never descend to the mean vulgarity which characterises so much of the writing of the present day.

There is no reason why legal arguments or judicial judgments should not be expressed in good English. There is every reason why they should. The advocate who can impart a literary flavour to his address adds to its persuasiveness and attraction; "Nor pleads he worse who with a decent sprig of bay adorns his legal waste of wig." Exotic flowers of oratory are not suitable adornments for our modern Law Courts, but the Temple has never disdained to deck its plots with the classic blossoms of the English flower garden. It is of even more vital importance that those who sit in judgment should have a mastery not only of law but of letters, so that they may be able to use with ease and freedom—and I should like to add, with distinction—the vehicle of language in which their decisions must be conveyed. The draftsman comes to take a joy in his sheer craftsmanship. I venture to think that there are few higher intellectual pleasures than success in the task of expressing an argument or a conclusion in just precisely the right language, so that the thought is caught and poised exactly as we would have it. Clear thinking always means clear writing and clear writing is always good writing.

And so I come back to the point from which I set out that alike for the preservation of our position as a learned profession and for the promotion of efficiency in the art we practise, it is essential that the lawyer should be steeped in literature and keep his mind constantly refreshed and renewed by contact with the great thinkers of the past. So only can he attain to true eminence.

LAW AND LANGUAGE

Presidential Address to the Holdsworth Club of the Students of the Faculty of Law in the University of Birmingham, May 1931

TO the legal profession, above all others, words and their meanings are a matter of supreme concern. The lawyer, indeed, may not unfairly be described as a trafficker in words. They are his staple, his stock-in-trade, and the annual turnover of the profession must far outstrip the almost astronomical figures of the Bankers' Clearing House. For all day and every day the lawyer is using words, whether he is framing a conveyance or a contract, advising a client about his affairs, arguing a case, writing a judgment or opinion, preparing the report of a decision—judges, counsel and solicitors are constantly making use of words, written or spoken, and are constantly endeavouring by the use of words to convey their meaning to others.

I do not pause to consider whether the service rendered to the community by dealers in words is as valuable as that which is rendered by those who follow the more creative callings, the architect, the shipbuilder, and the like. "Words", we are reminded, "are the daughters of earth, things are the sons of heaven." But this at least is certain, that it is of the utmost importance for the lawyer, if he is to perform adequately his duty to his clients and to the public, that he should possess a special skill in the use of language. It is not, of course, with words in themselves that he is concerned, as is the etymologist and, to some extent, the literary artist. For him "it is not necessary", as Vice-Chancellor Kindersley said (in construing the word "money" in a will), "to go into the derivation of the word, for that sort of reasoning would not assist in the administration of justice.* For the lawyer the importance of words lies in the fact that they are the vehicle of the law. In statutes, reports, and textbooks he finds the law in static form set out in words; in judgment, argument and draft he seeks to express the law in dynamic form, again in words. For the formulation, the exposition and the application of law the only medium is language, and success or failure in these endeavours is dependent on the skill and precision with which the lawyer handles his medium.

The surprising thing is that so little conscious and systematic study is in these days devoted by the legal profession to the art of the right use of language. In classical times it was otherwise. In Greece and Rome much time and much thought were given to the technique of words, and the schools of the grammarians were the training ground of the lawyer. We can still learn much from the precepts of the Attic orators and the treatises of Cicero and Quintilian.

The art of words is a difficult art and a fine art, and the practice of it brings pleasure as well as profit. It is not, however, the aesthetic aspect of language that is of primary interest to the lawyer, though Sir Frederick Pollock is right when he says that not even the draftsman of an ordinary lease can produce really good work "unless he has a share of artistic feeling in the eminent sense, and takes a certain artistic pride in the quality of his

* *Barrett* v. *White* (1855), 24 L.J., Ch. 724, at p. 726.

workmanship apart from the reward he will get for it".
It is rather the utilitarian and practical side of the art
which interests the practitioner. Let him not dismiss the
matter as merely theoretical. It is a matter of business.
No experienced lawyer will belittle the importance of
accuracy and precision in the record of his transactions
and the expression of his arguments, or fail to recognise
how indispensable it is to appreciate the exact meaning
of the words he uses. It is not inappropriate that the
Law Society should have adopted the word "Interpret"
as its telegraphic address!

The student of law soon realises that of all things
words are the most uncertain and ambiguous. "The
greatest sophism of all sophisms", according to Bacon,
"is the equivocation and ambiguity of words and
phrase."* Dryden says the same thing in verse:

> As long as words a diff'rent sense will bear,
> And each may be his own interpreter,
> Our airy faith will no foundation find:
> The word's a weathercock for every wind.†

Indeed, such is the imperfection of the human vocabulary
that hardly any word has a precise and definite meaning
except the terms used in mathematics and the physical
sciences. The terminology of the law labours in a special
degree under this disability because of the nature of its
subject-matter. The infinite diversity of human relationships with which the law has to deal transcends the
limited resources of language, which is always trying to
overtake the complexities of life and business and reduce
them to categories. Hence the paradox presents itself

* *Advancement of Learning*, Bk 2.
† *The Hind and the Panther*, ll. 462 *et seq.*

that the science whose main object is the achievement of order is most open to the accusation of indefiniteness and uncertainty in its pronouncements.

It is only the inefficient craftsman, however, who quarrels with his tools. The efficient workman will rather address himself to their mastery. Let me read you the admirable admonition of the author of the famous *Essay on the Human Understanding*. "I know", says Locke in his Epistle to the Reader, "there are not words enough in any language to answer all the variety of ideas that enter into men's discourses and reasonings. But this hinders not but that when anyone uses any term he may have in his mind a determined idea which he makes it the sign of and to which he should keep it steadily annexed during that present discourse. Where he does not or cannot do this he in vain pretends to clear or distinct ideas: it is plain his are not so; and, therefore, there can be expected nothing but obscurity and confusion where such terms are made use of which have not such a precise determination." Addressed to mankind in general, this exhortation has a very special application to the lawyer. It may be said without exaggeration that at least half the contests of the law have their origin in the ambiguous use of language. The imperfections of the human vocabulary are as lucrative to the legal practitioner as our physical frailties are to the physician. Many of these controversies over words are no doubt inevitable owing to the inherent defects of the instrument which perforce we must use, and cannot be entirely eliminated even by the most skilful, but, on the other hand, much the larger number of them arise from perfectly avoidable slipshodness and want of precision in thought and expression.

Law and Language

The subject of the lawyer's use of language is thus one which may profitably engage our consideration for a little. There is one interesting aspect of it on which I do not propose to enlarge, for it would take me into fields of investigation foreign to my present purpose, but it is worth mentioning. I mean the peculiar virtue attached to the use of certain words as solemnities. In the ceremonial ritual of all peoples in primitive times we know that a mystic potency was attributed to particular words and a whole branch of folk-lore is devoted to the study of spells and charms. The law has not been entirely free from this tendency. It is in the historical formalities attendant on transactions in real property that the ritual use of special words finds its best illustrations. The element of symbolism was by the nature of things imported into such transactions, for corporeal "traditio" is not possible in the case of land as it is in the case of personal chattels. And with the prescribed legal ceremonial the use of certain words was always associated. The omission of these "words of style", as they are called, was fatal. Let me give an example from the history of Scottish conveyancing. In Scots law from early times there was one word the use of which was indispensable to constitute an effectual transfer of heritable property, and that was the word "dispone". So recently as 1874 the House of Lords had to consider the consequences of its omission, in the case of *Kirkpatrick's Trustees* v. *Kirkpatrick*.* It there appeared that Mrs Kirkpatrick had on 4 March 1867 executed a trust disposition and settlement in which she used in the dispositive clause with regard to certain

* (1874) 1 R. (H.L.) 37, reported as *Alexander* v. *Kirkpatrick* in L.R., 2 Sc. App. 397.

property the familiar array of words, I "give, grant, assign, convey and make over", but omitted to say "I dispone". The deed was held to be ineffectual to convey her heritable property. Lord Chancellor Cairns bases his judgment on the ground that the deed "has not in it that word of art and style of efficacy according to Scotch law, I mean the word 'dispone', and it has been held unanimously by all the judges of the Court of Session that as the law stood at the time this deed was executed the want of the word 'dispone' was fatal to the deed as a conveyance of heritable property". This insistence on the use of a particular word to effect a particular legal result is not peculiar to Scots law. The Lord Chancellor goes on to say: "It may appear to be a very technical view to hold the presence or absence of a single word of this kind to be efficacious or fatal in a deed conveying heritable property, but your Lordships must bear in mind that according to the law of England also there are other words, I apprehend, not of greater importance, the presence or absence of which will be found to have an equal effect on the validity of a deed." I am not expert in the mysteries of English conveyancing, but I have no doubt that the Lord Chancellor was thinking of the virtues attached by it to such words as "demise", "heirs and assigns", and so forth. Mrs Kirkpatrick's omission to "dispone" her property as well as to give, grant, assign, convey and make it over would not now be visited with the penalty of nullity, for the Conveyancing (Scotland) Act of 1874,* enacted by section 27 that "It shall not be competent to object to the validity of any deed or writing as a conveyance of heritage coming into operation after

* 37 and 38 Vict. c. 94.

the passing of this Act on the ground that it does not contain the word 'dispone', provided it contains any other word or words importing conveyance or transference or present intention to convey or transfer." So another good plea has been consigned by the Legislature to the law's lumber room. There are still, however, I believe, cases in which it is as necessary to legal efficacy to use the correct verbal incantation as it was to employ the words "Open Sesame" to cause the door of the treasure cave of the Forty Thieves to roll back.

The requirement that prescribed words and formulas must be used to achieve certain legal results was not entirely a matter either of mere primitive mumbo-jumbo or of professional pedantry. It had a purpose. It was intended to secure deliberation and certainty. The law said: If you wish to accomplish a particular result, this is the way to do it; if you do it in that way, no question can arise and all the controversies which are so apt to surround questions of intention will be avoided. In Scotland, if you used the word "dispone" you conveyed the property; if you did not, you did not, and there was an end of it. Now under the statute of 1874 any word importing conveyance or transfer will do, but how much vaguer and more open to question is this concession to the linguistic frailty of those who wish to make a grant of their landed property! I confess to being rather an admirer of the discipline which required people to be accurate, precise, and formal in their important transactions and visited departure from the rules with penalties. Lord Cockburn once said: "Words acquire the character of being words of style solely because, from their expressing a thought necessary or usual for the

153

occasion, they can never be safely omitted. 'I hereby dispone' is a piece of style because without it there would be no disposition. When a man reserves power to revoke a deed and says in a subsequent writing, 'I revoke that deed', the force of these words is surely not weakened by saying that they are so precise, necessary, and conclusive that they have become words of style. No insignificant word ever becomes a matter of style."*

I leave this digression on what I may term spellbinding words and return to my main purpose, which is to discuss the general topic of the lawyer's use of words. "Most of the disputes in the world arise from words", said Lord Mansfield.† The experience of every practising lawyer will confirm this saying. I know for myself that for the past thirty years and more a great part of my daily business has been to give opinions, to argue or to decide as to the meaning of words. These disputes are by no means always barren logomachies. Great questions of principle may turn upon a word and valuable rights and interests depend on the meaning assigned to it. The difficulty of interpretation arises, as I have said, from the imperfection and inexactitude of language as a vehicle of ideas. If words are the currency of our business, they suffer from the defects which have always affected human currency. Their value in exchange is unstable, and they not only undergo changes in time but at any one moment their precise content is often indeterminable.

One of the great controversies of the law will serve as an illustration. I refer to the determination of the

* *Leith* v. *Leith* (1848), 10 D. at p. 1159.
† *Morgan* v. *Jones* (1773), Lofft. 176.

meaning of the word "minerals" in the Clauses Acts, and particularly the Railways Clauses Consolidation Act of 1845.* As you know, when a railway company buys land for the construction of its line there is implied in the statutory form of conveyance an exception of the mines and minerals in the land purchased. These remain the property of the vendor. This was, no doubt, designed to save the railway companies the expense of purchasing valuable underlying minerals when all that they required was the use of the surface. There is a code which provides for what is to happen when the owner of the retained minerals wants to work them, and the railway company, if it is afraid that its line may subside if it is undermined, has to pay compensation if it exercises its right of stopping the workings. Hence a whole series of leading cases has arisen in which the railway companies have maintained that particular materials were not minerals, and, consequently, belonged to them under their conveyances, while the landowners on the other hand have contended that these materials were minerals reserved to them which they were entitled to extract or for the non-working of which they must be compensated. The word is an admirable example of ambiguity. There is no definition of it in the statutory code, and, consequently, the Courts have been called upon to adjudicate upon one substance after another. What is to be the criterion? It is obvious that the familiar distinction between animal, vegetable and mineral which sufficed for the parlour games of our youth could afford no adequate guide. Is fireclay a mineral or merely part of the ordinary substance of the earth? Is building sandstone a mineral

* 8 and 9 Vict. c. 20.

or like ordinary stones and rock part of the common structure of the ground? To the former question the House of Lords answered that fireclay was a mineral; to the latter, that sandstone was not a mineral. Other cases have arisen about whinstone, china clay, brick clay, and so forth. The criterion ultimately prescribed by the House of Lords was that those things are minerals which are so described in "the vernacular of the mining world, the commercial world, and landowners". This may be a practical test and probably as good as any that could be devised, but it obviously relegated each case to be determined by evidence of usage. And it gave rise to another interesting question. If vernacular usage is to be the test we know that such usage varies from one generation to another. As at what date are we to ascertain the usage? The point came up in a litigation between the Marquis of Linlithgow and the North British Railway.* A canal which subsequently came to be owned by the railway company was constructed in the early part of last century partly through Lord Linlithgow's lands and traverses the well-known Linlithgow shale field. The statute authorising the construction of the canal was passed in 1817 long before the Clauses Acts, but its terms gave rise to the same question as I have just indicated. The landowner desired to work out the oil shale under the canal or to be paid for it as a mineral, while the railway company maintained that it belonged to them as part of the land conveyed to them. Possession of the land was taken by the original canal undertakers in 1818, but no conveyance was actually executed till 1862. Here were the makings of a first-class controversy.

* 1912 S.C. 1327; 1914 S.C. (H.L.), 38.

Law and Language

If vernacular usage was to be the test, was it to be the vernacular of 1817 when the Act was passed, or the vernacular of 1813 when possession was taken, or that of 1862 when the conveyance was executed, or that which was current when the question came before the Courts? The question was critical, for mineral oil became known as a commercial commodity only after Young's famous patents, the pioneer patents of the great modern oil industry, were taken out in the 'fifties of last century. Before that time shale was regarded merely as rubbish and of no value to anyone. A most interesting body of evidence on the history of mineral oil extraction was collected, and I remember Professor Gregory, the well-known geologist, furnished a remarkable reconstitution of the state of geological science at different periods on the subject of the properties of shale. The Scottish Courts held that the crucial date was the date of the actual transference of possession in 1818, and that at that date shale was not known as a mineral in the vernacular of the mining world, the commercial world, and landowners. The case went to the House of Lords, but there the interesting questions to which I have alluded were not dealt with, for in their disappointing way they found another ground in the terms of the statute for deciding the matter in favour of the railway company. There could be no better example of the uncertainty of language for, as you have seen, it was not merely a question of ascertaining the meaning of a term but a question as well of determining the date at which the meaning was to be ascertained.

Probably the most notorious instance of the difficulty of interpreting even the simplest words is to be found in

the famous case of *Powell* v. *Kempton Park Race Course Co.,
Ltd.,** where the controversy related to the meaning of
a "place opened, kept or used" for the purposes pro-
hibited by the Betting Act, 1853. The locality—I must
not say place—under discussion was a railed-in enclosure
adjoining a race course, to which enclosure the public
were admitted on payment of an entrance fee and to
which bookmakers resorted for the purposes of their
business. Such an array and such a division of eminent
judicial minds has seldom been seen. Taking all the
Courts which considered this momentous question, I
find on the one hand Lord Russell of Killowen, L.C.J.,
Rigby, L.J., Lord Davey and Lord Hobhouse in favour
of finding that the enclosure came within the scope of the
Act, while of the contrary and prevailing opinion were
Lord Esher, M.R., Lindley, Lopes, A. L. Smith and
Chitty, L.JJ., Lord Chancellor Halsbury and Lords
Watson, Macnaghten, Morris, Shand and James of
Hereford. The Lord Chancellor in his judgment sets out
the statutory words that required to be construed in an
analytical table, and deals with the problems which each
word raises. In Lord James of Hereford's speech a good
example of the process of interpretation is exhibited.
"There must", says his Lordship at p. 194, "be a defined area so marked out that it can be found and recognised as 'the place' where the business is carried on and
wherein the bettor can be found. Thus, if a person betted
on Salisbury Plain there would be no place within the
Act. The whole of Epsom Downs or any other race
course where betting takes place† would not constitute

* [1899] A.C. 143.
† Incidentally, observe the double use of the word "place"!

158

a place; but directly a definite localisation of the business of betting is affected, be it under a tent or even movable umbrella, it may be well held that a 'place' exists for the purposes of a conviction under the Act." The enclosure in question, his Lordship went on to say, might therefore physically speaking under certain conditions constitute a place, but even if so he held that it was not opened, kept, or used for the purpose of the owners, occupiers, or users of it betting with persons resorting thereto.

Many other examples of this uncertainty in the meaning of words will occur to you. The undiscriminating use of the conjunctive "and" and the disjunctive "or" has given rise to many a contest, and Jeremy Bentham devotes to the ambiguities of the latter monosyllable some devastating criticism. "May" and "shall" have almost a legal literature of their own. The amount of money which has been spent in trying to ascertain what is an "accident" within the meaning of the Workmen's Compensation Acts must now have reached a surprising total. The arguments and disquisitions on this topic enshrined in the law reports are an excellent commentary on my thesis. The question readily lends itself to metaphysical subtleties, and the whole theory of chance and design is involved. The layman is always exhorting the lawyer to use ordinary language which the people can understand, and when this legislation was first introduced we were assured that it was expressed in simple terms which would reduce litigation to a minimum. You see the result of this endeavour in the endless disputes which have arisen in the Courts over such apparently straightforward words as "wages", "suitable employment", "able to earn", "incapacity", and the like in which this so-called commonsense legislation abounds. An interesting contrast is afforded by the Succession Duty Act, 1853,* one of the most technical enactments in the statute book, which has earned high praise as an almost perfect example of the legislative art. So logical is its structure and so precise is its use of language, that the number of reported cases to which it has given rise is remarkably small considering the important interests it affects. But it is not easy reading.

Only last week you may have noticed reported in adjoining columns of *The Times* two cases in the King's Bench Division in one of which the question was what was meant by the word "cream" in a statute, while in the other the question was what was meant by the apparently tautological expression "non-working holidays" in a charter party. In the former† the Court held that Messrs J. Lyons and Co., Ltd., who had sold certain articles with the label "Lyons' Swiss Rolls, Chocolate Sponge (Cream Filled)", had not contravened a statute which forbids the sale, under a description including the word "cream", of any substance purporting to be cream unless the substance *is* cream. In the latter case‡ Roche, J., expressed the view that the mere fact that work might possibly be done on a holiday did not turn that day into a working holiday but that a working holiday was a holiday on which men worked without any substantial addition to their ordinary wages; in other words, the

---

* 16 and 17 Vict. c. 51.

† *J. Lyons and Co.* v. *Keating, The Times*, 7 May 1931. ([1931] 2 K.B. 535.)

‡ *Owners of S.S. Panagos Lyras* v. *Joint Danube, etc., Agencies of Braila, The Times*, 7 May 1931. (47 T.L.R. 403.)

kind of holiday with which we lawyers are only too painfully familiar.

Thus every day we see the Courts engaged in elucidating the meaning of the English language. These problems are likely to increase rather than to diminish in number in view of the growing tendency of the Legislature to enter upon regions which were formerly regarded as outside its province and to regulate every incident and transaction of our daily lives. The modern legislator, concerning himself with all the day-to-day affairs of the social life of the people, cheerfully imports into the statute book the inaccurate and colloquial language of the street and the market-place with only the most casual appreciation of what he is doing, and so we have questions as to whether catering is a trade,* and as to whether a chemist who sells lysol in an automatic machine at the door of his shop is conducting this business himself.† So complicated and various is our daily life that the Legislature which would seek to regulate its every activity would require to be endowed with superhuman knowledge and imagination in order to provide for every case, and even with these gifts it would find human language inadequate for its purpose. Whatever may be our political views, it is consoling to reflect that the increasing intervention of Parliament in the life of the people by means of imperfectly framed statutes will, at any rate, save many lawyers from swelling the ranks of the unemployed.

I fear, indeed, that the tasks which are being set to our

* *R.* v. *Minister of Labour, Ex parte National Trade Defence Association, and Others* [1932] 1 K.B. 1.
† *Council of Pharmaceutical Society, etc.,* v. *Watkinson* [1931] 2 K.B. 323.

highly skilled Parliamentary draftsmen in these days are becoming more than they can perform, for it is only possible to frame an intelligible and workable statute when its promoters have a clear and definite idea of what it is that they wish to express in the language of enactment, and such clear and definite ideas are far from being commonly possessed by the promoters of much of our modern legislation. Witness the recent breakdown in Parliament of a Bill which sought to amend the law of trade disputes. The learned Attorney-General proposed what he described as "simple words". They included the expression "the primary object" of a strike or lock-out; indeed the pivotal words of the Bill were these words: "the primary object." I doubt if any words more difficult of judicial interpretation and application could be found in the dictionary, and yet it was proposed to use them in a matter in which precision and certainty are pre-eminently desirable. The Attorney-General's happy quotation from *Through the Looking-Glass* in the earlier part of his speech—a quotation which is also prefixed to Stroud's *Judicial Dictionary*—seems to me peculiarly apposite to his own proposal. "'When *I* use a word,' Humpty Dumpty said, in rather a scornful tone, 'it means just what I choose it to mean, neither more nor less.' 'The question is,' said Alice, 'whether you *can* make words mean so many different things.'"

In much less exalted spheres this problem of attaining precision in the use of language equally presents itself. Suppose you are trying to draw up the rules for a students' union or a tennis club. You probably proceed to provide that members may introduce as guests persons belonging to their families. Then the trouble begins. What is a member's family? Does it mean his children, as when you say of a man that he has no family? Or does it mean those who live in family with the member, which may include his sisters, his cousins, and his aunts, or any one else who happens to reside under the same roof with him? Does it include his grandparents and his grandchildren? And so on and so on. This is no travesty. Those of you who have tried your hand at such tasks will have more sympathy, perhaps, with the unhappy Parliamentary draftsman who is required to produce overnight a measure for the better regulation of the ice-cream trade or some of the other lofty topics of jurisprudence with which the Legislature nowadays busies itself. He has to remember in Mr Justice Stephen's words that "it is not enough to attain to a degree of precision which a person reading in good faith can understand; but it is necessary to attain, if possible, to a degree of precision which a person reading in bad faith cannot misunderstand. It is all the better if he cannot pretend to misunderstand it."

As I have indicated, one of the chief functions of our Courts is to act as an animated and authoritative dictionary. It is for the Courts, we are told, to say what the statute or the contract means. The words used by one set of persons have to be interpreted by another set of persons. It is a difficult task enough, and perhaps none the less so that one of the cardinal rules is that you must not ask the person who used a particular word what he meant by it. The testator who leaves his "books" to a public library cannot be asked if he meant by that word to include his valuable stamp collection for the best of all reasons that he is now beyond the reach of examination, even if his evidence were otherwise admissible. And in construing an Act of Parliament the legislators who passed it cannot be asked to state on oath what they meant by particular words in it—for which they must often be devoutly thankful. Even the debates which have preceded the enactments of a statute must not be looked at, however surreptitiously. At least they must not be referred to in Court.

The extent of the task thus laid upon the Courts, and upon those who have to advise the public outside the Courts, may be gauged from the four admirable volumes of Stroud's *Judicial Dictionary*, a work already mentioned, for which we have all reason to be grateful, and which I wish was regularly brought up to date, for if you will look at the *Annual Digest* under "Words" you will see that every year adds new judicial interpretations to the English language. In the *English and Empire Digest* some 120 columns of the index are devoted to "Words and Phrases".

How is this duty of interpretation to be performed? "Is not the judge bound to know the meaning of all words in the English language?" asked Baron Martin, judiciously adopting the rhetorical and non-committal interrogative, in *Hills* v. *London Gas Light Co.*,* to which he added the merciful qualification: "or if they are used technically or scientifically to inform his own mind by evidence and then to determine the meaning?" Happily, we are not left entirely without guidance, for certain rules have been formulated for our assistance, though these rules themselves, being in turn expressed in words, are not always certain in their application.

* (1857), 27 L.J. Ex., 63.

Law and Language

There is first of all what has been termed the Golden Rule that in construing all written instruments the grammatical and ordinary sense of the words is to be adhered to unless that would lead to some absurdity or some repugnance or inconsistency with the rest of the instrument, in which case the grammatical and ordinary sense of the words may be modified so as to avoid that absurdity and inconsistency, but no further. This rule, originally formulated by Burton, J., afterwards received the high imprimatur of Lord Wensleydale, and has been again and again approved. It is a rule of good sense and sounds impressive, but, like another gold standard of which we hear much in these days, it may be criticised as effecting less than it professes. For the grammatical and ordinary sense of a word may vary, as we have seen in the case of so common a word as "family", and may also be different at different times, as we have seen in the case of the word "minerals". And how is the judge to know what is the grammatical and ordinary sense of every word? Fortunately he is permitted to consult the dictionary, and no work is more appreciated in the Courts than Murray's monumental *New English Dictionary*.* But even its aid often fails him, for it presents an embarrassing choice of meanings in many instances.

I could spend much time in discussing the various

* See *Spillers, Ltd.* v. *Cardiff Assessment Committee* [1931] 2 K.B. 21, for a delightful judgment of Lord Chief Justice Hewart on the meaning of "contiguous to" in Section 3 (3) of the Rating and Valuation (Apportionment) Act, 1928, in which he deprecates a too sweeping condemnation of the language of the Legislature, reminding us that the Courts see only its pathological side. The Lord Chief Justice in this case invokes the aid of Dr Johnson, who probably "employed the English language with a more anxious precision than any other man who ever lived", as well as of the *New English Dictionary*.

canons of interpretation which have been devised to aid the process of ascertaining the meaning of words. There is the famous *ejusdem generis* rule which prescribes that when you find an enumeration of specific items followed by general words you must examine the specific items to see if they belong to a genus or class, and if they are found to do so then the general words must be read as confined to other items of the same genus or class. If the expression to be construed were "dogs, cats and other animals", the genus might be said to be domestic animals, and the phrase would be reasonably read as excluding lions and tigers, though they are also animals. The rule fails, however, where the enumeration of the specific items is so heterogeneous as to disclose no common genus.

Another rule is embodied in the words *noscitur sociis*, which I may render by the jingle "words of a feather flock together". The meaning of a word is to be judged by the company it keeps. This is really a particular case of the general rule of interpretation which directs us to read all passages in a writing as controlled by their context. Divorced from their context both words and sentences may be made to mean something very different from what their authors intended, as we can see in the extracts which politicians quote from their opponents' speeches or publishers quote from the reviews in the Press.

A famous canon is afforded by the logical principle *expressio unius est exclusio alterius*, of which Coke also gives the alternative form *expressum facit cessare tacitum*. Of this rule, Lopes, L.J., said: "It is often a valuable servant but a dangerous master." It is based on the fact that every affirmation implies a negation, every frontier

166

excludes what it does not include. Illustrations of its application may be found, for example, where a statute which prescribes a particular method of doing something is held to prohibit by implication all other methods, and where a specific enumeration of items evidently intended to be exhaustive is held to exclude all items not specifically enumerated.

I must not fail to notice a method of interpretation much favoured by the Legislature, whereby the draftsman of a statute provides in an interpretation section a special dictionary of the terms employed in the measure. Some of these efforts in modern times are not a little surprising, and we find Parliament telling us that quite familiar words are for the purpose in hand to be deemed to include the most unexpected things. "These interpretation clauses", says Crompton, J., "are often the parts of the Act most difficult to be understood."* But they are a useful expedient if they are framed with a due regard to the advice given by Lord Thring in his work on *Practical Legislation*. "Definitions", he says, "require to be carefully considered, as a misuse of them is a frequent cause of ambiguity. It should be recollected that a word once defined preserves its meaning throughout the whole Act—a truism frequently overlooked in practice. A word should never be defined to mean something which it does not properly include—e.g., 'piracy' ought not to be defined to include 'mutiny', and so forth. The fewer the definitions the better, and, as a general rule, the draftsman should endeavour to draw his Act without definitions and insert them only when he finds that they are absolutely necessary. The proper use of definitions is to

* *Evelyn* v. *Whichcord* (1858), El. Bl. and El. 126, at p. 133.

include or exclude something with respect to the inclusion
or exclusion of which there is a doubt without such a
definition, and no attempt should be made to make a
pretence of scientific precision by defining words of which
the ordinary meaning is sufficiently clear and exact for the
purpose of the Act in which they are used." This is sound
advice, and I could wish it were more often observed.

And then, of course, the Interpretation Act, 1889,*
must always be borne in mind with its famous enactment that "words importing the masculine gender shall
include females and words in the singular shall include
the plural and words in the plural shall include the
singular", besides a host of other definitions, all carefully guarded with the prefatory warning "unless the
contrary intention appears".

But it is superfluous to set out all the aids which have
been devised for our assistance, for they may be found collected, discussed, and illustrated in that most fascinating
of legal textbooks—I use the epithet advisedly—Beal's
Cardinal Rules of Legal Interpretation. As regards the special
department of statute law, we have also the classic treatises of Maxwell and Hardcastle, the latter now known
by the name of its editor, Craies, while Norton on *Deeds*
is an admirable guide in its own province. To these I
refer you, and I can promise you that you will find them
good reading, which cannot be said of many law books.

From the earliest times the technical terms of our art
have been gathered and explained in law dictionaries,
a form of compilation now largely superseded by our
digests and encyclopædias. One of the earliest of these
dictionaries is Skene's *De Verborum Significatione,* of which

* 52 and 53 Vict. c. 63.

168

my edition is dated 1681. It professes to be an exposition of the "Termes and Difficill Wordes conteined in the Foure Buikes of Regiam Majestatem and uthers, in the Acts of Parliament, Infeftments; and used in Practique of this Realme; with Diverse Rules and Common Places or Principalles of the Lawes". There is much curious and forgotten lore in its pages. I am glad to see that Mr Cowley, the County Librarian of Lancaster, has under-taken the preparation of a bibliography of such works. In a recent issue of the *Law Journal* he gave a preliminary list and appealed for assistance in his enterprise, which I hope he will receive. His list included several law dictionaries previously unknown to me, but it omitted Skene and, rather remarkably, the well-known work of Dr John Cowell, sometime the King's Majesty's Pro-fessor of the Civil Law in the University of Cambridge, who published in the seventeenth century his monu-mental volume entitled *The Interpreter or Book containing the Signification of Words, wherein is set forth the true meaning of all or the most part of such words and terms as are mentioned in the Law Writers or Statutes of this victorious and renowned Kingdom requiring any Exposition or Interpretation: a work not only profitable but necessary for such as desire thoroughly to be instructed in the knowledge of our Laws, Statutes, or other antiquities.* The worthy professor sets a high standard for us. "Indeed," he says in his Address to the Reader, "a Lawyer professeth true Philosophy, and therefore, should not be ignorant (if it were possible) of either beasts or fowls or creeping things nor of the trees from the Cedar in Lebanon to the Hyssop that springeth out of the wall."

It is not, however, with the technical words of our craft that I am so much concerned. These have attained a reasonable scientific precision. It is for a more accurate and scholarly use by the practising lawyer of our ordinary vocabulary in his daily work that I plead. We have a matchless inheritance in our mother tongue, and a great tradition in its use handed down from the Bible and Shakespeare through a long list of masters to our own day. Let us see to it that we do not suffer it to be debased in our time, and that in our generation the legal profession shall continue to merit the proud distinction of being pre-eminently the learned profession.

THE ETHICS OF ADVOCACY

Read before the Royal Philosophical Society of Glasgow,
February 1916

AFRIEND at present in Malta sent me recently a cutting from the daily paper of the Island. It contained a report of the celebration by the Malta Chamber of Advocates of the feast of St Ives, the patron Saint of the legal profession. It is interesting to learn that, notwithstanding the din and turmoil of war-like activities amidst which they are now living, the Advocates of Malta, on 17 December last, duly attended solemn High Mass in accordance with ancient precedent, at the altar dedicated to their Saint in the University Church at Valetta. This picturesque incident, like the annual service at Westminster Abbey which precedes the opening of the Law Courts in London, serves to recall what is too often forgotten, that the practice of the law is more than a mere trade or business, and that those who engage in it are the guardians of ideals and tradi-tions to which it is right that they should from time to time dedicate themselves anew.

It may surprise some to learn that any lawyer should have attained to canonisation, and they may cynically hint that the *advocatus diaboli* cannot have studied his brief to much purpose before he addressed the tribunal of cardinals in the case of St Ives of Brittany. But the records of "The Advocate of the poor", as he was called, appear to have been such as amply to justify his place in the Saints' Calendar, for no one has ever been credited with more zeal in pleading the cause of the humble and oppressed, and he left behind him a tradition of beneficence and uprightness which lives to this day.

Yet even in the case of this lawyer Saint, the popular prejudice against his profession was only grudgingly overcome, and at his yearly festival the people still sing this refrain:

> Advocatus sed non latro
> Res miranda populo,

which I may freely render:

> An advocate but not a thief,
> A thing wellnigh beyond belief.

In pictorial art, too, the Saint is commonly represented with a cat beside him as his symbol, for the reason, as Mr Baring-Gould tells us in his *Lives of the Saints,** that the cat is regarded "as in some sort symbolising a lawyer who watches for his prey, darts on it at the proper moment with alacrity, and when he has got his victim delights to play with him, but never lets him escape from his clutches".

I propose on the present occasion to discuss, I hope impartially, the ethical grounds of the prevalent and persistent popular prejudice against the legal profession, and in this connection to examine the unwritten code which regulates the professional conduct of the advocate. The task I have set myself is perhaps not ill-timed. In these days when all our preconceived ideas and standards have been so rudely shaken by the shattering of civilisation in Europe, every one of us feels himself to be standing upon his trial in the forum of conscience. Our former easy acceptance of the daily routine of our lives

* Vol. v, p. 305.

no longer satisfies us. We each and all of us feel that we must justify ourselves anew. We cannot rest till we have retried by the more rigorous standards which this time of stress has set up the manner of our daily lives and vocations. The times demand resurveys and revaluations.

I scarcely think that at this time of day I need embark on a general justification of the profession of advocacy as a public institution. Ever since the State decreed that men must cease to settle their disputes with the vigorous arguments of fist and club, the administration of justice has been the prime concern of the State. In order to enable this primary function of government to be efficiently discharged, the experience of every civilised community has shown that it is indispensable to have a class of men skilled in advising and aiding the citizen in the vindication of his rights before the Courts to which the State delegates the task of dispensing justice in accordance with the law of the land. As social life grows more and more complex, as the relations of men grow more and more manifold, as the enactments by which the legislature seeks to keep pace with and regulate the constantly developing progress of the community become more and more elaborate and technical, the value of the part which the advocate is called upon to play in the social system becomes more and more apparent. The danger indeed in a democratic state is that his value may be over-estimated and the sphere of his activities unduly extended, so that he is tempted to take upon himself functions for which the very excellence of his technical aptitudes unfits him.

Justice is not a simple thing. I do not hesitate to say that in a large number of the actual cases which come before our higher Courts it is next to impossible to say in favour of which side ideal justice would decide. The Courts must decide one way or the other, for it is the business of the State to see that disputes take end. Indeed it is sometimes more important that there should be finality than that perfect justice should be interminably sought. But the essential thing is that no case should be decided without each party to the dispute being afforded the fullest opportunity of presenting his side of it to the Court. Common law and statute law alike, so long as they stand recorded in decisions and Parliament Roll, are, as Herbert Spencer would say, merely static. They are rules for the adjustment of human relations based no doubt on experience. But experience is always in the past. The law formulated in the light of past experience becomes dynamic when it has to be applied to the events of the present. In the Law Courts history never repeats itself. No two cases are ever the same. No lawgiver can be so prescient as to anticipate all the contingencies of human life. It is in the process of applying and adapting abstract law to the concrete cases of the moment, in all their diversity of circumstances, that the function of the advocate comes into play, and the contribution that he thus makes to the development of the body politic is a more important one than is commonly realised.

Law is not an exact science, as Lord Halsbury reminds us. Despite the majesty and gravity with which its administration is properly invested, it is a very human affair after all. It has to do not with scientific axioms or scientific formulae, but with the everyday concerns of ordinary citizens. The raw material of the cases that come into Court is composed of the struggles and rivalries, the desires and emotions to which human relationships give rise. This material cannot be analysed with the cold precision of the chemist in his laboratory. Considerations of equity and expediency mingle themselves with the more exact matter of the law. Justice cannot be laid to the line or equity to the plummet. The material is too intractable, too psychological, if you will, to be dealt with by any such mechanical process. You cannot argue against the mathematical fact that one and one make two. But in the human affairs with which the Law Courts deal the problems are not like this. There is almost always something to be said either way. And it is of the greatest importance that that something should be said, not only in order that each party may leave the judgment seat satisfied that, whatever has been the decision, the case has had a fair hearing, but in order that the Court may not reach its judgment without having had in view all that could be urged to the contrary effect. In order that the decisions of the Courts may give satisfaction to the parties and at the same time command public respect and acceptance, they must proceed upon full arguments on both sides. For it has long been proved that the most effectual and only practicable method of arriving at the rights of a dispute is by critical debate in the presence of an impartial third party, where every statement and argument on either side is submitted to the keenest scrutiny and attack. Where every step on the way to judgment has been tested and contested, the chance of error in the ultimate decision is reduced to a minimum. The better the case is presented on each side, and the keener and more skilful the debate before him, the more likely is it that the judge will reach a just and sound judgment. That is why it has been said that a strong Bar makes a strong Bench. It is, then, as contributing an essential element to the process of the administration of justice that the profession of the advocate discharges a public function of the highest utility and importance. Alike to the citizen seeking justice and to the Courts administering it, the existence of a class of trained advocates possessing knowledge of the law, skill in the orderly presentation of facts, cogency in logical argument, and fairness and moderation in controversy, is indispensable. These qualifications cannot be acquired without training and study. Those who seek proficiency in the exercise of them must devote their lives to the task. In short, advocacy must be their profession.

Now the qualifications which I have enumerated as distinctive of the efficient advocate sound one and all excellent and praiseworthy. And yet the advocate remains suspect in the public eye. From the beginning of history this has been his lot. Gibes at the expense of the hired disputant are as old as the days of Greek comedy. They still afford cheap entertainment to the cynic. No personal excellences, no intellectual ability, no moral probity on the part of the individual advocate can succeed in eradicating from the mind of the public their instinctive mistrust of his profession. The mercenary character of his forensic triumphs is constantly cast up against him. So long ago as 1629, an early traveller from England, in describing a visit which he paid to the Court of Session, narrates that the advocates there plead in Scotch before the judges, and "in the then time of their pleading their clients will put a double piece or more, with an ordinary fee for the poorest, and will say to their advocates, 'thumb it, thumb it', and then will the advocates plead according as they feel it weigh".* The repugnance of the popular mind to the idea of paid advocacy is still represented at the present day by the law which gives the advocate no legal right to payment. He cannot sue for his fees for work done; they are regarded purely as honoraria. But I venture to think that this is an honourable distinction, for it recognises the fact that the advocate in exercising his profession is discharging a public duty which it would not be fitting to place upon a mere business footing.

Now what is the explanation of the deeply rooted popular prejudice against the paid profession of advocacy? It is simply due to the peculiar nature of the advocate's work, and to the inability of the popular mind to understand it. Put bluntly, the charge is that no advocate can be a sincere and honest man in the performance of his daily business. This is the perennial ethical indictment against the profession. In other callings it is admitted that there are insincere and dishonest men. But these are the exceptions. In the case of the advocate it is his profession to be insincere if not, indeed, dishonest. This is a profound misconception, but it is an inveterate one. Let us examine the grounds on which it is based. In the first place the charge is based on the fact that the advocate by the rules of his profession has, theoretically at least, no choice in the selection of the cases he takes up. The ordinary man espouses a cause because he believes in it. The advocate takes up his cases because he is

* *Our Journall into Scotland*, 1629, p. 31. Edinburgh: David Douglas, 1894.

paid to do so. How can he sincerely support a cause which he has adopted not because he believes in its justice but because the brief has been handed in at his door with the appropriate fee?

A great newspaper controversy recently raged in the columns of *The Times* over the question of the right of an advocate to refuse to accept a brief duly tendered to him which he is not prevented by other prior engagements from accepting. Two eminent counsel at the English Bar, who were also members of Parliament, accepted instructions to appear in the Law Courts on behalf of certain public men to whom they were politically opposed, and whose character had been attacked in connection with matters which had aroused the bitterest party feelings. *The Times* led off the discussion in a leader in which it said: "A counsel may be bound according to professional etiquette to accept a brief in any Court in which he usually practises provided the fee be reasonable; and the two eminent counsel in question, it is argued, were only doing what they must do in conformity with these professional rules. That plea does not satisfy the ordinary man." But the point taken was not that it was wrong for these counsel to appear for the particular clients in question because they could not sincerely plead their case; it was rather that the rule which requires an advocate to give his services to any client who retains him is not and ought not to be an absolute rule, but should give way when obedience to it would involve dereliction of higher duties to the State. It was suggested that by taking up these cases the counsel in question disabled themselves from the performance of their duty as members of Parliament to their constituencies and to the public. The question as to the absolute nature of counsel's duty to serve all comers is an interesting one, but it is rather beside the question I am now discussing. So far as Scotland is concerned, the matter is dealt with in a sensible rule of Court of 27 May 1532—as old as the Court of Session itself—which runs: "No advocate without very good cause shall refuse to act for any person tendering a reasonable fee under pain of deprivation of his office of advocate." What is a very good cause is left undefined, but the qualification safeguards the exceptional cases in which all would admit that the advocate is excused—as, for example, if it was sought to compel him to appear against his own father or other near relation. For my present purpose it is enough that in ordinary daily practice the advocate, as a distinguished judge put it, is "in the position of a cabman on the rank bound to answer the first hail".

It is an odd circumstance that the very fact which is by some made the first point in the indictment against the advocate's sincerity is by others exalted as one of the chief glories of the profession. "That the services of counsel are open to every member of the public alike, and that it must be first come first served, is the rule, as I understand it," says the judge I have just quoted, "handed down to us by long generations of men who have left the reputation of the Bar of England for integrity, fearlessness, and impartiality unrivalled in the world." In the eloquent language of Erskine, spoken in 1792, in his defence of Tom Paine: "From the moment that any advocate can be permitted to say that he will or will not stand between the Crown and the subject arraigned in the Court where he daily sits to practise, from that moment the liberties of England are at an end. If the advocate refuses to defend from what he may think of the charge or of the defence, he assumes the character of the judge; nay, he assumes it before the hour of judgment, and in proportion to his rank and reputation puts the heavy influence of perhaps a mistaken opinion into the scale against the accused, in whose favour the benevolent principles of the English Law makes all presumptions, and which commands the very judge to be his counsel." (*State Trials*, xxii, 411.)

If it be accepted that it is the paramount duty of the advocate to place his services without fear or favour at the disposal of all who may require them, then, says the plain man, as the advocate cannot believe all his clients to be always in the right, he must have to maintain many cases in the justice of which he does not believe. How can he be sincere and honest in the advocacy of them? What a revolting position to be placed in, exclaims the plain man, to have to use all your resources of knowledge and skill in order to endeavour to impetrate from the Court a decision which you are convinced would be unjust! Surely Swift was right when with his mordant pen he described the Bar as "a society of men bred up from their youth in the art of proving by words multiplied for the purpose that white is black and black is white, according as they are paid". It is in this dramatic fashion that the essential immorality of the advocate's profession presents itself to not a few minds.

The answer is as old as the arraignment. It might be enough to refer to the illustrious names of the great leaders of the Bar in the past, and to ask: Were they all ignoble hirelings engaged in the sordid business of prostituting their great abilities in the promotion of injustice and untruth? If the nature of their calling be so ignoble, how comes it that their names are inscribed in the nation's Roll of Honour among the foremost champions of truth, honour, and liberty? Surely there is a strange inconsistency here. The explanation is to be found in the complete misconception on the part of the public of the true rôle of the advocate.

In ordinary life what a man says is presumed to be and ought to be the honest expression of his own beliefs, and those whom he addresses are entitled so to understand. What the plain man finds it difficult to appreciate is that in advocacy what the advocate says is not presumed to be, and ought not to be, the expression of his own mind at all, and those whom he addresses are not entitled to believe, and do not believe, anything of the sort. In pleading a case an advocate is not stating his own opinions. It is no part of his business, and he has no right to do so. What it is his business to do is to present to the Court all that can be said on behalf of his client's case, all that his client would have said for himself if he had possessed the requisite skill and knowledge. His personal opinion either of his client or of his client's case is of no consequence. It is the business of the judge or the jury to form their opinion of his client and his client's case. It is not for the counsel himself to prejudge the question at issue. His duty is to see that those whose business it is to judge do not do so without first hearing from him all that can possibly be urged on his side.

In their public and private utterances outside the Courts advocates are judged of course by the same standards as other citizens who are not advocates, and are expected when they speak to express their own opinions with the candour required from all honest men. But, in the words of the present Attorney-General, "when they speak as advocates every cultivated person in the world knows that, discharging a function vital to the very existence of civilised society, they give trained but strictly representative expression to the contentions of their clients". Lord Eldon puts it thus: "He (the advocate) lends his exertions to all, himself to none. The result of the cause is to him a matter of indifference. It is for the Court to decide. It is for him to argue. He is, however he may be represented by those who understand not his true situation, merely an officer assisting in the administration of justice, and acting under the impression that truth is best discovered by powerful statements on both sides of the question." (*Ex parte Lloyd*, 5 Nov. 1822, Montagu's Reports, p. 70 note.)

Now what is there morally reprehensible in taking one or other side in the contest which is to issue in judgment? You may entertain the private opinion that you have the weaker side in fact or in law. What has that to do with it? Is the weaker side not to get a chance? Perhaps the side which the advocate personally thinks to be the weaker may turn out to be in truth the stronger, and may in the end justly prevail. There is no advocate but has often had that experience. And why should the services of the advocate be regarded as tainted because he is paid for rendering them? That they should be so regarded is in a sense a curious left-handed tribute to the Bar, for I think that the idea arises from the feeling that the kind of services which an advocate renders to his client are not properly measurable in money. That is true. The client often confides to his advocate's hands all that he holds dearest—his goods, his reputation, his happiness, and sometimes even his life. Such a trust seems to transcend the ordinary commercial relations of debtor and creditor. But if the profession of advocacy is to exist, I see no dishonour in the advocate living by the exercise of it. The making of gain should not be his object; if that is his object, the fields of commerce afford far more golden opportunities. But he is fairly entitled to the due reward of the labour and skill which he expends, and I think it will be conceded that in no department of life does the making even of a sufficient competence involve the expenditure of more unremitting toil.

Once then the vital point is realised that the advocate in Court is engaged not in expressing his own views of the case, but in presenting and marshalling all that can be said in favour of his client's view of it, all room for the charge of insincerity against the advocate disappears. He is no more open to the accusation of duplicity than is a member of a debating society to whom has been assigned by lot the task of supporting the affirmative or negative of a particular thesis. But indeed the whole problem was long ago disposed of by the trenchant common sense of Dr Johnson in a memorable and often-quoted passage, which I cannot do better than quote once more:

BOSWELL: "But what do you think of supporting a cause which you know to be bad?"

JOHNSON: "Sir, you do not know it to be good or bad till the judge determines it. You are to state facts clearly; so that your thinking, or what you call knowing, a cause to be bad must be from reasoning, must be from supposing your arguments to be weak and inconclusive. But, Sir, that is not enough. An argument which does not convince yourself may convince the judge to whom you urge it; and if it does convince him, why then, Sir, you are wrong and he is right. It is his business to judge; and you are not to be confident in your own opinion that a cause is bad, but to say all you can for your client, and then hear the judge's opinion."

BOSWELL: "But, Sir, does not affecting a warmth when you have no warmth, and appearing to be clearly of one opinion when you are in reality of another opinion, does not such dissimulation impair one's honesty? Is there not some danger that a lawyer may put on the same mask in common life in the intercourse with his friends?"

JOHNSON: "Why, no, Sir. Everybody knows you are paid for affecting warmth for your client, and it is therefore properly no dissimulation: the moment you come from the Bar you resume your usual behaviour. Sir, a man will no more carry the artifice of the Bar into the common intercourse of society than a man who is paid for tumbling upon his hands will continue to tumble upon his hands when he should walk upon his feet."

In dwelling at such length upon this topic I fear I have been exhibiting the characteristic of the "legal mind", which, it has been said, "chiefly consists in illustrating the obvious, explaining the self-evident, and expatiating on the commonplace". But the misconception which I have been discussing is so persistent, and involves so vital an attack upon the ethical position of the advocate, that I have thought it worth while to combat it again, even at the risk of seeming to slay the slain.

The Ethics of Advocacy

But if it be conceded that there is nothing intellectually immoral in the profession of advocacy, it must on the other hand be equally conceded that there is no sphere in which more subtle ethical problems present themselves in practice for solution. The very nature of the advocate's task involves this. If no profession is nobler in its right exercise, so no profession can be baser in its abuse. And hence the advocate is bound by a host of unwritten obligations, which are designed to maintain the integrity of his professional conduct. The code of honour of the Bar is at once its most cherished possession and the most valued safeguard of the public. In the discharge of his office the advocate has a duty to his client, a duty to his opponent, a duty to the Court, a duty to the State, and a duty to himself. To maintain a perfect poise amidst these various and sometimes conflicting claims is no easy feat. Transgression of the honourable obligations which these duties impose upon the advocate is not like making a mere mistake in business. It involves infringement of his moral duty. It is a matter of conscience. And his offence cannot be hid, for all his work is done in the presence of his brethren and the public. His conduct is always exposed to the searching if salutary scrutiny of many critics.

The delicacy of the advocate's duty may well be illustrated by taking the hackneyed problem of what he is to do when he is retained for the defence of an accused person who has confessed to him his guilt, but nevertheless persists in pleading not guilty. This is a problem which the layman has always delighted in posing to the advocate. It was brought prominently into the arena of public discussion in the famous trial before the Central

Criminal Court in 1840, in which a foreign manservant named Courvoisier was accused of the murder of his master, Lord William Russell. The murdered man was found dead in bed with his throat cut. His watch and rings and a number of other personal possessions were found to be missing, and also a quantity of valuable plate. Some of these articles were found concealed in Courvoisier's pantry, and this and other circumstantial evidence pointed almost conclusively to him as the perpetrator of the deed. He was arrested and put on his trial. Charles Phillips, a well-known barrister of those days, was retained for the defence. In the course of the trial a dramatic incident occurred. No trace of the missing plate had been found by the prosecution, but while the case was in progress a communication was received by the Crown from an hotel-keeper, who had been reading an account of the trial in the newspapers, to the effect that a parcel had been left with him shortly before the date of the murder by a foreigner whom he had previously employed as a waiter, but whom he had only known by his Christian name. The hotel-keeper identified Courvoisier as his former employee who had deposited the parcel with him. The parcel was opened and was found to contain the missing plate. This discovery supplied the final and conclusive link in the chain of evidence connecting Courvoisier with the crime. Thereupon Courvoisier requested his counsel to confer with him—and now I quote from Phillips's own account of the incident:

"I have sent for you, gentlemen," said he, "to tell you I committed the murder!" When I could speak, which was not immediately, I said, "Of course then you are going to plead guilty?" "No, Sir," was the reply, "I expect you to defend me to the utmost." So perturbed and distressed was Phillips as to his duty in this appalling situation, that he sought an interview with Baron Parke, who, although not trying the case, had been sitting on the Bench with Lord Chief Justice Tindal. At this interview Phillips tells us that Baron Parke "requested to know distinctly whether the prisoner insisted on my defending him; and, on hearing that he did, said I was bound to do so, and to use all fair arguments arising on the evidence. I therefore retained my brief."* The advice was unquestionably right, but the difficulty of following it to the letter imposed a task of extreme delicacy upon Phillips. His manner of discharging it brought upon him a storm of virulent criticism. It was said that though he knew that his client was the murderer, he nevertheless sought to suggest to the jury that the guilt lay with another of Lord William's servants whom he of course knew to be innocent, and further that he called the Deity to witness that his client was innocent. Here are the words of his peroration:

"But you will say to me, if the prisoner did not do it, who did it? I answer, ask the Omnipotent Being above us who did it. Ask not me, a poor finite creature like yourselves. Ask the prosecutor, Who did it. It is for him to tell you who did it, and until he shall have proved, by the clearest evidence, that it was the prisoner at the Bar, beware how you imbrue your hands in the blood of that young man."

It is a pretty problem whether in speaking these words

* *Correspondence between Samuel Warren and Charles Phillips.* London: L. King, 1849. (Pamphlet in the Advocates' Library.)

187

and other words which he used in the course of his address to the jury, Phillips stepped outside the legitimate bounds of his duty. The concluding words at least of the passage I have quoted seem unexceptionable. It is fair to say that the presiding judge subsequently expressed the opinion that Phillips had discharged his difficult task without transgressing the limits within which he was bound in the circumstances to confine himself. The interest of the case lies for our present purpose in the public discussion to which it gave rise, and which did much to define with precision the duty of an advocate so situated. All were agreed that he would not have been entitled to suggest that any one else was guilty of the crime, and that he certainly would have had no right to pledge to the jury his own belief in his client's innocence. To have done the first of these things would have been to do a cruel wrong to the innocent; to have done the latter would have been to perpetrate a fraud. Indeed no counsel is ever entitled to express his own belief in his client's innocence. The moment he does so he steps outside his rôle of advocate.

As it happens, this very question has recently been before the Council of the English Bar, which was invited last year by the Shanghai Bar Committee to express an opinion for the guidance of the profession on the question of "the propriety of counsel defending on a plea of not guilty a prisoner charged with an offence, capital or otherwise, when the latter has confessed to counsel himself the fact that he did commit the offence charged". The reply of the Bar Council, approved by Sir Edward Carson and Sir Robert Finlay, is instructive. The topic is dealt with under two heads, according as the confession has been made before the trial on the one hand, or on the other hand during the trial or in such circumstances that the advocate cannot withdraw without seriously compromising the position of the accused.

In the former case the Bar Council state that "it is most undesirable that an advocate to whom the confession has been made should undertake the defence, as he would most certainly be seriously embarrassed in the conduct of the case, and no harm can be done to the accused by requesting him to retain another advocate".

In considering the duty of an advocate in the latter case the Bar Council point out that it is essential to bear in mind "(1) That every punishable crime is a breach of common or statute law by a person of sound mind and understanding; (2) that the issue in a criminal trial is always whether the accused is guilty of the offence charged, never whether he is innocent; (3) that the affirmative rests on the prosecution." The duty of the advocate for the accused is "to protect his client as far as possible from being convicted except by a competent tribunal and upon legal evidence sufficient to support a conviction for the offence with which he is charged.

"The ways in which this duty can be successfully performed with regard to the facts of a case are (*a*) by showing that the accused was irresponsible at the time of the commission of the offence by reason of insanity or want of criminal capacity; or (*b*) by satisfying the tribunal that the evidence for the prosecution is unworthy of credence, or, even if believed, is insufficient to justify a conviction for the offence charged; or (*c*) by setting up in answer an affirmative case."

Confession of guilt by the accused to his advocate does

189

not "release the advocate from his imperative duty to do all he honourably can do for his client, but such a confession imposes very strict limitations on the conduct of the defence. An advocate 'may not assert that which he knows to be a lie. He may not connive at, much less attempt to substantiate, a fraud.' While, therefore, it would be right to take any objection to the competency of the Court, to the form of the indictment, to the admissibility of any evidence, or to the sufficiency of the evidence admitted, it would be absolutely wrong to suggest that some other person had committed the offence charged, or to call any evidence which he must know to be false having regard to the confession, such, for instance, as evidence in support of an alibi, which is intended to show that the accused could not have done, or in fact had not done the act; that is to say an advocate must not (whether by calling the accused or otherwise) set up an affirmative case inconsistent with the confession made to him. A more difficult question is within what limits, in the case supposed, may an advocate attack the evidence for the prosecution either by cross-examination or in his speech to the tribunal charged with the decision of the facts. No clearer rule can be laid down than this, that he is entitled to test the evidence given by each individual witness, and to argue that the evidence taken as a whole is insufficient to amount to proof that the accused is guilty of the offence charged. Further than this he ought not to go."

I have quoted at such length from this Report because, so far as I know, it is the fullest and most authoritative, as well as the most recent, analysis of what is always put forward as the supreme test problem in the ethics of advocacy. I venture to think that no advocate who, in the difficult situation figured, faithfully adheres to the above ruling of the Bar Council will have aught with which to reproach himself. The fact is, however, that a broad question of professional conduct such as I have been discussing does not really raise so much ethical difficulty as do many of the more subtle questions which arise in daily practice. The manner in which he solves these is the truest and shrewdest test of the advocate. His failure to solve them aright brings discredit, not only on himself, but on his craft. For the solution of these daily problems no absolute code can be laid down. They are left to the advocate's honour, and I am proud to say that they are generally safely so left.

Let me give some instances. Written pleadings are frequently sent to counsel for revisal containing serious allegations of fraud, dishonesty, or misconduct. The consequence of lodging such pleadings in Court may be to cause irreparable injury to the person thus publicly accused. For an advocate to allow such charges to be launched with his name attached to them without the fullest investigation would be to abuse the absolute protection against actions for slander which the law affords to counsel. Counsel is not worthy of that protection unless he justifies it by the most scrupulous care in his written or oral attacks on character. He must insist upon being supplied with all the information which is thought by his client to justify the attack, and then he must decide for himself whether the charges made are such as can be justifiably made. In exercising his judgment in such a matter the advocate is fulfilling one of the most delicate duties to society which his profession casts upon him. It is no small responsibility which the State throws upon the lawyer in thus confiding to his discretion the reputation of the citizen. No enthusiasm for his client's case, no specious assurance from his client that the insertion of some strong allegations will coerce a favourable settlement, no desire to fortify the relevance of his client's case, entitles the advocate to trespass, in matters involving reputation, a hair's-breadth beyond what the facts as laid before him and duly vouched and tested will justify. It will not do to say lightly that it is for the Court to decide the matter. It is for counsel to see that no man's good name is wantonly attacked.

Again, suppose that your opponent's leading witness has to your knowledge many years ago been guilty of some offence, but has long outlived it and by honourable conduct completely wiped out all public recollection of it. Your client perhaps urges you to ask him in cross-examination a question reviving this long-erased blot upon his escutcheon in order to discredit his present evidence. What are you to do? If the witness to the best of your judgment is giving his evidence truthfully and fairly, you will decline to deal a cowardly blow at him through his past.

Or take in turn a question involving counsel's duty to the Court. Suppose that in the course of your researches you have discovered a ruling judgment against you on the point you are arguing, but that neither the opposing counsel nor the judge is aware of its existence. Must you draw the attention of the Court to this adverse precedent, although to do so may prove fatal to your client's case which you are in a fair way to win? Or should you say to yourself that it is for the opposing counsel to find the case, and if he fails to do so that is his affair? Have you any duty to prevent the judge from giving a decision in your favour contrary to the law which is binding upon him? The situation is complicated by the fact that it is not always possible to say whether the damaging precedent you have discovered is exactly in point or not. It may be distinguishable. My own opinion, though I know I am here on debatable ground, is that it is the duty of an advocate, if he is satisfied that the adverse precedent he has come across is directly in point, to draw the Court's attention to it, come what may, and to do his best to differentiate it, or to induce the Court not to follow it. The Court is entitled to rely on counsel's not misleading it. On a question of fact the duty of counsel in the matter is absolute. Woe betide the advocate who follows the hint of a certain unscrupulous leader who is credited with having said to his junior, "The law is clear and the judge knows it; the facts remain at your disposal". On a question of law the duty of the advocate to the Court is more complicated than on a question of fact. The judge is presumed to know the law, and in any case the particular law applicable to the case in hand is not like a matter of fact capable of precise ascertainment. It is a matter for argument. But the argument must be fair to the Court, and while counsel has no duty to argue his opponent's case or to bring forward authorities supporting his opponent's contentions, he has in my opinion a duty to see that the Court does not proceed to judgment without having before it a previous ruling decision which is exactly in point.*

---

* Since the above was written Lord Chancellor Birkenhead has stated that the House of Lords "expects—and indeed insists—that authorities

Then take one illustration of the duty which a counsel
owes to the counsel on the other side. Suppose, as not
infrequently happens, a brother advocate has come to
you for assistance in a troublesome case in which you are
not yourself engaged, and discusses with you the doubts
and difficulties which are pressing upon him, and then
suppose that you find yourself retained as counsel on the
opposite side. The rule is clear that you must not avail
yourself in Court of what you have previously learnt in
confidence from your opponent, however tempted you
may be to do so, and however advantageous to your
client such breach of confidence might be. Or, again,
you may have come to some arrangement with your
opponent as to the conduct of the case which you subsequently find is going to prove to your detriment. The
arrangement is unenforceable, for it is a matter of honour
only. Nevertheless you must rigorously adhere to it unless your opponent consents to release you. There is no
more heinous offence at the Bar than a breach of the
confidence which counsel are entitled to place in each
other. The nature of their business is such that more than
in any other profession the members of the Bar must be
able to rely implicitly upon each other's sense of honour.
It is a trust which is seldom if ever betrayed.

Lastly let me take an illustration of a rarer kind involving counsel's duty to the State. A great counsel once

which bear one way or the other upon matters under debate shall be
brought to the attention of their Lordships by those who are aware of
those authorities. This observation is quite irrespective of whether or not
the particular authority assists the party which is so aware of it. It is an
obligation of confidence between their Lordships and all those who assist
in the debates in this House in the capacity of counsel." *Glebe Sugar
Refining Co.* v. *Greenock Harbour Trustees*, 1921, S.C. (H.L.) 72.

placed counsel's duty to his client so high as to surmount even his duty to his country. Here are the words used by Brougham in his defence of Queen Caroline before the House of Lords:

"I once before took occasion to remind your Lordships, which was unnecessary, but there are many whom it may be needful to remind, that an advocate, by the sacred duty which he owes his client, knows in the discharge of that office but one person in the world—that client and none other. To save that client by all expedient means, to protect that client at all hazards and costs to all others, and among others to himself, is the highest and most unquestioned of his duties; and he must not regard the alarm, the suffering, the torment, the destruction which he may bring upon any other. Nay, separating even the duties of a patriot from those of an advocate, and casting them if need be to the wind, he must go on reckless of the consequences, if his fate it should unhappily be to involve his country in confusion for his client's protection."

I venture to differ from this high authority. The advocate does not cease to be a citizen by becoming a counsel. He is himself in a sense a servant of the State. He takes the oath of allegiance on his admission to the Bar. His very privileges are conferred upon him by the State. The interests of his country must be paramount with him as with every true citizen over every other concern. This does not mean that he must not defend a citizen charged with high treason. Far from it. Nor that it is unpatriotic of him to defend a client charged with a breach of the laws for the defence of the realm. It is as important to the State as to his client, nay more so, that there should be no conviction of such an offence except upon fully tested evidence after a fair defence. But suppose counsel could only successfully defend his client by using and disclosing information in his possession of vital importance to the enemy with whom his country is at war? He should, of course, endeavour to have the case heard *in camera*. But if he fails to accomplish this, what then? I present you with the problem as a supreme illustration of the ethical difficulties in which a counsel may find himself involved.

I have chosen at random these varied examples of the cases of conscience which arise in the daily practice of the Bar. I could have given a hundred others. But these will serve to make my point that the ethics of advocacy are concerned with singularly complex and subtle problems of conduct. You may ask how it is possible at all to conduct a business which is fraught with so many difficulties. The truth is that so settled are the traditions of honour and fair dealing which the Bar observes and such is the atmosphere which long observance of these traditions has created, that those who have absorbed these traditions and live in that atmosphere acquire unconsciously a sense of what is due to their calling and are scarcely aware of the code of honour which daily guides them, so much has it become their second nature. It is in this fine sense of professional duty that the existence of the Bar finds its chief justification. It is its faithful adherence to its high ideals which renders it not unworthy of the lofty encomium of the great French Chancellor d'Aguesseau who described the Order of Advocates as: "Un ordre aussi ancien que la magistrature, aussi noble que la vertu, aussi nécessaire que la justice."

The Ethics of Advocacy

And now let me in conclusion refer briefly to a topic rather psychological than ethical, of which we have heard a good deal in public lately. I mean the effect of the profession of advocacy upon the mental attitude of those who practise it. I am not concerned to deny that the continuous practise of advocacy has a certain effect upon the habit of mind of the advocate. His nature is inevitably subdued to what it works in, like the dyer's hand. As practice and experience render him more and more useful and skilful in his own sphere, the very specialisation of his abilities tends to disqualify him for other spheres of intellectual or practical activity. His mind is constantly preoccupied with the presentation of facts and arguments relating to things which other people have done or are doing. A recent acute critic* who in no unfriendly fashion describes lawyers as an order of men admirable in their private and professional capacities, trusty friends, delightful companions, stricter perhaps than any other civil profession in all rules of honour, nevertheless strenuously deprecates their predominance in public life. "Lawyers", he says, "see too much of life in one way, too little in another to make them safe guides in practical matters. Their experience of human affairs is made up of an infinite number of scraps cut out of other people's lives. They learn and do hardly anything except through intermediaries." He admits the value of their contribution to the conduct of public affairs, but he would not allow them a position of control. This is shrewd criticism. It is true that the legal mind is apt to over-estimate the efficacy of words. When a problem presents itself to the advocate he is apt to approach it from

* *Ordeal by Battle.* By F. S. Oliver, p. 201.

the point of view of seeking not necessarily the best practical solution, but the solution which will best lend itself to verbal justification. When facts are put before him he instinctively proceeds to interest himself in arranging them in an attractive pattern for oral presentation. He is apt to ask himself with regard to a proposed course of action—How will this state? rather than —How will this work? and, as Bacon puts it, to "desire rather commendation of wit, in being able to hold all arguments, than of judgment in discerning what is true: as if it were a praise to know what might be said and not what should be thought". (*Essays*, xxxii, Of Discourse.)

I am disposed to concede that there is an element of truth in this diagnosis. The advocate cannot escape the defects of his qualities, any more than any one else can. The criticism is directed not against the advocate as advocate, but rather against the advocate who puts off his gown and enters another arena. It is the engrossing and absorbing nature of his professional work which must be his excuse if he sometimes forgets that he is not still wearing his gown when he leaves the Courts and essays other activities—commercial, administrative, or political. But the further consideration of this attractive topic of discussion would lead me far from my subject to-night.

It has been my endeavour during the past hour to study with you rather the special character of the ethics of conduct which guide the advocate in the exercise of his profession. I hope I have demonstrated afresh, if fresh demonstration were needed, that so far from the profession of advocacy requiring its practitioners to lay aside either their probity, their candour, or their honour, there is no profession in which the possession of these very qualities is more essential, or more likely to lead to eminence and success, no profession in which the want of these qualities in one of its members renders him more of an outcast. No one ever stated the duty of the advocate in truer or more eloquent words than fell once from an Irish Judge in the great cause of *The Queen* v. *O'Connell*.* With his words of vindication and exhortation I leave the reputation of the Bar in your hands. "He (the advocate)", says Mr Justice Crampton, "is a representative, but not a delegate. He gives to his client the benefit of his learning, his talents, and his judgment; but all through he never forgets what he owes to himself and to others. He will not knowingly misstate the law— he will not wilfully misstate the facts, though it be to gain the cause for his client. He will ever bear in mind that if he be the advocate of an individual, and *retained* and remunerated (often inadequately) for his valuable services, yet he has a prior and perpetual *retainer* on behalf of truth and justice; and there is no Crown or other licence which in any case or for any party or purpose can discharge him from that primary and paramount retainer."

* 1844, 7 Irish Law Reports, at p. 313.

SOME OBSERVATIONS ON
THE ART OF ADVOCACY

Address to the Birmingham Law Students' Society,
December 1933

I HAVE chosen a spacious subject this evening, so spacious that you will find it hard to convict me of irrelevance. But I promise to exercise within reasonable limits the *jus spatiandi* which it confers on me and to explore with you only a few of the vistas which it opens up.

In its widest sense the art of legal advocacy is the art of so presenting a case to a tribunal in writing or in speech as to secure if possible a desired decision. I should be disposed briefly to call it "the art of persuasion", the earliest classic definition of rhetoric, were it not that Quintilian, that great master of our science, protests that this definition is both too wide and too narrow. And besides, there is perhaps truth in the criticism that it suggests that to persuade at any price is the aim of the advocate, a view certainly open to serious ethical objections. Subject, however, to all reservations on the score of morality, a topic which I am not going to discuss on this occasion, I think we may accept the statement of the Greek grammarian Apollodorus that the first and all-important task of forensic oratory is "to persuade the judge and lead his mind to the conclusions desired by the speaker" (Quintilian, II. 15. 12).

If I were to select the rule which in my estimation

Some Observations on the Art of Advocacy

above all others should govern the presentation of an argument in Court, it is this—always keep steadily in mind that what the judge is seeking is material for the judgment or opinion which all through the case he knows he will inevitably have to frame and deliver at the end. He is not really interested in the advocate's pyrotechnic displays: he is searching all the time for the determining facts and the principles of law which he will ultimately embody in his decision.

I remember a friend of mine on the Bench once discussing with me the advocacy of a certain counsel. He came into Court briskly, spoke well and vigorously and at reasonable length, and indeed exhibited all the outward evidences of what is known as "a good appearance". He left the Court receiving the congratulations of his junior and the thanks of his client. All seemed well. "But", said the judge, "when I came to write my judgment in my study at home that night I found I had a blank note book. The speech apparently so successful had contributed just nothing to assist me in my task. On analysis I found it to consist chiefly of robust commonplaces and confident assertions." On the other hand how often a halting address, delivered with every fault of manner and diction but manifestly the result of careful thought and thorough research, will command the respect of the Bench and provide the judge with the very material he wants. Counsel's task is to help the Court— to help the Court to reach a decision in his client's favour. I used always to have before me the vision of the judge sitting down at his desk to write his judgment after all the stir and excitement of the debate was over. Extreme propositions confidently advanced at the Bar do not help him then. He wants the clear phrase, the moderately stated principle, the dispassionate array of facts which may appropriately find a place in his judicial finding. It is a good exercise to think out how, if you were the judge and not the advocate of your client's cause, you would yourself frame a judgment in your client's favour. Then model your speech on these lines. You will be surprised to find how often the grateful judge when he comes to give judgment will adopt the very words of an argument so presented. You have furnished him with the materials of judgment; he will be predisposed to use them because they are at hand and the more so if your opponent has adopted a less helpful though possibly more showy method of advocacy.

After all, the problems of pleading are all problems of psychology. One mind is working on another mind at every point and all the time. The judicial mind is subject to the laws of psychology like any other mind. When the judge assumes the ermine he does not divest himself of humanity. He has sworn to do justice to all men without fear or favour, but the impartiality which is the noble hall mark of our Bench does not imply that the judge's mind has become a mere machine to turn out decrees; the judge's mind remains a human instrument working as do other minds, though no doubt on specialised lines and often characterised by individual traits of personality, engaging or the reverse. It is well, therefore, for the advocate not only to know his case but to know his judge in the sense of knowing the type of mind with which he has to deal. *Mores quoque si fieri potest judicis velim nosse*—I should also wish, if possible, to be acquainted with the character of the judge, says Quintilian

202

(IV. I. 17). And he adds—"For it will be desirable to enlist their temperaments in the service of our cause, where they are such as are like to be useful, or to mollify them, if they are like to prove adverse, just according as they are harsh, gentle, cheerful, grave, stern or easygoing." I used to find *Who's Who* quite a useful volume to consult before addressing a Parliamentary Committee with whose members I was unacquainted. It is unwise to attack too violently the practices of landowners when that invaluable manual has informed you that a member of the Committee owns 30,000 acres, or to assail the methods of a trade in which it tells you that another member is engaged, or even to deride a recreation in which another member has artlessly confided to the public that he indulges.

But I was thinking of larger matters, not of mere prejudices or predispositions, when I said that the judicial mind is subject to well-known psychological laws. One of the most conspicuous, and perhaps one of the most creditable, of the instincts of all intellectual minds is a tendency to assist any one who confesses that he is struggling with a difficulty. I call it the instinct of rescue. There are occasions when it is worth enlisting on your side. When you know that your case is confronted with a serious difficulty in the shape of an awkward passage in the evidence or an embarrassing precedent, do not shirk it. Read the awkward passage with all emphasis or quote the authority without flinching, and point out the difficulty which it creates for you. You will almost invariably find that the first instinct of the judge is to assist you by pointing out that the evidence is less damaging to you than you represented or that the precedent is on examination distinguishable. The Court is favourably disposed by the absence of all concealment of the difficulty and is attracted by the very statement of the difficulty to address itself to the task of solving or alleviating it. A good man struggling with adversity always makes an appeal to the judicial as well as to every other generous mind! A solution which the judge himself finds for a problem, too, is always much more valuable to the advocate than one which he himself offers to the Court, for the Court is naturally tenacious of its own discoveries and your opponent who ventures to challenge its solution finds his adversary, not in you, but in the Court—a much more serious matter! But there is another reason for adopting the course I have recommended. It is sound tactics, as Quintilian pointed out over eighteen centuries ago, *Non inutilis etiam est ratio occupandi quae videntur obstare*—it is a good plan to antici- pate the points that you think are going to be made against you (IV. 1. 49). You will now probably tell me that my disquisition on this aspect of advocacy is super- fluous for it is already part of our proverbial philosophy, and that I might have expressed my advice with much greater simplicity in the homely recommendation "take the bull by the horns". I should, however, add that the expedient of disarming your opponent by anticipating him is one to be used with discretion; it is not always possible to adopt it, nor is it always desirable to resort to it. Circumstances alter cases. Nor is it always well to dwell too emphatically on the bad points of your case —you may defeat your object by satisfying the judge that they really *are* fatal to you. I only desire to indicate the utility of these methods of advocacy in suitable instances.

Some Observations on the Art of Advocacy

One principal, however, is of universal application. There can be no good advocacy that is not orderly in its presentation. It is a well-known fact that a skilful exposition of a case often largely supersedes the necessity for argument. I have indeed heard it said of an artist in advocacy that he never argued his cases; he merely stated them. So orderly and adroit was his arrangement of his statement that the conclusion which he wished to be drawn appeared inevitable. The colloquial retort— "I'm not arguing with you, I'm telling you"—has a subtler application than its users generally appreciate. In this connection I venture to impress upon all whose ambition it is to be successful advocates that they should not neglect the mechanical side of preparation. Orderliness in the arrangement of the documents in a case has far more importance than is generally realised. Which of us has not seen the discomfort and confusion produced by a paper going amissing just at the moment when it is wanted, or the irritation of the judge when he finds his copy of documents differently paged or arranged from counsel's copy? The thread of the argument is interrupted, tempers are upset, and half the effect of a good speech may be irretrievably lost. All this can be avoided by a little forethought and system. I shall give you an example of what I mean. I remember once having to give before a tribunal a long historical explanation of the development of an important chapter of our administrative law. It necessarily involved constant references to a whole series of statutes and to a mass of blue books and Government Reports. I knew what would happen if some uniform system of arranging all this material were not devised. No two members of

205

the tribunal would ever be looking at the same document, half the time would be occupied in looking for missing copies, and before I was done a general state of confusion would have resulted. So I told my instructors to obtain from the King's Printers a complete set of all the Acts I was going to refer to and to bind them up in a single volume, paged consecutively with a cover of a distinctive colour, and to do the same for all the Blue books and reports. I prepared my notes with these before me. The result was that I had only to tell the tribunal to look at the red volume page so and so or the blue volume page so and so. If I may say so without disrespect, the system was fool-proof. Consequently the minds of the tribunal were never diverted from following the case by futile fumblings among a pile of disordered productions and the argument proceeded in comfort. All this, you may say, is very elementary, not to say menial. But, believe me, it is of real importance. Attention to these apparently trivial details has a much greater effect on the fortunes of a case than is imagined. When what I may call the mechanical apparatus of a case works easily and well, the mind of the judge is inevitably favourably impressed. He follows easily what is presented to him in orderly fashion and he is predisposed to accept as sound what is so well-ordered. Even the judicial mind is not immune from the attraction of the path of least resistance. There is also the satisfaction and ease enjoyed by counsel in handling his case, which in turn results in a better and more effective address. I speak from the fullness of my heart when I say that I have seen more trouble in Court over disorderly papers than from any other cause. So I decline to treat as a triviality beneath counsel's notice this matter of the tidiness and accessibility of the documents in the case.

I should like also to emphasise the importance of citing your authorities clearly and accurately, a matter to which my friend, Mr Singleton, draws attention in his recently-published Lectures on *Conduct at the Bar*. You should have on a separate sheet of paper a list of all the cases and textbooks to which you are going to refer, and when you are going to cite them you should announce them by name slowly and deliberately, giving the year, volume, series and page of every case quoted, so that the judge may have time to take down the reference. I have seen much time wasted and much irritation engendered by a failure to observe this simple rule.

As you will have observed from one or two passing quotations which I have already made, I have recently been looking into Quintilian's *Institutio Oratoria* or *Institutes of Oratory*. Both that great work and Cicero's well-known dialogue *De Oratore* are amazing repositories of information and suggestion on the art of pleading. But they suffer to some extent from over-sophistication. An art is always decadent when it becomes too self-conscious, and the over-elaboration of the analysis of the pleader's art in the later classical period is an indication that it was losing spontaneity and becoming too artificial. All the same it is remarkable to find how fully alive were these ancient experts to all the refinements of advocacy. There is no artifice practised by the pleader of to-day which you will not find discussed by them. And amid much that seems to us merely scholastic or pedantic there are many sound observations. One topic with which they deal at great length is the use of humour in debate. The

Greek orators, too, devoted much attention to the topic "concerning laughter". *Urbanitas opportuna reficit animos* says Quintilian (IV. 1. 49)—timely wit refreshes the mind. But it can do much more than merely refresh jaded spirits. As he says himself in another passage *Rerum autem saepe maximarum momenta vertit ut cum odium iramque frequentissime frangat* (VI. 3. 9).—It frequently turns the scale in matters of great importance, as for instance when it dispels, as it often does, hatred or anger. Even a seventeenth-century Scottish Calvinist admits that "there is a faculty of laughing given to men, which certainly is given for use, at least at some times; and diversions are sometimes needful for men who are serious and employed in weighty affairs" (Hutcheson's *Exposition of the Book of Job*, 1669, p. 389). I doubt if any one has ever succeeded in defining humour, but we all know it when we hear it and it is certainly one of the most valuable parts of the pleader's equipment. It has a curious and almost incalculable psychological effect—I had nearly said physiological. Take a situation such as not infrequently arises in the course of a serious encounter in the Law Courts, when the atmosphere has grown tense and electrical and the nerves of judge and counsel are alike on the stretch. Suddenly someone interposes a happy stroke of wit. The effect is instantaneous. *Solvuntur tabulae risu*. The tensity is relaxed and—an odd thing—cannot, at least immediately, recur. Laughter is invincible as a solvent. We use the phrase "irresistibly funny" quite correctly. What is truly humorous cannot be resisted—the laugh will out, however solemn we may be, indeed the more certainly the more solemn we are or are trying to be. The wit of the Law Courts is commonly derided as being of poor quality, appreciated when it comes from counsel because anything is a relief from the tedium of legal argument, and when it comes from the judge because it is expedient to simulate an obsequious enjoyment. It is true that poor enough efforts sometimes pass muster and that much legal humour is esoteric and loses its flavour when transplanted from the purlieus of the law. But I am thinking of the really witty phrase and the really humorous sally which at a critical moment may save a situation from disaster and win more genial consideration for a case in jeopardy. Somehow or other the muscles of the grimmest judicial countenance, once they have relaxed in genuine merriment, can never recover their stern tautness. So it is well to have in one's forensic quiver a few barbless shafts of humour to use at discretion.

My friend, Mr Condie Sandeman, formerly Dean of the Faculty of Advocates in Edinburgh, whose recent death we all lament, was a master of the kind of epigrammatic wit I have in mind. I may recall a couple of instances of it. One afternoon at a quarter past three he rose to address the Court. The Lord President asked him how long he would take. "Three-quarters of an hour", he replied. "Very good," said the Lord President, "we have just that amount of judicial time available for you this afternoon; pray proceed." As the Dean was speaking the Court interposed so frequently that at last the Lord President said—"It would be hardly fair, Mr Dean, to keep you to your allotted forty-five minutes in view of the amount of discussion to which your interesting argument has given rise." "My Lord," replied the Dean, "I had allowed for that in my estimate"! On another occasion, this time in the House of Lords, one of their Lordships, employing a familiar judicial expedient, said to the Dean: "May I put your case for you thus—" and proceeded to state the Dean's case in such a way that it was difficult for him to say that it was not his case, though he knew that if he assented he would immediately find himself in difficulties. "My Lord," said the Dean, "while fully appreciating the benevolence which has prompted your Lordship to come to my assistance, may I be permitted, for reasons which your Lordship will understand, to state my case in my own way?" Alas, we cannot all turn a phrase so neatly.

Bathos above all things must be avoided. The classical instance is that of the advocate Glycon who to move the hearts of the jury produced a weeping boy as one of his witnesses. Unhappily for the success of this dramatic coup the boy, when asked why he was weeping, instead of giving the arranged answer blurted out that his pedagogue had pricked him. In Racine's inimitable comedy, *Les Plaideurs*, you will find an admirable example of the failure of a similar artifice, but much too French for me to venture to rehearse it here. Theatrical appeals rarely succeed. There are great moments in great cases where some dramatic licence is justifiable, but they are rare, and Quintilian wisely advises us to remember not to put the mask and buskins of Hercules on a small child (VI. 1. 36).

Now let me say a little about the form as apart from the substance of pleading. I believe that no advocate can be a great pleader who has not a sense of literary form, and whose mind is not stored with the treasures of our great literary inheritance upon which he may draw at will. The fortune of an argument depends much more than is commonly realised on the literary garb in which it is presented. A point made in attractive language sticks in the judicial memory. You must avoid the commonplace without falling into the bizarre. Originality is effective but eccentricity merely repels. There is much in the way in which a speech is started; as the French with their infallible instinct put it, *c'est le premier pas qui coûte*. You want to arrest attention from the outset. And so we find Quintilian and the other ancient experts dwelling at length on the exordium. He is a bad pilot, he says, who wrecks his ship when putting out from the harbour (IV. 1. 61). It is, perhaps, a moot point whether you should state your best point at the very outset—put your best foot foremost. Quintilian says—*Festinat enim judex ad id quod potentissimum est* (IV. 5. 10)—The judge is always in a hurry to reach the most important point. But I am not sure that he should always be gratified. There is something to be said for keeping your best vintage till your guests have been duly prepared for its reception. But of this I am convinced, that you should make it your aim to interest your judge from the very start. Even the driest topic can be made interesting with a little imagination and ingenuity. To be interesting is almost as important as to be logical. Let me in passing just mention a habit of some advocates which is peculiarly exasperating to the judge. Who has not heard counsel when faced with a difficulty endeavour to postpone the evil day by the time-worn phrase "I'm coming to that"! You know and the judge knows that he never will, if he can help it. There was one very eminent counsel who is said to have emitted more promissory notes of this kind than any counsel before him and to have redeemed fewer of them. The better course is to deal at once with the point put to you. The question indicates the train of the judge's thought: he will not be diverted from it by your evasion. Have it out there and then, even although you may have to desert the progress of your argument for the moment. You can work back to your main theme with a little dialectic skill.

Let there be balance and proportion in your argument. Some advocates give as much time and trouble to the exposition of their bad points as of their good points. There is no worse fault. The judge will soon be unable to see the wood for the trees. A counsel who used laboriously to argue before the Court every point, good, bad and indifferent, which was placed before him by his industrious solicitor, observed cynically that he had in consequence lost many cases but had never lost a client. I do not commend this policy. In the arrangement of your points you ought not to exhaust all your best material at the beginning, or else you may decline to a lame conclusion, than which there is nothing less impressive. *Ne a potentissimis ad levissima decrescat oratio* (Quintilian, v. 12. 14). The natural order is to place first the points arising on the facts, displaying their salient features, then the points of law, and, finally, the general equitable considerations which tend to satisfy the conscience of the Court that justice is on your side.

It would be attractive to dwell on the manners of the advocate, the importance of courtesy to one's opponent, respect towards the judge and fairness to all. But this is too large a region upon which to enter now. One other piece of advice, however, I may cull from Quintilian, as true to-day as ever it was: *Bonus altercator vitio iracundiae careat* (VI. 4. 10)—The good debater must avoid the fault of temper. Calmness and coolness are his best equipment, if he is to serve his client well.

And now you will not resent it if I bring these desultory observations to a close on a more serious note. There are some who would malign the art of the advocate as dishonest and morally degrading. The taunt is as old as Plato, and so is its refutation. There is no calumny more unfounded. It is an art truly beset with perils but there is no sphere in which gifts of character and uprightness are more sure of recognition and reward. It has been practised by some of the noblest men in the long and glorious annals of our country. Practised with the high sense of honour which has always characterised the Bar in our country, it is the sure bulwark of justice and liberty. "I, for one," says Quintilian, "restrict the name of orator and the art itself to those who are good" (II. 15. 1).

LORD CHANCELLOR
BIRKENHEAD

I. HIS JUDICIAL WORK

The Empire Review, October 1923

"The parts of a judge are four: to direct the evidence; to moderate length, repetition or impertinency of speech; to recapitulate, select and collate the material points of that which hath been said; and to give the rule or sentence." Bacon's *Essays*, LVI, Of Judicature.

THE Lord Chancellorship differs in its attributes from all other judicial offices. Its unique character was emphasised by Lord Birkenhead himself in the recent discussion on the propriety of Law Lords taking part in current political controversies. It is indeed typical of the anomalies of our Constitution, which prides itself on the jealous separation of the legislature, the executive and the judiciary, that our highest judicial functionary should nevertheless be also the Chairman of the Upper Legislative Chamber and a member of the Cabinet, the supreme executive of the nation. To become Lord Chancellor therefore does not involve the renunciations which are becoming and indeed imperative in the case of other judicial appointments. This consideration doubtless availed to reconcile Sir Frederick Smith to the acceptance of the Great Seal, for neither his age nor his temperament were such as to render attractive to him the idea of retirement from the arena of active public life. "The Bench", a veteran lawyer once said, "is very like Heaven; it is a place we all hope to go to some day—but not to-day." Lord Birkenhead in 1919 at the age of 46 would not have welcomed a call to even the most exalted judicial Elysium. The shelf, as the irreverent might say, would have afforded too limited and secluded a platform for the display of his universal gifts. But the Chancellorship was a different matter. If it was not Heaven, it certainly was not the shelf. When the Great Seal was delivered to Sir Frederick Smith on 14 January 1919, he thereby not only attained the highest legal preferment, but also retained the right of participating in the most dignified and authoritative fashion in the government of the country. Perhaps he also anticipated the enjoyment, in Bagehot's words, of "that great pleasure in life, doing what people say you cannot do". For it must be admitted that the legal profession and the public at large viewed at first with some misgiving the entrusting of the highest judicial office in the land to one whose previous career had given no special promise of fitness for its duties. The new Chancellor's participation in politics had been marked by brilliance rather than by gravity. Vigorous powers of onslaught and a pretty turn of ironic and occasionally barbed wit had distinguished his championship of the causes he had espoused. Less was known of his amazing and rapid industry, his dynamic legal intellect and his instinctive sense of justice.

The new occupant of the Woolsack was not long in converting his critics into enthusiastic admirers. Plainly, a Daniel had come to judgment. It was not so much a case of the office making the man as of the office affording the opportunity for the exhibition by its holder of qualities hitherto unsuspected, or, at least, imperfectly appreciated. This paper is not concerned with Lord Birkenhead's resounding success as Speaker of the House of Lords; its purpose is to consider the drier topic of his strictly judicial work as Lord Chancellor. In this no less exacting though more technical sphere he at once established an unchallenged predominance. It was a searching ordeal to be called upon to preside over the deliberations of the Supreme Courts of Appeal for the United Kingdom and the Empire, composed as these Courts were of the ablest and most experienced judicial minds of the day, including an unusual array of ex-Lord Chancellors, but, alike in the House of Lords and in the Judicial Committee of the Privy Council, Lord Birkenhead acquired from the outset an easy supremacy. The transition from addressing a tribunal as counsel to presiding over it as chairman is apt to be an embarrassing one, but he compassed it without a perceptible jolt. Though in years far younger than any of his colleagues, he was accepted by them as their president with immediate loyalty. There was no trace of the assertiveness of the new broom in his attitude. He seemed to take his place on the Woolsack as though to the manner born. His relations with his judicial brethren and with the Bar were irreproachable, and won from both instant recognition.

We have heard far too much in the past of the supposed ethical difficulties which beset the path of the advocate. To judge from the extensive literature on the subject a layman might be tempted to believe that the life of a barrister is a series of contests between his duty and his conscience. On the other hand, the judge's life is conceived to be free from all such conflicts, and indeed to be concerned chiefly with the avoidance of the injustices into which counsel is perpetually engaged in enticing him. The truth is that the functions of a judge require for their proper discharge powers of ethical discrimination every whit as nice as those of the highest minded advocate. Counsel's task consists in exposition and argument. These are relatively simple matters. To tell a story truly and fairly requires only an accurate and honest mind; to argue a case persuasively needs only a reasonably equipped armoury of law and logic, some powers of imagination and a happy gift of selection. But decision is a much more momentous affair than either exposition or argument. Exposition may aid, and argument may influence, decision, but after all it is the judge who is responsible for the decree which rules the fortunes of the parties in their status or their property. It is not a simple matter to do justice; it is even more difficult to convince the parties to a litigation or the wider public that justice has been done. The judicial oath of office imposes on the judge a lofty duty of impartiality. But impartiality is not easy of attainment. For a judge does not shed the attributes of common humanity when he assumes the ermine. The ordinary human mind is a mass of prepossessions inherited and acquired, often none the less dangerous because unrecognised by their possessor. Few minds are as neutral as a sheet of plate glass, and indeed a mind of that quality may actually fail in judicial efficiency, for the warmer tints of imagination and sympathy are needed to temper the cold light of reason if human justice is to be done. If law were an exact science, and judgment were to be laid to the line and righteousness to the plummet, then justice might be

a mechanical product, but amidst the incalculable complexities of human relationships the administration of
justice can never be of this character. To quote the
ancient and impressive formula, the judge in pronouncing
his decision must be ripely advised, and have God and a
good conscience before him. His task is not merely to
select one or other of the two conflicting views submitted
to him. He has to make his own contribution from the
garnered stores of his experience and research. He must
purge his mind not only of partiality to persons, but of
partiality to arguments, a much more subtle matter, for
every legal mind is apt to have an innate susceptibility
to particular classes of argument. Hume Brown used to
say that a man cannot jump off his own shadow, but the
judge must try his best to do so. The great contests of the
law are always nicely balanced. A cool and steady hand
is required to hold the balance true. The over-con-
scientious judge is apt to torture his mind by wondering
whether he has exhausted all the study and given all the
consideration which entitle him to proceed to judgment.
An eminent judge said that during the first ten years in
which he held office he always feared he was wrong,
during the second ten years he always was sure he was
right, and in the last ten years he did not care whether
he was right or wrong. The criticism may be hazarded
that each of these attitudes of mind was wrong.

But it is not only in the grave matter of judgment that
the judge is tested. His conduct of the proceedings before him in Court affords a gauge of his ethical equipment for the judicial office. Courtesy and patience must
be more difficult virtues to practise on the Bench than
might be imagined, seeing how many otherwise ad-

mirable judges have failed to exhibit them; yet they are essential if the Courts are to enjoy public confidence. Not a few judges have failed to lay to heart Bacon's admonition: "It is no grace to a judge first to find that which he might have heard in due time from the Bar." Mr Justice Wills, who was not free from this defect, no doubt appreciated the irony of the counsel who remarked to him: "Your Lordship is even a greater man than your father. The Chief Baron used to understand me after I had done, but your Lordship understands me before I begin."

To be a good judge thus calls for the exhibition of high ethical as well as intellectual qualities. But to be a great judge demands in addition the indefinable gift of genius. The time has fortunately not yet come for estimating the place which Lord Birkenhead will finally occupy in the legal annals of our country. An unusual opportunity has, however, just been afforded to us of estimating the quality of his judicial work during his recent Lord Chancellorship by the collection in a single volume of most of the judgments delivered by him during his tenure of office. The collection is not a judicial anthology. It is simply a compilation of cases important and unimportant in the decision of which Lord Birkenhead took part as Chancellor, and each case is presented, after the consecrated manner of the Law Reports, with rubric, narrative and judgment. For this very reason the volume affords to the technical student a better means of appreciating Lord Birkenhead's work than if it had contained merely a series of choice extracts possibly more attractive to the general reader. It may be said at once that a perusal of this mass of judicial exposition and argument leaves on the mind an impression of remarkable competence. These recorded judgments all convey the sense of easy and admitted mastery, to borrow one of Lord Birkenhead's own phrases from his address to the American Bar Association the other day. The difficulties which encompass the task of judgment and which have been no more than hinted at on a preceding page are here seen surmounted by a mind consummately equipped with just those aptitudes which are so much more easily recognised than described. It must, of course, always be remembered that the great majority of these judgments were delivered on appeal from lower Courts in which the facts and the law had already been sifted more than once by able precursors. But this circumstance it is which renders them of such value. In the final Court the way is cleared for the ultimate conflict of principles, and scope is afforded for the authoritative exposition of the law. Here law is in truth made as well as applied, here the broadening of our law from precedent to precedent is visibly in progress. The high province of a Supreme Court is to control and develop the law so as to enable it to keep pace with and yet moderate the changing social and economic conditions of the nation.

The first thought which strikes one in looking through these five hundred pages is the extraordinarily multifarious character of the topics which within so short a period of time came up for consideration in the Courts of ultimate appeal. Commercial disputes about charter parties and marine insurance, collisions at sea, contracts as affected by the war, workmen's compensation, restraint of trade, interpretation of wills, conveyancing

problems, matrimonial disputes, the effect of drunkenness on criminal responsibility—upon such varied subjects and on many others Lord Birkenhead was called
upon to pronounce. We realise once more that to the
law *nil humanum alienum*. The fate of the cases which came
up for review is interesting from the statistical aspect.
There are here recorded 38 cases from the Court of
Appeal in England; in 26 of these the judgment below
was affirmed, and in 12 the judgment below was varied
or reversed. Of 15 appeals from the Court of Session
in Scotland, 5 were dismissed, 9 sustained and 1 com-
promised. Of 11 Irish appeals, 6 were dismissed, 4 sustained, and 1 adjourned without decision. One decision
of the Court of Criminal Appeal was reversed, while in
the Privy Council 3 appeals from the Dominions were
dismissed, and 1 sustained, and 1 appeal from the
Lincoln Consistory Court was dismissed. Of 3 reported
matrimonial petitions taken by the Lord Chancellor as
a judge of first instance, 2 were dismissed and 1 granted.
One petition to the Committee of Privileges was dismissed. In justice to the Scottish Court of Session it
should be explained that three of the decisions reversed
were on the same point of workmen's compensation law.
The ingenious may calculate the odds against an appellant.

It is difficult to select from this bulky mass of legal exposition, much of it highly technical, samples fitted to
illustrate Lord Birkenhead's judicial method. What most
interests the lawyer is often most repellent to the layman.
All, however, can join in appreciating the great and
courageous judgment which the Lord Chancellor delivered early in his career on the subject of the legality

of bequests for masses for the repose of the soul of the testator. For the best part of a century it had been accepted as a commonplace that such bequests were invalid as being for superstitious uses, and the Court of Appeal, following precedent, had refused to sustain a series of legacies left by a Catholic testator for masses. The matter was open for reconsideration in the House of Lords which had never previously been called upon to pronounce on it, but in view of the existing authorities on the subject most lawyers would have deemed the appellant's task an uphill one. Lord Birkenhead's historical analysis of the law is an admirable example of judicial reasoning. He sums up the result in a series of paragraphs showing that at common law such masses were not illegal, that they became illegal by the passing of the Acts of Uniformity, but that in consequence of the Catholic Relief Act of 1829 the taint of illegality was removed. Once it was demonstrated that the law now recognises the Catholic religion as one which may be practised in this country without any penal consequences or breach of the law, the principle *cessante ratione, legis cessat lex ipsa* could properly be allowed free play, and the conclusion is irresistibly reached that a bequest for masses for the soul of the dead ceased to be impressed with the stamp of superstition when Roman Catholicism was once more permitted to be openly practised. The Lord Chancellor carried with him in his enlightened decision all his colleagues except Lord Wrenbury. The courage of this judgment is manifest to every lawyer, and it has a special value as illustrating the class of case in which the House of Lords is prepared to reconsider what has long been regarded as settled law. "If there were in fact an unbroken line of authorities dating back 300 years, then it would have been a matter for grave discussion whether this House, in accordance with well-recognised principles, would consent to break that chain. The authorities, however, are only uniform in result. Some depend upon statutes, some on the principle that no religion other than that by law established can be recognised and protected by the Courts, while others depend upon a misunderstanding of the ancient decisions." Reconsideration of the whole question was thus permissible. The House not long before had decided that a bequest in favour of the Secular Society was not illegal, and the Lord Chancellor, in a characteristic passage, thus referred to this circumstance: "Unwilling as I am to question old decisions, I shall be able," he says, "if my view prevails, to reflect that your Lordships will not within a short period of time have pronounced to be valid legacies given for the purpose of denying 'some of the fundamental doctrines of the Christian religion', and have held to be invalid a bequest made for the purpose of celebrating the central sacrament in a creed which commands the assent of many millions of our Christian fellow-countrymen."

As an example of Lord Birkenhead's handling of legal doctrine, his judgment in the case of the S.S. *Volute* on the subject of contributory negligence is of outstanding merit. The doctrine is one which is apt to go off into metaphysical subtleties and scholastic refinements. The general principle is clear enough. A person cannot complain that he has been injured through the negligence of another if by his own negligence he has contributed to his injury. But the fact that the injured person has him-

self been negligent does not disentitle him to redress unless his negligence is directly associated with the injury
he has sustained. There is obviously room here for much
legal controversy in particular cases. Lord Birkenhead
illuminated the topic with a broad flood of common-
sense light. Simultaneity of the two acts of negligence is
discarded as a decisive test. The real test is whether
the negligent acts of both parties form "parts of one
transaction" resulting in the injury. If the negligent
acts of the plaintiff and the defendant are so closely involved the one with the other in time, place and circumstance as to render them in combination the composite
cause of the injury, the plaintiff has no right to redress.
The lucidity of Lord Birkenhead's exposition of the principles of this difficult branch of law elicited from Viscount Finlay, one of his colleagues, an encomium such
as is rarely heard in the restrained atmosphere of the
House of Lords. "I have nothing to add", he said, "beyond this one sentence, that I regard the judgment to
which we have just listened as a great and permanent
contribution to our law on the subject of contributory
negligence and to the science of jurisprudence."

Possibly, the judgment of Lord Chancellor Birkenhead
which will be most often quoted in the future is that in
which he defined the precise limits within which the plea
of drunkenness is admissible as a defence to a criminal
charge. He traces the gradual development of the law
on the subject from the early days when drunkenness
was treated as an aggravation rather than a mitigation.
The Court of Criminal Appeal had held that the question for the jury was whether the accused was incapable
through his drunken state of knowing that what he was

doing was likely to cause serious injury, or in other words was incapable of foreseeing or measuring the consequences of his act. This view the Lord Chancellor characterised as unsound. The true test was whether the accused was in such a state as to be incapable of forming and entertaining the requisite criminal intent. He thus enunciates the law: "Where a specific intent is an essential element in the offence, evidence of a state of drunkenness rendering the accused incapable of forming such an intent should be taken into consideration in order to determine whether he had in fact formed the intent necessary to constitute the particular crime. If he was so drunk that he was incapable of forming the intent required he could not be convicted of a crime which was only committed if the intent was proved. This does not mean that the drunkenness in itself is an excuse for the crime, but that the state of drunkenness may be incompatible with the actual crime charged, and may therefore negative the commission of that crime." Malice prepense is of the essence of the crime of murder; where there is no capacity to form any intent there can be no such malice prepense. Particularly valuable is the Lord Chancellor's discrimination between the defence of insanity (whether induced by alcoholic excess or otherwise) and the defence of drunkenness. The whole judgment is a model of clear and authoritative judicial exposition on a topic of cardinal legal importance.

There is one judgment in this volume which exhibits perhaps better than any other the remarkable power of assimilation which Lord Birkenhead possesses. A dispute had arisen in Scotland between the Crown and the landowners holding directly of the Crown regarding the feudal payments which the Crown was entitled to exact from them in respect of their tenure. A test action was raised to try the question, which was one of prime importance, involving very large pecuniary consequences. The arguments which occupied over seven days were of the highest technicality, necessitating an investigation of the whole history of the feudal system in Scotland and the most crabbed niceties of Scottish conveyancing. The very vocabulary of the case was strange to English ears. Yet in his judgment Lord Birkenhead moves with assured tread through this difficult territory previously unexplored by him, and expounds the law of Scotland with accurate and exhaustive learning. To many Scottish conveyancers the achievement seemed a veritable *tour de force*, and it is all the more remarkable in that the whole grounds of the judgment of the Court of Session were discarded early in the hearing, although the decision was affirmed. The Lord Chancellor manifested a special interest in Stair and Erskine, the great institutional writers on Scots law, to whose works he was then introduced, and greatly admired their spacious and logical style of legal exposition. Their writings have no exact counterpart in the law of England.

It would be attractive to discuss many of the other judgments in this volume, but it must suffice only to mention one or two more. The long examination of the evidence in the notorious case of Archdeacon Wakeford, which led the Lord Chancellor to agree with the verdict of guilty found in the Consistory Court, is an example of detailed work on facts seldom surpassed. The selection and arrangement of the salient points in the great mass of evidence was obviously undertaken by Lord Birkenhead with zest, and the result is a piece of constructive reasoning of convincing cogency. His method of dealing with expert testimony, a very different class of evidence, is perhaps best exemplified in the case in which sitting alone he had to decide whether it was possible that a husband could be the father of a child born to his wife 331 days after he had left her and gone abroad. Lord Birkenhead decided, after a full discussion of the scientific evidence, that having regard to the present state of medical knowledge and belief he could not hold it to be impossible. The petition, addressed by Viscountess Rhondda to the Committee of Privileges, claiming the right to sit and vote in the House of Lords in virtue of the Sex Disqualification (Removal) Act of 1919, gave Lord Birkenhead the opportunity of stating his reasons for disallowing the claim in an interesting and, in parts, trenchant disquisition on constitutional law. His judgment in another *cause célèbre*, the case of Mrs Rutherford, shows the Lord Chancellor once again disentangling a complicated problem of fact fraught with painful human issues, and at the same time contributing valuable observations on the subject of legal evidence. A case which is unfortunately not included in the present collection was the occasion of a statement by the Lord Chancellor on the duty of counsel to bring before the House all authorities which bear one way or another upon the matters under debate, and of which counsel are aware, quite irrespective of whether or not the particular authority assists the party who is aware of it. This statement gave rise to no little discussion at the time and did not command universal assent. It has long been a moot point of professional ethics at the Bar whether counsel owe to the Court a duty to cite adverse authorities of which the other side is unaware. In the particular case there can be no question that the House ought to have had from counsel on one or other side a reference to the relevant statutory enactment which they omitted to mention, not intentionally but because they did not happen to be aware of it until it was discovered by one of the Lord Chancellor's colleagues. But the general question of counsel's duty, and whether that duty is different in the House of Lords from what it is in the lower Courts, is too large a one upon which to enter here.

This volume, into which the present article can only pretend to have dipped, will serve to convince its readers of the great value of Lord Birkenhead's contributions to the law during the period from January 1919 to October 1922, in which he occupied the Woolsack. His grasp of principle, his gift of analysis, and, perhaps most conspicuously, his beautifully lucid style can here be admired for all time. But no more than the herbarium can preserve the grace of the living flower can any such collection of judgments reproduce that quality which so pre-eminently distinguishes Lord Birkenhead's judicial work, the quality of conveying to all who resort to him for justice the assurance that their case will be heard with the fullest understanding, with the most earnest desire to hear all that can be fairly urged on either side, and with a courtesy and patience unwearied till the last plea has been adequately explored. No one ever left the bar of the House of Lords during his Chancellorship without feeling that the case had been tried out to the last ounce of its merits. That is a satisfaction only less than the satisfaction of victory, nay, perhaps, greater, for it can be shared by winner and loser alike. It would not be too much to claim for the judgments of Lord Chancellor Birkenhead what was said of those of Sir Matthew Hale that "the parties themselves, though interest does too commonly corrupt the judgment, were generally satisfied with the justice of his decisions, even when they were made against them". And it should be remembered that no Lord Chancellor during his term of office has done more to remove the reproach of the law's delays. In his speech at the Lord Mayor's Banquet on 9 November 1919, Lord Birkenhead recalled "the words of, perhaps, the greatest charter of the liberty of the subject: 'To none will we deny, to none will we delay, justice'", and added that to delay justice was in nineteen cases out of twenty to deny justice. His own record shows how fully he had laid this truth to heart.

II. A REVIEW OF HIS "FOURTEEN ENGLISH JUDGES"

The Empire Review, February 1926

The Judges of England, for the most part, have been unfortunate in their biographers, and, perhaps, not least so when they have attempted autobiography. There is no doubt a distinguished exception to the rule in Atlay's *Victorian Chancellors*. But most of the judicial "Lives" on our shelves exhibit all the dullness of uninspired propriety. This was not the conspicuous fault of Lord Birkenhead's predecessor to whom Sir Charles Wetherell referred as "my noble and biographical friend who has added a new terror to death". His offences lay in other directions. An anonymous critic of Lord Campbell's famous work, after a devastating onslaught upon the unhappy author, puts in this damning plea in mitigation: "A charming style, a vivid fancy, exhaustive research were not to be expected from a hardworked barrister."

The reproach commonly levelled at the qualities of legal authorship has been redeemed. The characteristics of the present work are precisely "A charming style, a vivid fancy, exhaustive research." Nothing quite like it has appeared before, for it appeals at once to the initiated and to the general reader. When Montesquieu described the judges of the nation as inanimate beings who act only as mouthpieces to pronounce the law, he was far wide of the mark. Each of these fourteen judges is here seen instinct with personality. They live as well as judge, and they are the greater judges just because they lived so vividly. In a sense, the events of a legal career of eminence are apt to have a certain sameness, and, however thrilling they may be to contemporaries in the law, it is difficult to render them exciting to the mind of unprofessional posterity. But, while all these fourteen judges were successes, each in his own way, no one could complain of the monotony of their careers as here depicted. The intimate and discerning view of their lives which we may now share with Lord Birkenhead reveals an astonishing diversity of personality and attainment. Each makes his own quite distinctive contribution to the galaxy. But all are servants of the same exacting mistress, the Law of England. "One judge looks at problems from the point of view of history, another from that of

philosophy, another from that of social utility, one is a
formalist, another is a latitudinarian, one is timorous of
change, another dissatisfied with the present; out of the
attrition of diverse minds there is beaten something
which has a constancy of uniformity and average value
greater than its component elements." (Cardozo's
Nature of the Judicial Process, p. 177.)

These portraits err neither on the side of adulation nor
on the side of depreciation, but preserve an appropriately judicial balance of discrimination. It is said
that an eminent judge, who was not a little proud of his
recently painted portrait, once invited a colleague to
come and see it. As they stood before the masterpiece
the subject of it asked the customary questions: "Now,
what do you think of it? Do you find it like me?"
"Painfully like", was the devastating rejoinder. The
adverb would be quite out of place if applied to these
likenesses, though here and there Lord Birkenhead
seems, as was said of Sargent, to bring to the surface
unsuspected qualities in his subjects.

The peculiar merit of this presentation of the life
and work of these fourteen great lawyers is its technical
precision. The literary man who writes about the law
distresses the lawyer by his technical deficiencies; the
lawyer who writes about the law distresses the literary
man by his deficiencies in style. Here we have literary
art of an engaging and refreshing quality wedded to
technical accuracy. The layman may, perhaps, be a
little repelled by the summaries of each judge's notable
decisions. But why should he? He has never before had
a chance of reading in intelligible language the history
of the great judgments which have built up the fabric of

the law and he should be grateful. The experts of the Law Reports will recognise an adept in their mystery of writing rubrics.

The order is chronological; it is an apostolic succession. We are bidden to await, in a later volume, a classification of the *ten* greatest judges in order of merit. Which of the fourteen will fall out? Mansfield, at least, is assured of a place, for the article on him concludes with this sentence: "No list of the *six* greatest judges whom the British Empire has produced could exclude the brilliant name of Mansfield." The class is becoming progressively exclusive. The portrait of Mansfield is, perhaps, one of the best in the gallery. We learn of his great work in establishing the Common Law of England, but we are not allowed to forget that he was a Scotsman caught young, and we are also admonished to remember what he owed to his brilliant predecessors. I venture to think that if he had a complaint to make of his treatment it would be on the score of the omission of any reference to the resounding judgment in which "not only on the plain and open principles of justice, but from regard to the public and from regard to this misguided Corporation itself" he forbade the City Fathers of Edinburgh to desecrate the most beautiful street in the world by the erection of buildings on the south side of Princes Street. The law may not be beyond cavil, but we may applaud the result.

The portrait of Lord Halsbury we can judge from a nearer standpoint. It is lifelike and a great tribute to a great character. But, on the point of his stubborn pertinacity, a Scots Appeal may be recalled in which, when counsel had advanced with becoming diffidence a proposition of English law, he made the caustic comment: "It will take a great deal to persuade me that that is the law of England." By good fortune, authority from the venerable archives of Vesey Junior was available. The capitulation was as gracious as the attack had been formidable: "Pray proceed. What was good enough law for the Chancery Courts in 1794 is good enough for me."

It would be an attractive task to attempt to compile from these studies a portrait of the perfect judge, by a process of selection and elimination of the diverse merits and demerits of these fourteen. But the difficulty would be to set the standard. Bacon himself set one and failed to attain it. Thomas Fuller furnishes eleven maxims conformity to which, he would have us believe, provides the touchstone of judicial merit. And then, there is Lord Dun's little book of *Friendly and Familiar Advices*, in which he devotes twenty-seven pages to his "Advice to the Judge". "The necessary qualifications for a judge", he tells us, "are in part natural and partly to be acquired." This distinguished platitude he enlarges with much pious elaboration. But his platitude is quite true. And the supreme interest of these studies consists in observing the natural characteristics of these great personages in the process of their development and training, and the effect upon them of their varying fortunes. Each character in turn is discussed and appraised with mingled justice and urbanity. Whether each estimation will be accepted as final is another matter. There is always an appeal to posterity, but for our time these judgments, however provocative of discussion (and that is a merit), will be difficult to overturn.

The temptation to enlarge upon the interest of these biographies must, however, be resisted here, for all but two of them first appeared in *The Empire Review*, and a conventional rule curbs the reviewer's eulogies in such circumstances.

III. AN INTRODUCTION TO HIS "LAST ESSAYS"

Published in 1930

Lord Birkenhead never stood in need of the services of an usher to cry "Oyez, Oyez" before him. Whatever he had to say on any topic was always assured of a hearing. It is therefore superfluous to introduce these further gleanings from the varied fields of his intellectual activities with any commendation of them to the attention of the reader. Whatever subject engaged his interest Lord Birkenhead contrived to make attractive by the freshness and the courage of his approach to it, and not the least merit of his views has always been their provocativeness. He never left a topic where he found it. But if he delighted in controversy, it was in controversy not as a means of obstruction to thought, but as a means of progress in thought. The papers here collected will be found to be eminently characteristic of his method and his mind, and many will be glad to have them thus preserved.

But if introduction is superfluous, it is fitting that a few words of valediction should preface this volume. It seems strange, almost incredible, that one should have to write of Lord Birkenhead in the past tense. We cannot easily realise that the vivid flame of his spirit has been quenched in death. His was so living, so commanding, a personality that it seemed superior to the fate of ordinary mortals. There was in truth something dæmonic about him which marked him out from all the men of his time. When he joined any gathering it was not merely, as with most of us, that there was one more person in the room; his advent seemed to affect the whole spirit of the meeting as the addition of a single element may alter the nature of a chemical composition. But no one can yet attempt to estimate adequately the place which Lord Birkenhead held in the life of his country or to compute the sum of his many-sided activities. To complete the record many hands would require to collaborate. For to some he was best known as a politician and a statesman, to others as a consummate advocate and brilliant Lord Chancellor, to others again as a lover of books and literature, and to yet others as a man of the world, devoted to sport and good fellowship, while to the intimate circle of his friends he revealed qualities of loyalty and generous affection of which the public were little aware. For how true it is, as Maurois says in his "Life" of that other great statesman with whom Lord Birkenhead has been so often compared: "La face éclairée des hommes reste presque toujours cachée à ceux qui ne les connaissent que dans la vie publique."

To each of us according to our bent one or other facet of his career presents itself as of specially attractive lustre. It is natural that I should think of him first and foremost as a servant of the law. He showed that devotion to the law was no narrowing thing. The dingy view of law as an affair of musty precedents and disingenuous wranglings was never his. He found in the pursuit of the law a liberalising and a fascinating profession. The intellectual training which it affords, its readiness to question all things without fear or favour, the opportunities of public service to which it opens the way, the good fellowship of its fraternity—all these he realised and enjoyed, and by all these he profited. To him law was never a mere technical art. He saw it as the supreme regulator of human relationships, and he never forgot, as many do in these days, that justice above all other matters is the prime concern of government. He would have agreed that "the final cause of law is the welfare of society".

The qualities which go to make up a great lawyer are diverse, and there are corresponding diversities of greatness among the names which adorn our legal roll of honour. Of Lord Birkenhead's excellence it may be said that it lay not so much in mere learning as in his attitude of mind. His triumphs in the forensic arena have often been recounted and even already are assuming that legendary character which invests so soon the tales of men of law. The fame of a great advocate, like that of an actor, seldom long survives and by the nature of things soon becomes a mere tradition. It is in judicial work alone that the lawyer can hope to secure for himself a permanent reputation. In the Law Reports which enshrine his judgments he may secure a measure of immortality. But the Law Reports, however monumental, fail in one respect. Of the men who delivered the decisions they record, nothing is told us beyond the bare dates of their tenure of office. How often we should like to have not only the decision, but also some knowledge of what manner of man the judge was who pronounced it! Judges have not only to decide cases; they have to conduct the business of their courts, and the method of the administration of justice is scarcely less important than its products.

If I were to select one attribute of Lord Birkenhead's genius in the judicial sphere as his especial virtue, it would be his method of dealing with the cases which came before him as Lord Chancellor. It is no secret that his appointment to the Woolsack was viewed with some apprehension by many who knew only of his achievements in other and very dissimilar spheres. But from the very first he established himself as a master of the business of judging in the estimation of that critical body, the Bar, and in the no less critical estimation of his colleagues.

To the advocate arguing before him Lord Birkenhead imparted some of his own inspiration. He was so obviously attracted by the matter in hand. On any topic which you could persuade him was worthy of his attention he wanted to know all that could be said and to be satisfied in proceeding to judgment that he had everything he should know. In the art of advocacy the first essential is to interest the judge in the problem presented. It is not always easy to do so, for the long routine of judicial work is apt to dull the receptiveness of the mind. Lord Birkenhead was always responsive. He gave the advocate the impression that he was really interested and found intellectual pleasure in the development of the case. No one left his Bar without feeling that every one of the points in the case which merited attention had been understood and appreciated and would

237

receive its due consideration. He never resisted or ob-
structed argument, but he always controlled it. It is no
part of a judge's business to suffer fools gladly—or perhaps at all. But it is his business to see that the advocate
gets every chance to state his client's case and not to let
the imperfections of the advocate prejudice a just cause.
It is often the judge's own fault if he does not get the
assistance which he should have from the Bar. Lord
Birkenhead got the very best out of those who were
privileged to plead before him, and he did so because
he knew how to manage debate. Counsel before him
felt as I should imagine a well-trained horse feels when
it knows that a master is handling the ribbons. Irrelevance was checked and tediousness dispelled, but all
that tended to advance the progress of the case was
encouraged. He had his reward from the Bar, as every
great judge has, for those who were asked for their best
gave of their best. And he won also by his consideration
and courtesy that other reward from the Bar which does
not always fall to the lot of great judges, the genuine and
respectful affection of all its members. Truly, as a great
authority has said, "There is no guaranty of justice except the personality of the judge."

Lord Birkenhead's Chancellorship was all too brief.
Appointed on 14 January 1919, he delivered up the seals
on 25 October 1922. A second term of office subsequently offered to him was not accepted. Yet within the
compass of less than four years he securely established
his position as one of the greatest and most distinguished
of those who have occupied his historic office.

Of his achievements in other spheres I am not competent to speak. He had in these other spheres his suc-

cesses and his failures, but if his failures as well as his successes are recalled let it also be remembered that it is only at the tree loaded with fruit that people throw stones. In the sphere of law there are no failures to record, and surely one may say, with Kipling, that "recognition by one's equals and betters in one's own craft is a reward of which a man may be unashamedly proud". And if it is doubtful whether he had any equals and certain that he had no betters in his own craft, let us substitute the recognition of his brethren as the tribute which he earned so surely and valued best of all.

THE PROFESSIONAL MIND

The Maudsley Lecture delivered before the Royal Medico-Psychological Association, May 1934

IN devoting to the foundation of a memorial lecture-ship a portion of Dr Maudsley's bequest, the learned Society which I have this afternoon the honour to address made an indulgent concession to the laity in prescribing that the lecture to be delivered should in alternate years be of a scientific and of a popular character. This year it is the turn of the popular lecturer—a rôle which I have assumed with some trepidation. The distinction drawn is an ominous one. It seems to suggest that to be scientific you must be unpopular, and to be popular you must be unscientific. But is there necessarily so absolute a dividing line between the two domains? I hazard the view that it is possible to be at once both popular and scientific. No doubt there is still a tendency in learned circles to deride what is known as popular science, but that is an inheritance from the days of the cheap and inaccurate manuals which used to be written by imperfectly informed persons, pretentiously professing to enlighten the masses on the truths of science. Nowadays, science has become more condescending, indeed almost affable, to democracy. The approach has come from both sides, for democracy is now better educated, and science is now more expert in the art of exposition. The advent of the internal combustion engine, of wireless telegraphy and of many other

practical applications of science to daily life has created
a new and widespread interest and aptitude on the part
of the general public in the acquisition of accurate
scientific knowledge, particularly among the younger
generation. At the same time the physicist, the chemist
and the biologist have found it possible and worth while
to impart much of their learning to wider audiences.
Science is daily entering more and more into the lives of
the people, with the consequence that its social, economic
and political implications are being more and more
realised by its professors. The President of the Royal
Society has reminded us that we live in an age when the
advance and development of scientific knowledge are
continually creating new social and economic problems
of the utmost importance, and has emphasised the necessity of bridging the gap between the scientist and the layman by every possible means. The British Science Guild,
now doing such excellent work, was founded some thirty
years ago by Sir Norman Lockyer for the express purpose
of promoting the application of scientific method and
results to social problems and public affairs. The market-
place can doubtless never supersede the laboratory, but
the scientist no longer disdains to take his wares to
market.

However, I think I know what is meant by the admonition that I must, on this occasion, deliver a popular
address. Every science has a general as well as a technical aspect. The technical side must always be for the
expert, and for him alone; the general side is of interest
to every intelligent citizen. I have chosen my subject
with this distinction in view. I shall not discourse on the
legal technicalities which beset and sometimes embarrass

the psychiatrist, the only technical department of medical psychology of which I can profess any knowledge. But I shall ask you to consider with me for a moment certain phenomena which, while they fall within the province of your special study, are at the same time matter of common observation and interest; I mean the phenomena exhibited by various types of the professional mind in its daily working—not excluding, incidentally, your own, for I recognise that I am addressing an audience of professional men.

My subject would, I believe, have commended itself to the very eminent specialist whom these lectures commemorate, for deeply versed, as he was, in the abstruse and recondite problems of a difficult branch of science, he was ever ready to recognise that his most valuable data were to be found in the ordinary human activities around him. Certainly few scientists have been more successful in illumining their writings with illustrations drawn from literature and daily life.

The choice and the practice of a profession have, as all will agree, a decisive and pervasive influence on a man's whole mental outlook. I use the word "profession" here in no narrow sense. I do not limit it to the three old-established professions of the Church, the law and medicine, though the practitioners of these three distinctive professions provide the best clinical material for study. I am thinking for the moment in wider terms of the mental characteristics exhibited by those who have chosen and practise a particular vocation, be it that of a clergyman, a lawyer or a doctor, or be it that of a politician, a banker, a teacher, a merchant or an industrialist. The first question we always ask about a new acquaintance is, What does he do? The answer gives us the first clue to the kind of man we have to deal with, for wide as are the individual differences among the members of a profession, there are always common elements which are shared by all who belong to it. Our habits are controlled, our thoughts canalised, our prejudices formed by the profession we practise, so true is it that "man's nature is subdued to what it works in, like the dyer's hand". Even our place of residence may be dictated by our vocation, as witness the Temple, "where studious lawyers have their bowers", and Harley Street, sacred to Æsculapius.

I do not know enough either of physiology or of psychology to describe the growth of the professional mind in terms of those sciences, but I may adopt and adapt the language which Dr Maudsley uses in discussing the larger topic of the inculcation of morality. He describes the process as one of moral manufacture, and points out that the whole purpose of education in morals is to produce a nature in which moral action shall have become, not a matter of uncertainty and deliberation, but automatic. Each moral act by the law of nervous action renders the next more easy, and so a man's nature is gradually modified. When a habit of nature has thus been formed, the desire of the organism is to display that function which is embodied in its nature, and the pleasure of gratifying that desire becomes itself a sufficient motive. Imitation plays its part, too, for man, as Gabriel Tarde, the eminent French sociologist, reminds us, is essentially an imitative animal: "He imitates his forefathers, that is custom; he imitates his neighbours, that is fashion; he imitates himself, that is habit." It is by some such means that the process of our professional training and experience gradually moulds our minds and characters until our reactions become largely instinctive. And so we say, for example, of a man, "Oh! he's a lawyer; you know how lawyers always look at things." I regret that the implication in the case of my own profession is generally disparaging.

From the earliest times the practitioners of a particular art have always shown a tendency to draw apart from the rest of the community and to constitute themselves a separate class or fraternity, with their own ceremonial rites and shibboleths. The widest of all caste cleavages in former days, and still a wide one, was that between the clergy and the laity, between those devoted to sacred things and those devoted to secular things. Indeed the very word "layman" is most often used in popular parlance to denote one who is not a cleric. This fundamental differentiation between clergy and laity runs through the whole history of our law. Within the ranks of the laity in turn many associations grew up of men united by a common calling. The merchant and trade guilds, surviving into our own time as city companies, were typical examples of the segregation of the followers of particular arts and crafts. The lines of demarcation, both social and professional, were much more rigidly drawn in former times, and the resulting mutual exclusiveness produced much more distinctive types of person. Nowadays the barriers are broken down and men of all careers mix with each other. This is a more excellent way of living. But there still remain and will always remain certain typical attributes which the lifelong pursuit of a particular calling engenders. Such differences and peculiarities lend colour and interest to social life, and the followers of each vocation have their own distinctive contribution to make to the variety as well as to the welfare of the community. Moreover, in these days of exaggerated and explosive nationalism, it is important to foster all those bonds which tend to unite men of common pursuits irrespective of geographical boundaries. There is a remarkable passage in Professor Whitehead's *Adventures of Ideas*, in which he describes the widening range of modern professional interests: "Professions", he says, "first appear as customary activities largely modified by detached strains of theory. Theories are often wrong; and some of the earlier professional doctrines erred grievously and were maintained tenaciously. Doctrines emerged as plausible deductions and survived as the wisdom of ancestors. Thus the older professional practice was rooted upon custom, though it was turning towards the intellectual sunlight. Here and there individuals stood out far in advance of their colleagues. For example, in the fourteen hundred years separating Galen from Vesalius, the standard of European medical practice was not to be compared with the attainments of either of these men. Also, more than a century after Vesalius, Charles the Second of England, on his deathbed, was tortured by physicians employing futile remedies customary at that time. Again, as a designing engineer Leonardo da Vinci was unequalled until the advent of Vauban and James Watt. In the earlier centuries, the professional influence, as a general sociological fact, was mainly a welter of bygone flashes of intelligence relapsing into customary procedures. It represented the continual lapse of intellect into instinct. But the cul-

245

mination of science completely inverted the rôles of custom and intelligence in the older professions. By this inversion professional institutions have acquired an international life. Each such institution practises within its own nation, but its sources of life are world-wide. Thus loyalties stretch beyond sovereign states." I have quoted at such length from Professor Whitehead because he puts so much better than I could do the new conception of the professions, particularly the learned professions, as exercising not a narrow and sectional influence, but an influence both broad and catholic, which traverses national frontiers unimpeded by tariffs and quotas, and which, by promoting free trade in all beneficent discoveries, advances the welfare of humanity at large.

While we may claim that devotion to a common calling tends to create a sense of professional brotherhood throughout the civilised world, and thus widens and liberalises the minds of its practitioners, there is, on the other side of the account, a mental tendency resulting from immersion in a profession which is not so meritorious, and that is the tendency to resist all changes. Those who, by the expenditure of much time and labour, have acquired facility and expertness in the practice of the system they have so painfully mastered, are naturally disinclined to scrap what they have found to work well enough. They are reluctant to make the effort of examining, and still more of adopting, new ideas which may prove uncomfortably subversive. The beaten path is so much easier to tread, and experience has so often shown that alleged new lights are only will-o'-the-wisps leading into a morass. I am tempted to instance the hostility which has been frequently shown to the discoveries of the great pioneers in medicine, but in this gathering it will be more discreet, as well as more courteous, to refer to the inveterate conservatism of my own profession, which has almost passed into a proverb. Or I may instance the Civil Service, and cite the case of one of our great Government Departments, the Admiralty, which in 1826, when an eminent inventor placed before it a project for electric telegraphy, curtly informed him that "telegraphs of any kind are now totally unnecessary", and again in 1830 felt it to be its duty to discourage the introduction of steam as calculated to strike a fatal blow at the naval supremacy of the Empire. The truth is that no profession, no calling, is immune from this tendency. The prophet has always been greeted with a volley of stones, for, again to quote Professor Whitehead, "routine is the god of every social system". He who would upset that routine is treated as a heretic and blasphemer. There is a good side as well as a bad side to this instinct. It is not all obscurantism. Without the stability of routine the social fabric would inevitably disintegrate, and resistance to innovation is part of the essential protective armour of civilisation. The same Scriptures which lament the stoning of the prophets bid us prove all things and hold fast that which is good. Happily in our day open-mindedness is becoming more prevalent, and there is on all sides a greater receptivity of new ideas.·

On the debit side of my reckoning I must also include a charge which has always been laid against the professional mind, and that is its proneness to prefer the interests of the craft to the interests of the community. It is another way of putting the criticism with which

I have just been dealing. Changes are often advocated in the general interest which are inimical to the interests of those engaged in a particular calling, who are apt to resist those changes, not on their merits, but for purely selfish reasons. This is one of the less desirable products of the trade union spirit. Examples will readily occur to you of what I mean, but again I had better be discreet. My great compatriot, Adam Smith, was very critical of professional and trading corporations, and was unkind enough to say that "People of the same trade seldom meet together, even for merriment and diversion, but the conversation ends in a conspiracy against the public or in some contrivance to raise prices. It is impossible, indeed, to prevent such meetings by any law which either could be executed or would be consistent with liberty and justice. But though the law cannot hinder people of the same trade from sometimes assembling together, it ought to do nothing to facilitate such assemblies; much less to render them necessary." I wonder what he would have thought of the innumerable congresses and conferences which in these days are constantly being held by every trade, calling and profession. I am afraid he would often find in a perusal of their proceedings little to dispel the truth of his indictment. There is more lip-service nowadays to lofty social motives, but the pursuit of selfish aims under the guise of the public good is not an unknown phenomenon. I see that the Carnegie Foundation for the Advancement of Teaching in their last *Annual Review of Legal Education* describe "the tendency of organised minorities honestly to identify their own interests with those of the public at large" as being "an inescapable feature of democratic procedure".

248

The Professional Mind

I could wish that the adverb "honestly" were as well deserved as it is charitable.

There is in these days an increasing resort, in all departments of life, to the particular type of professional man known as the expert. The maladies of the world have become so acute that the specialist has had to be called into consultation. In medicine the specialist has long been a familiar figure, but we have now specialists in every branch of human affairs. The reason, doubtless, is that the field of knowledge has become so vast that no individual can hope to become master of more than a corner of it. Hence, when a public problem arises in any particular province of administration, whether it be water supply, or bacon imports, or London traffic, or the foreign exchanges—just to take some instances at random—the demand always is for the expert to be put in charge, or at least to be consulted. The results are not always happy. The expert mind, as a species of the genus professional mind, is apt to have failings as well as excellences. The attainment of a highly specialised knowledge of one isolated subject tends to create a certain arrogance of assurance. It is not unnatural to assume that if you know *more* about a subject than any one else you know it *better* than any one else. But is that necessarily so? It might be so if human life and human knowledge were divided up into water-tight compartments, and it were possible to deal with each compartment by itself. But we cannot isolate any one factor in the social organism. The interrelations of the parts with each other and with the whole are infinitely complex. The result is that the conclusions of the specialist, however convincing they may seem to him within his own sphere, have often to be corrected and modified when brought into relation with wider considerations. Then there is the constitutional tendency of experts to differ, so unjustly associated in the proverb with the medical profession only. The faith of the public, for example, in political economists has been rudely shaken by the discordant advice which they have tendered since the war for the treatment of the ailments of the body politic. This proneness of experts to differ is easily explicable. Even the most arrogant expert would not lay claim to complete knowledge of his subject; he has probably devoted himself to one aspect of it to the exclusion of others, and has been led to form certain opinions from what is, after all, only partial knowledge. Having formed these opinions for himself, he develops a parental affection for them which becomes emotional rather than scientific. As we say, "there is no reasoning with him".

On the other hand, the value of specialised knowledge is incontestable, being the product, as it is, of intensive research and experience quite beyond the range of the ordinary practitioner. One of the most interesting problems of the day is how best to utilise the expert in the public interest. In the Law Courts we have tried three methods. First, and most conspicuously, experts are called in by the parties as witnesses in support of their respective contentions, where technical matters are involved. I have had a long and wide experience of expert witnesses, and despite the unkind things which have been said of them, I am prepared to pay tribute to the fairness which they in general exhibit. But the witness-box is a difficult place for the scientific man to occupy. It is wrong for him to be an advocate, and the contentious atmosphere of the courts is not always conducive to the calm and dispassionate exposition of truth. Probably it is quite salutary for the more pretentious type of expert to be exposed to an occasional rigorous cross-examination, but the irritation which that process causes him, especially if at the hands of an advocate for whose knowledge of the subject he has a supreme contempt, may well lead to the pronouncement of confident assertions which he may have occasion subsequently to regret. Fair cross-examination—and I emphasise the epithet—is one of the best means of eliciting and testing the truth, but not all cross-examinations are fair. Of one thing I am certain, and that is that no scientific man ought ever to become the partisan of a side; he may be the partisan of an opinion in his own science, if he honestly entertains it, but he ought never to accept a retainer to advocate in evidence a particular view merely because it is the view which it is in the interests of the party who has retained him to maintain. To do so is to prostitute science and to practise a fraud on the administration of justice. I remember being told by a very eminent civil engineer that when he received a retainer to give evidence for a client he used to reply that he did not accept retainers to give evidence for anybody, but that he would be happy to consider the matters on which his help was desired, and if he found that he could support the case he would be prepared to do so. The true rôle of the expert witness is to afford the court the best assistance he can in arriving at the truth, and if he bears this duty in mind he will never go far wrong.

A less perilous sphere for the exercise of the expert mind in the administration of justice is to be found in the utilisation of the expert as a referee, of which the best known example is the system of medical referees under the Workmen's Compensation Act. The medical referee is exempt from the temptations of the witness-box, and has to exercise the functions, not of a partisan, but of a skilled adjudicator. It is a highly responsible part to play, especially as Parliament has set the seal of finality on the medical referee's certificate, but I have no doubt that the duty is faithfully and conscientiously performed. The third method in which the law invokes the aid of the expert professional mind is by employing the expert as an assessor, that is to say, in a consultative capacity, as, for example, when the court sits with nautical assessors, who give their advice on any technical points of navigation arising. Here also the partisan element is eliminated, but in such instances the Court is not bound to accept the assessor's opinion. He is there to inform, not to decide.

Upon the whole, I am disposed to think that it is in some form of consultative capacity that the abilities of the expert mind are best utilised in the public service. The faculty of practical judgment is not always to be found in conjunction with scientific learning. The art of judgment is itself an art. The judge, the statesman and the business man may often be better able than the expert to reach a wise solution of a practical problem, even though it does involve technical matters, but it is essential that the requisite technical assistance should be at his disposal in the study of his problem.

So far I have been dealing with some of the characteristics of what I may call the professional mind in general. I propose now to consider some of the mental phenomena exhibited by the practitioners of the three learned professions, so-called because they possess pre-eminently the character of intellectual pursuits. These three traditional professions, however, as the American Bar Association *Journal* reminds us, "connote something more than mere learning joined to a special vocation. They have brought with them from the past an aura of devotion to the service of others, a sense of individual responsibility, a consciousness of a public function. These ethical implications of professional learning may have been reinforced by the times when so much of learning was confined to churchmen. At any rate, they exist in the case of the theologians, doctors and lawyers, and they thus give to their activities a special significance." Sir Walter Scott puts into the mouth of his inimitable Anti-quary the pregnant aphorism that "the clergy live by our sins, the medical faculty by our diseases and the law gentry by our misfortunes". It is odd to think that the main object in each case of the clergyman, the doctor and the lawyer is to combat the very thing which is the cause of his existence. But I think Jonathan Oldbuck took too pathological a view of the activities of the three great professions. The clergyman is not always in the confessional, the doctor by the bedside, or the lawyer in the courts.

The legal mind is the type of professional mind with which I am naturally most familiar. There is probably no professional type which throughout the ages has been more consistently the subject of depreciatory comment, not all of it unjustified. The main attack has always been that the practice of the law has a warping effect upon the moral nature of its practitioners. The advocate is supposed to be perpetually engaged in distorting the truth, in his efforts to make the worse appear the better reason. "How", asks your neighbour at dinner, "can a man be honest who defends a criminal whom he knows to be guilty?" "It is scarcely necessary to say", remarks Walter Bagehot, "that professional advocacy is unfavourable to the philosophical investigation of truth; a more battered commonplace cannot be found anywhere. To catch at whatever turns up in favour of your own case; to be obviously blind to everything which tells in favour of the case of your adversary; to imply doubts as to principles which it is not expedient to deny; to suggest with delicate indirectness the conclusive arguments in favour of principles which it is not wise directly to affirm —these, and such as these, are the arts of the advocate." It is not an engaging picture. But is it a true one? I can only say, speaking from a long experience, that the conception of the advocate as a kind of artful dodger who makes his living by stupefying his conscience is utterly remote from the truth. I would even venture to say that the lawyer encounters no more problems of moral conduct in his daily professional life than do the practitioners of any other art or business—perhaps fewer, for there is no profession which has a higher, a better recognised or a more rigidly enforced standard of honour. But I am not going to re-open to-day this time-worn controversy. The arguments on both sides are familiar and threadbare. I would only point out that the great bulk of the legal work of the country is administrative and non-contentious, requiring for its successful performance no perverse intellectual sublety, but just the ordinary workaday virtues of industry and honesty;

while, as for the contentious work of the Law Courts, I can assure you that an advocate who worked to Mr Bagehot's pattern would never win the esteem either of his brethren or of the Bench, and certainly would not attain to any eminence in his profession. But while I am satisfied that the practice of the law has no deteriorating effect on the moral character, I am not blind to the elements of truth in the popular caricature. The profession is one which undoubtedly tends to foster certain intellectual habits, which, when they become exaggerated, are not admirable. The business of the lawyer is preeminently with words, not with things, and preoccupation with words has its dangers. "Words", says Hobbes, "are wise men's counters; they do but reckon by them; but they are the money of fools." It is not a good thing to consider arguments from the point of view of how they can be stated rather than from the point of view of whether they are sound or not. There is a danger even in logic in human affairs. The practical problems of humanity are not solved by syllogisms or by neatly framed codes. I think there is a proneness in the legal mind to prefer formulas to facts and to place too much reliance on the power of words.

It is sometimes said that the lawyer's experience of life is apt to make him cynical. Let me give you the answer which Sir Walter Scott puts in the mouth of Counsellor Pleydell: "It is the part of our profession", says that eminent practitioner, "that we seldom see the best side of human nature. People come to us with every selfish feeling newly pointed and grinded; they turn down the very çaulkers of their animosities and prejudices, as smiths do with horses' shoes in a white frost. Many a man has come to my garret yonder that I have at first longed to pitch out at the window, and yet, at length, have discovered that he was only doing as I might have done in his case, being very angry, and of course very unreasonable. I have now satisfied myself that if our profession sees more of human folly and human roguery than others, it is because we witness them acting in that channel in which they can most freely vent themselves. In civilised society, law is the chimney through which all that smoke discharges itself that used to circulate through the whole house and put everyone's eyes out—no wonder that the vent itself should sometimes get a little sooty." I am content with my brother-advocate's defence.

Then another defect commonly attributed to the legal mind is that it is unduly critical. The lawyer's training is certainly apt to make him look for the weak points rather than the strong points of any proposition submitted to him. This critical habit is a useful quality in its proper place, but it often handicaps the lawyer in dealing with constructive proposals, where success can be attained only by disregarding risks. And so lawyers are not temperamentally well fitted for leadership either in politics or in business, in both of which spheres an adventurous spirit is essential. They may be admirable in deliberation; they are not so useful in action. In the State and in society the most useful function of the legal mind lies in the orderly and just regulation of human relations. The promotion of justice and order is surely a sufficiently important public service to satisfy any ambition. But I am forgetting the maxim of the law that no man should be a judge in his own cause, and so I will leave the legal profession to your better judgment, with a parting quotation from a great statesman who happily blends his praise with a discerning qualification: "The law", says Burke, "is, in my opinion, one of the first and noblest of human sciences; a science which does more to quicken and invigorate the understanding than all the other kinds of learning put together; but it is not apt, except in persons very happily born, to open and to liberalize the mind exactly in the same proportion." There I must leave it.

That mordant critic of our Universities, Mr Abraham Flexner, declares that "medicine and law are professions essentially intellectual and learned in character, and requiring for their cultivation the traditions, resources, facilities and contacts which exist within a university and nowhere else". I agree that the two professions have this feature in common, but the resemblance does not go much further. It seems to me that the outlook of the physician upon life must necessarily be widely different from that of the lawyer, for his service to humanity is of an altogether different order. According to the Statute of Henry VIII confirming the Letters Patent which established the Royal College of Physicians in 1518, none were to "be suffered to exercise and practise physic but only those persons that be profound, sad and discreet, groundedly learned and deeply studied in physic". I am glad that my own profession is not required to live up to so exacting a standard.

Sir Wilfred Grenfell tells us that in Labrador the Eskimos called him by a name which means "the man that has to do with pain". The effect on the mind of constant contact with human suffering cannot but be profound. The relation between a patient and his medical

adviser has an intimacy which does not subsist between
a client and his legal adviser, and it is a relation which
makes a call upon the emotions as well as upon the intellect. So far as the medical man is engaged in study
and research he is a man of science, and may be expected to exhibit in this connection the mental qualities
of accurate observation and induction which we as-
sociate with all men of science. But in the region of
professional practice calls are made upon him of a very
special nature. There is no exact science of therapeutics,
and its practice must be largely empirical. It has to deal
not only with the body of the patient, which can be the
subject of more or less accurate investigation, but also
with his mind—a much subtler business. Diagnosis requires not only knowledge, but reasoning power and
often imagination as well. Personality counts for a great
deal, and the mere presence of a trusted medical adviser
may be therapeutic by reason of the confidence he in-
spires. *Officium medici est confortatio animi*, says Petronius.
The demand thus constantly made upon the whole
physical, mental and emotional resources of the medical
practitioner creates a special type of character. This is
exemplified in the highest degree in those who, like the
members of this Association, have to minister to minds
diseased, for in this region of practice psychological
factors necessarily predominate. Moreover, the exacting
nature of the doctor's work and its irregular hours tend
to cut him off to some extent from ordinary social life.
He can seldom take part in public work. When Apollo
offered to confer all his accomplishments on Iapis as a
reward for his having cured Æneas, the aged physician,
we are told, chose rather the virtues of herbs and the

practice of healing and to exercise unfamed the silent arts. And it was Dr Johnson who said that the physician's part lies hid in domestic privacy and silent duties, and silent excellences are soon forgotten. No one probably has a wider knowledge of human nature than the doctor, but it is a specialised knowledge. Can it be said then that there is a distinct medical type of professional mind? I think there is, but it is not easy to put into words. The rôle which the doctor is required to play must react on his mental and moral make-up. I do not believe that his constant contact with suffering renders him callous, but he must acquire a certain calmness in the presence of the emergencies and tragedies of life which is apt to be mistaken for unconcern. His natural sympathies must be under control if he is to perform his work adequately. The very confidence which is reposed in him and the immunity from publicity which he enjoys may tend to make him professionally oracular. The tradition of spells and incantations dies hard, and prescriptions are still made up in hieroglyphics. On the other hand, the unselfishness and devotion to duty which are the very hallmark of the profession far outweigh any of the foibles which may be laid to its charge. It is perhaps in the medical man that the professional mind exhibits its finest flower. At any rate I envy the physician the epithet which is peculiarly his own and which gratitude and affection have bestowed on him, the epithet "beloved". I have never heard of a beloved barrister or a beloved solicitor.

Let me leave this, in the circumstances, rather embarrassing topic and turn to one other manifestation of the professional mind; I mean the clerical mind—perhaps the most distinctive type of all. By his profession the clergyman is in a peculiar degree removed from the rest of the world. Indeed it is of the essence of his vocation that he should be unworldly. He is called upon to dedicate himself to his work by vows which require of him a manner of life distinct from that of his fellow-citizens. The standards of conduct applied to him are more exacting than those applied to others. He must exhibit a walk and conversation becoming his high calling. Intellectually, too, he is set apart. By his profession he has circumscribed his freedom, for he has pledged himself to certain beliefs which he cannot question if he is to remain in his profession. The Church requires of her servants a conformity both ethical and intellectual, such as no other vocation demands. It is no discredit to a lawyer or a doctor to enter his profession from motives of personal ambition, but we feel it to be wrong for anyone to enter the Church unless he has a distinct call to her service. Yet the Church, too, is a profession, and clergymen are professional men, and the practice of his profession undoubtedly induces in the clergyman certain professional ways of looking at things, certain habits of mind, just as does the practice of other professions. The sanctity of his calling, while ennobling his aspirations, is not without its attendant perils. The intellectual dangers are dogmatism with its ugly companions, intolerance and persecution, and casuistry with its accompanying lack of candour. Clericalism and sacerdotalism are not attractive things. The corruption of the best is the worst. On the other side of the account we have to place the long record of saintly lives and noble characters which the annals of the Church contain. In this material world, often so sordid and so ugly, the profession whose calling requires its members to inculcate "whatsoever things are true, whatsoever things are honest, whatsoever things are just, whatsoever things are pure, whatsoever things are lovely, whatsoever things are of good report", renders an inestimable service, and those who consecrate themselves to such a task cannot but themselves acquire virtue from their labours.

It would be interesting to discuss the effects of other callings on their practitioners, and to analyse the special mental characteristics displayed by the teacher, the accountant, the politician and so forth. But I have done enough to make my point, which is only an instance of the general rule that specialisation of function necessarily produces specialisation of the organ charged with that function, or, in simpler terms, that the instrument adapts itself to its work. It must be the daily experience of those whom I am addressing to encounter the distinctive mental features of the different types of patients with whom they have to deal. They are worth studying, for treatment must be accommodated to the psychology as well as to the physique of the patient. But it was not the pathology of the professional mind which I set out to discuss. Such a topic, even if it were appropriate for a popular lecture, lies far beyond my competence. Rather I have sought to gather together and present to you a few of the impressions which have been left on my own mind by other minds, engaged in my own or in other occupations. The observation of one's fellow-men in thought and in action will always be the most fascinating of studies. Doubtless we each find our most acute critics among the members of our own profession, but equally it is in our own profession that we find the loyalty and comradeship which spring from interests, anxieties and successes shared in common. I may fittingly conclude with the memorable words of Bacon: "I hold every man a debtor to his profession; from the which as men of course do seek to receive countenance and profit, so ought they of duty to endeavour themselves by way of amends to be a help and ornament thereunto."

LAW AND THE CITIZEN

Broadcast National Lecture, delivered at a meeting of the Royal
Philosophical Society of Glasgow, April 1936

ON a former occasion, just twenty years ago,
when I was privileged to address the Royal
Philosophical Society of Glasgow, I chose for
my subject "The Ethics of Advocacy". I was at that
time immersed in the daily practice of the Law Courts
and I was concerned to vindicate the profession by which
I earned my livelihood from the aspersions commonly
cast upon it. Since then it has been my fortune to gain
some experience of the law from other and wider points
of view, and latterly in the serener atmosphere of the
judicial Bench my task has been to administer justice not
only according to the laws of England and of Scotland
but also according to the diverse legal systems of almost
every quarter of the civilised globe. I could wish that, as
compared with that occasion twenty years ago, my
knowledge had expanded as widely as my audience,
visible and invisible, has expanded to-night.

To action succeeds reflection. No one can give forty
years of his life to any pursuit without ultimately ques-
tioning himself about the meaning of his activities and
coming to a few conclusions as to what it has all been
about. So to-night I take a wider theme and propose to
share with you some reflections on the part which law
plays in the social life of the community.

In the three-quarters of an hour at my disposal it

263

would manifestly be impossible to discuss every aspect of so wide a topic. I shall not be able, for instance, to deal with the perennial problem of the relations of law and morality, of "sin" and "crime", or with the technical difference between civil and criminal law. As I imagine that there are comparatively few criminals, actual or potential, among my audience, I may be forgiven for omitting to discuss specifically the criminal law. It is of law generically as it concerns the law-abiding citizen that I propose to treat.

Nothing is more remarkable than the strange misconceptions which exist about the law. So few people have any clear ideas on the subject. It is a tribute to the genius of the great novelist, the centenary of whose best-known work we have just been celebrating, and to the pervasive influence of the daily Press, that to the ordinary citizen the mention of the law conjures up a confused vision of the Courts as portrayed in *The Pickwick Papers* and *Bleak House*, mixed with recollections of reports of sensational criminal trials and sordid matrimonial disputes. You all remember the lady who on visiting the Court of Chancery looked round and asked which was the prisoner. As for the study of the law, it is deemed a dismal and repellent pursuit whose mysteries no one would care to penetrate who was not paid to do so. Gibbon expressed the popular view when he said that "few men without the spur of necessity have resolution to force their way through the thorns and thickets of that gloomy labyrinth".

Law and the Citizen

LAW AS PART OF EDUCATION

For the prevalence of such conceptions or misconceptions of the law I am afraid that lawyers themselves are a good deal to blame. They are too often content to confine themselves to the technical routine of their profession and to regard with distaste if not disdain any attempts to examine and explain the true nature of the art which they practise. The law has thus come to be regarded as a matter for experts in whose mysteries the public are fortunate if they can escape entanglement.

It was not always so. There was a time when a general knowledge of the law was esteemed an indispensable part of every educated man's equipment. The famous *Paston Letters* written in the fifteenth century "afford ample evidence that every man who had property to protect, if not every well-educated woman also, was perfectly well versed in the ordinary forms of legal processes". It was in the same century that the Fifth Parliament of King James the Fourth of Scotland ordained that law should be taught in the Grammar Schools to the sons of barons and freeholders, so that they might have knowledge and understanding of the laws, through the which justice might remain universally through all the realm.

There must have been a sad falling from grace by Blackstone's day. That eminent authority, to whom Bentham paid the tribute of saying that he first taught jurisprudence to speak the language of the scholar and the gentleman, roundly declares in his *Introductory Lecture on the Study of Law*, delivered in 1765, that in the knowledge of the laws and constitution of their own country "the gentlemen of England have been more remarkably deficient than those of all Europe besides". It will be consolatory to part of my audience that he goes on to remark that in the northern parts of our island "it is difficult to meet with a person of liberal education who is destitute of a competent knowledge in that science which is to be the guardian of his natural rights and the rule of his civil conduct".

"AN ENTICING STUDY"

Now I do not for a moment suggest that every citizen should be an expert lawyer—an appalling thing to contemplate! What I do desire is that every citizen should have a general conception of the legal system under which he lives. Again to quote Blackstone: "It concerns every man to be acquainted with the rule to which he must conform his actions and to have a clear idea of the whole system of duties which he is to perform and of rights which he may exact." Every branch of knowledge has a technical aspect which is the province of the expert, but it has also general principles, which every educated person should know. The laws of the body politic are like the laws of the human body. It is for the skilled physician to master the technique of the science of medicine, but we must all, at our peril, possess a general working knowledge of the laws of health. I should be in favour of including in the curriculum of all our secondary schools some instruction in the general principles of law and government. If such instruction were intelligently given, it would be found to be anything but a dull subject. "Were law taught as a rational science," said Lord Kames, one of the most liberal minded of our eighteenth-century Scottish judges, "its principles unfolded and its connection with manners and politics, it would prove an enticing study to every person who has an appetite for knowledge."

The reason why the study of at least the principles of law ought to form part of any scheme of liberal education is because the law is the very foundation of human society, the very basis on which our civilisation is founded. Has it ever occurred to you to inquire how it is that the millions of human beings who crowd our cities and populate our rural areas manage to live together at all? If you think of them each individually compact of ambitions, passions, rivalries, and jealousies and all in competition for the necessities and the luxuries of life, and of the endless opportunities for conflict which their daily contacts present, how comes it, you may well ask, that we all go about our several vocations undisturbed and live our lives in peace and freedom? The main reason is that by the slow growth of law the warring instincts of mankind have been accommodated and subdued to order. We are not conscious of this influence regulating our lives and we have grown so accustomed to its operation that we no more think of it than we do of the air we breathe. But it is true all the same that it is as essential to our social well-being as the air is to our lungs. An eminent legal friend of mine once inelegantly compared our legal system to our main sewerage. We spend our days oblivious of its beneficent action until something goes wrong with it and then we realise from the unsavoury consequences how much of our comfort depends upon it.

Law and Other Things

"THE EFFECTIVE INSTRUMENT
OF PROGRESS"

The process of civilisation has been a process of evolving an ordered social life out of the chaos of savagery. Without this organisation of society, as Huxley graphically put it, "I should probably have had nothing but a flint axe and an indifferent hut to call my own; and even these would be mine only so long as no stronger savage came my way." In the evolution of our organised society the effective instrument of progress has been the law. It is not for nothing that we inevitably link together the words "law" and "order". As in the biological world it is the vertebrate structure which has enabled physical life to attain its highest forms, so in the social world it is the ordered structure of the law which has enabled society to attain its highest development. In either case the skeleton is invisible, but in neither case can we stand upright without it. Without the framework of the law in which our lives are set it would be impossible to carry on the infinitely diversified activities of modern humanity. Not a single day or hour of our lives is spent in which we do not benefit from the legal system under which we live. Let me take at random one or two instances of what I mean. You rise in the morning and take your daily bath—have you ever thought of the elaborate legal procedure which has preceded the simple operation of turning on the tap? The water supply which you so easily take for granted has been drawn from a river or pumped from underground sources or impounded on gathering-grounds miles away and brought

268

to your home by an intricate system of pipes. Think of all the rights and interests which have had to be dealt with before this result was achieved. Landowners may have had to be compensated for the use of their property, the rights of millowners, and of navigation and fishing, may have had to be considered, wayleaves obtained, streets opened and so on. The method by which all these complicated matters are adjusted is to be found in an elaborate legal code known as the Waterworks Clauses Acts, by which every step in the procedure is regulated. These Acts provide the general law on the subject of water supply, but our system of Private Bill legislation, of which the average citizen has only the vaguest idea, enables special provision to be made for the requirements of each area. To the Select Committees of Parliament is confided one of the most responsible of all jurisdictions, the duty of deciding the occasions and the terms on which private rights must give way to public needs. But that is not all; the scheme which brings the water to every household tap has to be administered and financed, and this in turn necessitates the utilisation of the vast apparatus of local government law, with its many branches—rating, inspection and the like. I could easily spend my whole allotted time to-night in telling you how the law of water supply has been evolved, and a fascinating subject it is. But I must content myself with asking you to realise to-morrow morning how large a share the law has had in providing you with the means of ablution.

Law and Other Things

A DAY'S CONTACTS WITH THE LAW

This, however, is only the beginning of your day's contacts with the law. You go downstairs and warm yourself at a gas or electric fire—another whole code of law lies behind the provision of these other public utilities, as they are called. You sit down to breakfast and enjoy the protection of the Food and Drugs Acts which see to it that your milk is pure and your butter unadulterated. You leave your home and set off to your work by 'bus or tram or tube; in taking your 2d. ticket you enter into one of the numerous legal transactions of which your day is full, for the taking of that ticket involves both you and the company or local authority who have undertaken to convey you to your destination in a whole series of mutual rights and duties. You arrive at your office or works and enter the sphere of your employment; at once you find yourself in another set of legal relations regulated not only by the common law but by all the statutes dealing with workmen's compensation, employers' liability, trade unions, the payment of wages and so forth. Perhaps you go out for your midday meal, whereupon you enter into a contract of sale and purchase of consumable commodities, and the Sale of Goods Act prescribes what are your rights in the matter of merchantable quality, implied warranty of fitness for human consumption and all the rest of it. And so I could follow you through all the doings of the day and show you how, without your ever giving it a thought, you are at almost every moment availing yourself of a social system built up and ordered by law, which in general works so smoothly that you take it all for granted.

Law and the Citizen

This, then, is what law does for the citizen; it provides him with a mechanism of life whereby all the incidents of his relations with his fellow-beings are regulated and the element of friction eliminated by definite and familiar adjustments.

LITIGATION AS A SYMPTOM OF FAILURE

Let me disabuse your minds of the idea that litigation is the essential feature of law. Litigation is rather a symptom of the failure of law. When one reflects on the millions of legal relationships which in a single day the manifold transactions and activities of our citizens involve and then on the number of cases which find their way into the Law Courts, it will be realised at once how minute is the percentage of instances in which disputes arise which call for judicial determination. An ideal system of law would provide in advance for every possible contingency, so that no dispute could ever arise. But no humanly devised code can attain such perfection, and even were the law always clear and definite its application to the infinite diversity of facts could not fail to give rise to occasional controversy. Thus conflicts of rights and wrongs and questions of disputed fact must inevitably arise which the Courts have to settle, but what I desire to emphasise is the operation of law as exhibited not in our tribunals but in the daily conduct of our lives. Litigation indeed may be said to represent the pathology of law as contrasted with its physiology.

But I must not make too large a claim on behalf of the law. Pervasive as is its influence, there is a large region of human conduct to which it is indifferent. As I have said, it provides the framework of our social life but within the security of that framework there is happily a wide sphere of human activity where spontaneity and individuality may have free and unfettered play—where, as we say, we can do as we like. The law does not prescribe—as yet at least—what we shall eat and drink (although there have been experiments in that direction) or whether we shall smoke or not smoke (except in certain places) or how we shall spend our leisure or how we shall conduct our ordinary family life, though even here there is a legal background. With such matters the law is unsuited to deal, for law is of necessity a formal, rigid thing; my metaphor of the skeleton may be once more invoked and its contrast with the living flesh. The standards of the law cannot be other than objective. It deals with men's acts and their consequences. As for their personal habits, feelings and emotions and all the intricate fabric of the life of the spirit, the law is too crude an implement to deal with these. What we think and what we feel, the realms of the intellect and of the heart, are not within the law's province. It is not concerned with the imponderables. As Lord Balfour once observed, "The three greatest things in the world, love, beauty and happiness, have this feature in common, that they are utterly incapable of measurement"; they are equally incapable of legal regulation. Yet without law none of them could be attained or enjoyed. Without the shelter and security which it affords, these finer elements in life could not exist. The law can protect what it cannot create. It cannot produce a beautiful landscape, but it can at least prevent it from being desecrated by advertisements. "It is true", as a former Duke of Argyll said, "that neither wealth nor health, nor knowledge, nor morality can be given by Act of Parliament. But it is also true that the acquisition of one and all of these can be impeded and prevented by bad laws as well as aided and encouraged by appropriate legislation."

WHERE LAW SHOULD NOT INTERFERE

It is well, then, to remember that there are limits to the beneficial operation of law, for there is in these days a tendency in some quarters to require the law to interfere in regions where it is wholly unfitted to operate. We see attempts in other countries to tyrannise by law over the private life of the citizen, even over his thoughts and his beliefs, with a revival of all the evils of persecution which such attempts engendered in the past; and among ourselves there are some whose zeal to dictate to others how they shall live their lives leads them to press for undesirable extensions of the law. So do not let us ask too much of law and let us see that it is confined to its own proper sphere. You can well have an excess of law. I note with interest that the various legislatures of the United States, a country which prides itself on being the land of the free, are credited with having passed over 60,000 statutes in five years.

The "reign of law" was a phrase which enjoyed a wide currency in the Victorian age. The phrase has recently come into vogue again, particularly in international matters. The conception which it embodies is the conception of certainty as opposed to arbitrariness. To know what we can lawfully do and what we cannot lawfully do; to be subject only to laws constitutionally enacted and enforced; to be certain that infractions of the law will be justly and impartially investigated and dealt with; to show respect for the rights of others; to observe good faith in the performance of our contracts, domestic or international; to possess the assurance of security in the enjoyment of our lives and property— these are the things which are denoted by the reign of law. History shows by what slow and painful processes this happy state was attained in our own country; it was only after centuries of contest that we achieved the supremacy of law over all alike, from the Sovereign to the humblest of his people. It is our duty and our privilege to maintain this priceless inheritance and to hand it on undiminished to our successors.

"SANCTIONS" BEHIND THE SYSTEM

I now pass to consider what, in the current language of the day, are the "sanctions" behind the legal system under which we live. Law is not merely static, not merely an ideal code of social conduct. It is dynamic; it acts. It is essential that it should be observed by all. Unhappy experience has proved that in every community there will always be law-breakers. We cannot blink the fact that there are forces of evil in the world—they are only too obvious—and no system of law, however perfect, can dispense with the aid of force. It may be that in Utopia the law might rely for its observance on the persuasion of its reasonableness. But we do not live in Utopia, and if the law is to be obeyed it must have behind it the power of enforcement against the disobedient. In every civilised nation the whole collective force of the government can in the ultimate resort be invoked in support of the law. In one hand Justice holds the scales; in her other hand she holds a sword. Behind the judge's seat stands the policeman; behind the policeman are arrayed the armed forces of the land. This is no less true of the civil law than of the criminal law. A judgment that cannot be enforced is a mere pious sentiment, and law without the power of compelling obedience is no law at all. "Law", wrote Huxley, "is the expression of the opinion of the majority; and it is law, and not mere opinion, because the many are strong enough to enforce it." I need not remind you at this moment of the difficulties which in this respect have arisen in the attempt to bring the nations of the world under the reign of law. We have had too poignant a demonstration of the impotence of law which lacks the power of enforcement. If war is to be eliminated from the society of nations as it has been eliminated from the society of individuals, then it is essential not only that there shall be a code of international conduct but also that there shall be the means of enforcing it. This is the great problem of the future of civilisation and the ultimate aspiration of law—to bring about among the nations the collective security which within the confines of each nation has been achieved among individuals.

But it is precisely because law is enforced and obedience to it compelled that it behoves us to be vigilant to see that our laws are just. Force may be and has been in the past employed for the enforcement of what is unjust as well as of what is just. The most hideous of all social menaces is injustice enthroned in power. Pascal, in one of the profoundest of his thoughts, thus exhorts us: "We must therefore put together Justice and Force; and therefore so dispose things that whatsoever is just is mighty and whatsoever is mighty is just."

"THE JOINT PRODUCT OF CUSTOM AND LEGISLATION"

Hence the immense importance to the citizen of the methods by which the law which governs his daily life is created and administered. Of the law of this country it may be said that it is the joint product of custom and legislation, of the common law and of the statutes of the realm. The former represents that body of authoritative usage which has been gradually secreted by experience. By a process of natural selection practices which have proved their utility and their consonance with public opinion have, through judicial decisions, consolidated themselves as the foundation of the common law of the land. But while the principles of our law have thus been evolved by a slow process of growth, they are not as the laws of the Medes and Persians. It is of the very essence of law that it should continue to be capable of change, as all living things must be. The main means of securing the adaptation of law to the varying complexities of modern life and its adjustment to changing views of social policy is by legislation, that is to say, by the pronouncements of the representatives of the nation in Parliament assembled. Legislation by representative bodies may be an imperfect method of producing a perfect system of law, and, no doubt, it sometimes works injustice, particularly to minorities, but it is the most practicable method which mankind has yet succeeded in evolving, and if, like all other human institutions, it has its defects it has at least this great merit, that it gives to every citizen the right to share, however infinitesimally, in the making of the laws which are to govern him. I would venture to emphasise how vital is the responsibility which is thus imposed on every individual, however lightly he may esteem this privilege. Full citizenship, as Aristotle defined it, lies in the right to take part in legislation and the administration of justice. Although in the modern State the citizen cannot take so direct a part in the making of the laws as the citizen of Athens did, he has still a share in the process. If he is dissatisfied with the law as it exists, he is entitled to use his vote and his influence for its reform. All reform of the law is ultimately brought about by the aggregate effect of the wishes of the people expressed through the exercise of the franchise. So the citizen has a duty to think about the law and to form his own opinion upon it. Common law and statute law alike derive their moral sanction from the consent of the people, evidenced in the former case by their acquiescence in customs which they have found convenient and equitable, and in the latter case by their participation in the process of its enactment.

WHAT PART SHOULD THE STATE PLAY?

Nothing is more interesting to the student of our social development than to note the different conceptions which have prevailed at different times of the part which the State, through its laws, should play in the regulation of the lives and activities of the individuals who compose it. The subject is one which falls within the domain of the science of politics rather than within that of the science of law, but the prevalent views upon it are of immense significance in the formulation of our laws. The whole social complexion of an epoch takes its colour from the conception which animates its legislators as to the proper sphere of their activities. No intelligent observer can fail to be struck by the immense change which in recent times has come over our ideas of what should be done by law, that is, by the State through the Statute book, in every department of human life. To appreciate this change you cannot do better than read Herbert Spencer's famous manifesto, *The Man versus the State*, published just half a century ago. Speaking in the name of enlightened Liberalism, he denounces in no measured terms "The New Toryism", which you will be a little surprised to find is socialism—"The Coming Slavery", "The Sins of Legislators" and "The Great Political Superstition". His whole thesis is that the welfare of the people was being gravely endangered by the inroads which the Government was making into regions which it ought to leave alone. He must have applauded the saying of Tom Paine, that eminent champion of the rights of man—"The more perfect civilisation is, the less occasion has it for government...it is but few general laws that civilised life requires." What Herbert Spencer denounced has now become common form. He was a true prophet in discerning the signs of the times, but even in his gloomiest vaticinations he could have had no conception of the contents of our modern statute book, composed as it is almost entirely of measures relating to housing, public health, unemployment and all manner of economic and social matters and condescending even

278

to such humble topics as pigs, eggs and bacon. This is neither the time nor the place, nor am I the person, to discuss the merits or demerits of this great change, but I must remind you that it is a change which, whatever its motive, is being effected by law, which is the vehicle of this changed social policy. What is germane to my subject and what is of profound interest to citizen and lawyer alike is the realisation of this new social use to which law is being put.

I have hinted already that all laws are not necessarily good laws. There are good laws and bad laws, and even the best of laws fall short of perfection. But there is one test of merit to which law is constantly and rightly subjected, the test of whether it is abreast of the enlightened opinion of the times. "Legislation", says Lecky, "is only really successful when it is in harmony with the general spirit of the age. Law and statesmen for the most part indicate and ratify, but do not create. They are like the hands of the watch which move obedient to the hidden machinery behind." To the collective spirit of his age each citizen contributes and thus the wisdom or unwisdom of our legislation depends ultimately upon the wisdom or unwisdom of the people. Hence the importance of an educated public opinion, for in the absence of this, our civilisation, like that of ancient Rome, may fall a victim to the *ardor civium prava jubentium.*

POSITIVE AND NEGATIVE LAW

Another noteworthy feature of modern law is the extent to which it has become positive rather than negative. The Ten Commandments are for the most part injunc-

279

tions not to do certain things. The commandments of modern Parliaments are almost entirely injunctions to do certain things. Negative law is concerned to see that the individual shall be protected from molestation in the pursuit of his own chosen activities. Positive law is concerned to direct his activities for him. Once again, it is for the citizen to decide how far he desires this new phase of law to be carried. My task is only to exhibit to him the present-day trend of law so that he may apply his mind deliberately to the problems which it raises and reach a considered judgment as to where his welfare truly lies.

But it is not only essential to have good laws. It is no less essential that they should be well administered. There are, unhappily, countries which possess the most admirable codes of law but where lawlessness is rife. We have for so long in this country been accustomed to a judicial system in whose efficiency and impartiality the people have confidence, that it has come upon us as a painful surprise to see in other countries, professing to be civilised, the judges made the instruments of the arbitrary and oppressive policy of the executive. The administration of the law must be absolutely independent of everything except the law. "To act in good faith and listen fairly to both sides", said Lord Chancellor Loreburn in a well-known leading case, "is a duty lying upon everyone who decides anything." Justice must be administered according to known and settled law and not according to caprice or as the instrument of any political policy or at the beck and call of any outside power. This is cardinal. Once the administration of justice is tampered with, once it becomes swayed by fear or favour,

the whole fabric of society is threatened. Let me quote
the words of Viscount Cecil of Chelwood. Speaking in
the House of Lords on 28 November 1934, he said: "For
my own part I believe that the independence of the
judges is by far the most important guarantee of the
liberty of the subject in this country that can possibly be
devised, and that the moment you allow, as in some
foreign countries recently has been done, the judges to be
at the mercy of the political power, you are destroying
the great guarantee of the freedom of the people of this
country."

THE ATTAINMENT OF JUSTICE

And now I would ask every citizen to reflect upon the
aims which should animate the law, both in its formation
and in its administration. First and foremost, the aim
of the law must be the attainment of justice, "the great
standing policy of civil society", in Burke's resounding
phrase. Justice is the meeting-place of law and ethics,
and the words with which Justinian, the greatest lawgiver the world has ever seen, begins his famous *Institutes*
—"Justice is the constant and perpetual will to give
every man his due"—might equally form the exordium
of an ethical treatise. There is no instinct more deep-
rooted in our moral being than the instinct of justice.
It is indefinable, like all the greatest things in life. But
we all possess it. There has been much controversy
among philosophers as to whether there is such a thing
as the law of nature, the law of natural justice. It is an
interesting but a rather barren controversy, for we all
know perfectly well that we have an inner voice which

bids us be just in our dealings with each other, however often we may flout its admonitions. Justice is indeed no "cloistered virtue", as my judicial brother Lord Atkin said only last month in a judgment of the Privy Council. It finds a sphere for its exercise in all our transactions with our fellow-men, from the most trivial of our daily doings to the most august international conventions. Its dictates are simple and straightforward and permit of no sophistication. The content of the conception of justice no doubt may vary from time to time, in different lands, at different stages of social development, but its categorical imperative is constant. Law as framed and administered by fallible human beings must always fall short of the ideal standard of justice, but the more law approximates to justice, as justice is for the time being conceived, the more gladly and readily will it be obeyed. This is the spiritual side of law, and as Disraeli in his Address as Lord Rector of Glasgow University in 1873 reminded us, "The spiritual nature of man is stronger than codes or constitutions. No government can endure which does not recognise that for its foundation, and no legislation last which does not flow from this fountain." In language no less sublime Froude, in one of his *Short Studies on Great Subjects*, declares that "our human laws are but the copies, more or less imperfect, of the eternal laws so far as we can read them and either succeed and promote our welfare or fail and bring confusion and disorder, according as the legislators' insight has detected the true principle or has been distorted by ignorance or selfishness". I have borrowed these passages from two of our great writers to adorn my discourse because they express what I believe to be the ideal of law with an eloquence which is far beyond my own compass.

IMPORTANCE OF LIBERTY

With justice is linked liberty, for the greatest injustice in the world is the unjust deprivation of liberty. The civilised nations have abolished slavery in the economic sense, but the world now presents the appalling spectacle of the creation of a far more deadly slavery—the slavery of the spirit. Freedom to think and to believe and to say what we deem right, subject only to the recognition of the same freedom on the part of others—that is the charter of liberty which our ancestors won for us, not without blood and tears. This freedom we now see threatened by new tyrannies which seek to reduce the citizen to a soulless unit, to moral and intellectual servitude. It is a subtle process; it takes many guises and disguises; and it may invoke high-sounding motives; but whether it takes the form of the dictatorship of a despot or the ruthless domination of one section of the community over all others, in whatever form it appears it is the sworn foe of justice.

What, on the other hand, are the rewards of the observance of these great principles of justice and liberty in the making and administration of our laws? By their observance, and only by their observance, will we attain to peace and welfare. There can be no peace where there is not justice; there can be no welfare where there is not liberty. It seems unnecessary to elaborate these truisms.

For my peroration I quote the stately words, as true now after the lapse of three centuries as when they were addressed by the Commons to James I and VI in 1610: "Amongst many other points of happiness and freedom which your Majesty's subjects of this Kingdom have enjoyed under your royal progenitors, Kings and Queens of this realm, there is none which they have accounted more dear and precious than this, to be guided and governed by certain rule of law, which giveth both to the head and members that which of right belongeth to them, and not by any uncertain or arbitrary form of government."